THE COMPLETE GUIDE TO MEXICAN BEVERAGES

THE COMPLETE GUIDE TO MEXICAN BEVERAGES

From Atole to Zambumbia

N. C. STEVENS

BLOOMSBURY ACADEMIC
NEW YORK • LONDON • OXFORD • NEW DELHI • SYDNEY

BLOOMSBURY ACADEMIC
Bloomsbury Publishing Inc, 1359 Broadway, New York, NY 10018, USA
Bloomsbury Publishing Plc, 50 Bedford Square, London, WC1B 3DP, UK
Bloomsbury Publishing Ireland, 29 Earlsfort Terrace, Dublin 2, D02 AY28, Ireland

First published in the United States of America 2026

Cover photos by N. C. Stevens, cover image iStock.com/Nadiinko
Cover design by Diana Nuhn

Library of Congress Cataloging-in-Publication Data
Names: Stevens, N. C. (Nicholas C.) author
Title: The complete guide to Mexican beverages : from atole to zambumbia / by N.C. Stevens.
Identifiers: LCCN 2026004624 (print) | LCCN 2026004625 (ebook) | ISBN 9798216389439 hb | ISBN 9798216389446 ebook | ISBN 9798216389453 epdf
Subjects: LCSH: Beverages—Mexico—History | Drinking customs—Mexico | Pulque—Mexico
Classification: LCC GT2883.M6 S74 2026 (print) | LCC GT2883.M6 (ebook)
LC record available at https://lccn.loc.gov/2026004624
LC ebook record available at https://lccn.loc.gov/2026004625

ISBN: HB: 979-8-216-38943-9
ePDF: 979-8-216-38945-3
eBook: 979-8-216-38944-6

Typeset by Deanta Global Publishing Service, Chennai, India
Printed and bound in the United States of America
For product safety related questions contact productsafety@bloomsbury.com.
To find out more about our authors and books visit www.bloomsbury.com and sign up for our newsletters

Quién a dar suma y número se atreve
A las tabernas que hay de esta bebida?
Qué esponja alcanza a lo que aquí se embebe?

—Bernardo de Balbuena, Grandeza Mexicana, 1604

CONTENTS

ACKNOWLEDGMENTS

Drinks are a cornerstone of hospitality in all cultures. Superlative in its drinking culture, Mexico is home to a warm and humbling ethos of hospitality. In researching the many drinks of Mexico, I have been accepted into the homes of welcoming strangers across the country, where I slept, ate, drank, and learned. I want to thank my many hosts and their families: Carlos in Monterrey, Oscar and Kahlo in San Luis Potosí, Luis in Tampico, Mauricio in Ciudad Guzmán, Jorge in Colima, Oscar in Ciudad de México, Jos in Puebla, Antonio in Tehuacán, Luis in Tuxtla Gutiérrez, and Mizael in Mérida. Their friendship, generosity, and guidance have been fundamental to realizing this project. Each of them has pointed me toward at least one beverage of interest.

To the many vendors, producers, and cantineros who took a moment to speak with me, I owe each of you a gratitude for sharing your flavors, insights, and traditions with me. I would like to especially thank Abel Pulido of Huapilla Tampico y Gran Día, Chef Nico Mejía, Genaro de Jarano and his family of Camellón de la Tuba, Jorge Velasco Rocha of La China Mestiza, Martín "La Gallina" of Laguna de Guadalupe, Abraham González of Pulquería Las Duelistas, Don Lázaro San Simon "El Ratón" of San Simón Tlatlahuquitepec, Sister Luísa de Jesus of the Convent of the Clarisas Capuchinas, Karen Mendoza and family of Coxcatlán, Enrique Galán and his wife of San Bartolo Coyotepec, Dulce Regalado of Juchitán de Zaragoza, Apícola Real Xtabentúnof Mérida, Don Luis of Meliponario U Naajil Yuum K'iin, María "Doña Nebi" Cruz of Maní, and the foremost expert on Mexico's fermented beverages, César Iván Ojeda Linares.

I would also like to acknowledge the important work that cultural institutions in and around Mexico do for culinary research: Biblioteca de la Gastronomía Mexicana of Fundación Herdez, Artes de México, Instituto Nacional de Antropología e Historia, Instituto Nacional de los Pueblos Indígenas, Consejo Nacional para la Cultura y las Artes, Hemeroteca Nacional Digital de México, and the many government and civil-society organizations that support cultural works. I have relied extensively on the output of these institutions and would be proud to have similar ones in my country.

Finally, a well-earned thank you to my family—Gib, Chet, Russ, Kirsten, Mom, and Dad—for accommodating my nomadism and helping to create our very own Pratt Street drinking culture! Kudos to Lisa Ben-Horin for editing so much of my early writing. And an eternal gratitude to Asiana for braving distance in love and seeing value in my exploration of the colorful world of drinks. This is a tiny testament to the magnitude of your support.

Mil gracias.

1

Introduction

The year is 1520. By the reckonings of the Aztec calendar, it is 2-Tecpatl—a year named after the sacred flint knife with which Mexica priests ceremonially remove beating hearts from sacrificial chests. Vendors in the markets of Tenochtitlán buy and sell as they have for nearly two centuries. Some take *nextamalli*, a dough of corn treated with ash, and boil it with water into a thick and nourishing drink called *atolli*.

Cacahuatl, cacao pods, exchange hands as barter in the marketplace and as a form of wealth in the upper echelons of the Aztec capital. Lords with land around the empire haul dozens of *xiquipilli*, sacks holding up to 8,000 cacao beans, across Lake Texcoco's causeways to the island city to pay tribute to the emperor. In the royal household, the hot surface of a clay *comalli* toasts the valuable nibs. A cylinder of volcanic stone called a *metlapilli* grinds the cacao against a *metlatl* into a buttery paste. The emperor and his elite entourage sip a drink of the bitter cacao whisked into water and flavored with sundry ingredients like vanilla, achiote, and aromatic flowers. They are drinking money.

On festival days, certain buildings around the capital city's Great Temple fill with priests sitting in circles around large rabbit-shaped vats of *octli*, the fermented sap of agave. They drink from reed straws and become intoxicated with the divine essence contained in the vessel. Some add particular roots, barks, seeds, and mushrooms to the brew, inducing visions, euphoria, and disorientation among the drinkers. This, too, is a divine experience.

Far to the east of Lake Texcoco, though, a new drink arrives on the shores of the land ruled by the Aztec Triple Alliance. An expedition of Spaniards, led by Hernán Cortés, brings European grape wine from Cuba to the coast of Veracruz. When Emperor Moctezuma's emissaries meet with the Spanish interlopers at the coastal bivouac of San Juan de Ulua, legend has it that they partake of the European vintage for the first time.

* * *

The year is 1620. The agave wine of the Aztecs, *octli*, has shed its sacrosanct sheen. Now, residents of New Spain buy and drink the wine with a new name—*pulque*. The Spanish viceroyalty is wary of the drunken vices that occur in the shops called *pulquerías*, yet still permits indigenous communities to license vendors to sell the fermented sap, so long as they pay their taxes. Despite the new regulations, many taverns still operate informally.

Chocolate, too, has lost some of its value. People no longer exchange the pods as if they were money. The increasingly diverse peoples of the city drink new versions of corn atole and chocolate modified with introduced products like cow's milk, cane sugar, and cinnamon. The Spanish Inquisition punishes the use of herbs and roots in beverages, citing the diabolical effects they have on the behavior of souls needing saving.

On the distant western coast, Filipino sailors fleeing from the harsh transpacific crossing of the Manila Galleon at ports like Acapulco introduce indigenous people to the technology of distillation. Vast coconut plantations provide ample sweet palm sap for fermentation and distillation. They call their fortified product *vino de cocos*. The memory of Ciudad de México's first brewery, which closed in the late 1550s, is all but forgotten. In the northern reaches of New Spain, frontiersmen produce true grape *vino* from European vines planted alongside native varieties in the suitable climes of Coahuila.

* * *

The year is 1720. The coffers of the colonial government depend heavily on taxes levied on the sale of pulque. Sugarcane plantations conquer vast expanses of eastern and central New Spain. Many *hacendado* landowners keep clandestine stills for making spirituous *aguardiente* adjacent to their *trapiche* sugar mills. But the Crown is keen to root out this untaxed liquor. It has been illegal to produce rum for a century; all of it is moonshining. Workers toiling on the sprawling cane haciendas live indebted to the owners. They drink the aguardiente for energy and succor. To make the harsh cane spirit potable, the laborers macerate it with local seasonal fruits, spices, and herbs to make liqueurs they call *curados*. Indigenous communities in the west of the colony use distillation to transform roasted agave wines into stronger, clearer spirits.

Catholic missionaries plant new vineyards along the Pacific Coast in the Baja Peninsula. The mission grape, hardly known in the vineyards of Europe, provides a source of sacramental wine for the Catholic mass in New Spain. On the continent, the Spanish Crown jealously guards a monopoly on the chocolate trade, dealing the exotic drink to the wealthy of Europe, where it is sipped in parlors in the most fashionable cities.

* * *

The year is 1820. Revolutionaries are waging a war against the Spanish Crown. Tight restrictions on growing grapes in New Spain in favor of imported Spanish wines have chafed locals like Father Miguel Hidalgo, who led an unsuccessful revolt 10 years prior. In fact, Spain has cut off the North American colony from nearly all trade with the rest of the world. Beer from northern European countries almost never reaches the eastern ports on Spanish ships. Tea, well-known in some parts of Europe, is not traded by the Spanish. Coffee, having grown well around the Caribbean, is only just establishing a foothold in the eastern regions of tropical Veracruz.

Haciendas to the east of the capital increasingly dominate the pulque trade. Wealthy men in Ciudad de México coordinate the planting of massive *magueyes pulqueros* on their land in the nearby state of Hidalgo. Distillers also legally produce cane and agave spirits in regions with established specializations.

* * *

The year is 1920. Industrial Mexican brewing is gnawing away at the pulque stronghold, as beer slowly replaces Mexico's ancestral beverage thanks to sanitation, shelf life, and industrial production. Mexico's first soda companies have sprung up in the shadow of the brewing industry, which provides them with bottles, caps, and carbonation. Mexican coffee exports rank among the highest in the world, with plantations in Veracruz, Michoacán, and Chiapas producing world-class Arabica beans.

Where the Yucatán Peninsula is not planted with fibrous henequen agaves used for making textiles, the karst landscape is awash with rum and the more refined *habanero*. Tequila resounds increasingly patriotic as the Mexican Revolution reignites pride in a homegrown identity. The entire world now consumes chocolate in solid form, ignorant of its liquid Mesoamerican origins.

* * *

The year is 2020. Mexico exports more beer than any country in the world. Mexicans also drink more soft drinks than any other population. While bars in Mexico boast some of the most critically acclaimed cocktails around, every up-to-snuff liquor cabinet outside of Mexico is equipped with a bottle of tequila. The Mexican agave spirits industry sells over 10 billion dollars of liquor a year. Everyone and their mother loves the margarita.

Pulque has made a quiet comeback in grungy urban circles where local traditions are valued. But many indigenous drinks have been neglected for centuries. Only in the most rural and remote regions of Mexico are native brews like *tesgüiño* and *nochocle* still produced, celebrated, and drunk.

* * *

Through five centuries of Mexican history, we trace how various ingredients and beverages came to be prominent factors in daily life and fell from favor—even into obscurity. Such an expansive review of drinking in Mesoamerica,

New Spain, and Mexico is possible only because the beverages of this land have consistently proven their power to fascinate. Accordingly, we inherit a rich canon of literature that discusses Mexican drinks.

The mythologies and codices of Mesoamerica held indigenous drinks like cacao and pulque as central conceits, even elevating them to the status of sacred substances. When the first Old World outsiders arrived in Mesoamerica, they often recorded their observations of drinking habits—even while systematically destroying them. The earliest and most prolific of the colonial chroniclers of New Spain, including the missionary Toribio de Benavente and the Franciscan Friar Bernardino de Sahagún, gave detailed accounts of pulque consumption, cacao preparation, atole vending, and the use of hallucinogenic plants and fungi.

The records of colonial New Spain, too, are unwavering sources of information on the gastronomical landscape of the viceroyalty and its increasingly diverse subjects, at times archiving detailed lists describing dozens of different local drinks. The Spanish Crown proved to be obsessed with what people were drinking over several centuries. Laws and edicts outlawed the production of spirits, legitimized the sale of pulque, subsidized the planting of vineyards, philosophized on the morality of drinking chocolate, and demonized the use of hallucinogens. Many drinks were considered illegal for much of the sixteenth and seventeenth centuries, though enforcement did not come about in a meaningful way until the late eighteenth century.[1] In 1755, on the eve of the tax-optimizing Bourbon Reforms, Spain even developed the *Juzgado de Bebidas*, an ad hoc tribunal meant to study and eliminate many of the alcoholic beverages consumed by the laypeople of New Spain.

In the wake of Mexican independence in the nineteenth century, a rich archive of newspapers, magazines, and state records continued to tell compelling stories about the rise of beer brewing, the Porfirian apogee of pulque, and the modernization of the spirits industry. Joel R. Poinsett, who would serve as the first US representative to independent Mexico, had roamed the young country in 1822. Sent by the Monroe Administration on a secret mission to feel out the United States's new neighbor and its leader, Iturbide, he wrote anonymously, "A small quantity of wine and brandy are consumed by the wealthy, but the ordinary drink of the people is the rum of the country, pulque, and vino mezcal, the brandy of the Maguey."[2]

Today, the beverages of Mexico remain superlative. Mexico drinks the most soda, exports the most beer, and mixes some of the best cocktails. Once again, academics, journalists, and bartenders have found themselves enamored with the drinks of Mexico. Yet it is impossible to appreciate the modern success of Mexico's beverage industry without understanding the historical, cultural, and technological factors that have allowed each drink to exist.

This book takes up the cup from which countless writers have drunk over the past five centuries since the fall of Tenochtitlán. It combines centuries of reporting on the development of drinking in Mexico with a twenty-first-century investigation into how many of the most popular and beloved drinks fare today. While dissecting the individual character and importance of over 100 unique beverages (some, like pulque, merit a lengthier discussion), we also explore broader trends in Mexican gastronomy. How have different plants come to play central roles in agriculture, nutrition, and economy? How have the arrivals or developments of new culinary technologies and techniques, from ancient nixtamalization to modern distillation, changed the way people feed and fete? How have different cultures contributed to such a vibrant array of socially salient drinks?

This book is also a recipe book. No, we will not teach you how to mix the best margarita or how to brew the most decadent hot chocolate. Instead, we will use the lessons of history as ingredients. We will take the natural endowments of the land—agave, corn, cacao—and we will mix them with foreign implants—wheat, sugarcane, grapes—in the great cauldron of *mestizaje*. We will measure out the effect of the law and water it down with the persistent insubordination of the masses. The seasoning will be that of the harvest cycle; the preparation time of centuries, layering each drink with nuance and complexity. All of this served in a dried gourd cup of cultural purport with a garnish of sundry linguistic, socioeconomic, and religious intrigues. Even today, Mexico's culinary influence on the world is underappreciated. This book will reacquaint the reader with the drinkable origins of globalized commodities like chocolate, corn, vanilla, pineapple, honey, cactus, oregano, chia seeds, peanuts, pumpkins, and more.

The reader will do well in understanding one central concept in Mexican culture. The idea of *mestizaje* represents the centuries of mixing between innumerable ethnicities and cultures that have coincided in the land between the Lacandon Jungle and the Sonoran Desert. The concept is not without its controversy. The process of forced cultural change began with Hernán Cortés's 1519 massacre in Cholula and continues today. History discounts the many unique and unknowable cultures of the groups who came to live in Mexico, imagining legal categories like the *castas* as representative identities of a gradually and benevolently mixed society. The continued hierarchy of race and heredity (within Mexico and internationally) has influenced and benefited from the culture of mestizaje more than anything else.

What mestizaje is meant to demonstrate here is that the collective language, gastronomy, and worldview of Mexico is not monolithic. These have developed over the centuries and become irreversibly entwined into something entirely new and ever-evolving. The story of Mexico's beverages is an example of the broader story of cultural intermingling and demarcation between Indigenous, European, African, Asian, and other influences.

In each of Mexico's drinks, we find a story that could exist nowhere else on Earth. In the collection of all of Mexico's drinks, we find a compelling story of Mexico itself.

2

Traditional Fermented Beverages

One of Mexico's richest and most diverse beverage traditions is that of fermentation. From the cactus wines of the country's northern deserts to the corn-dough drinks of the Guatemalan border, fermentation plays a fundamental role not only in what Mexicans drink today but also in what Mesoamericans have been drinking for millennia.

Traditional fermented beverages are part of an incredibly complex system of cultural knowledge that allows beverage makers to be masters of microbial metabolism. Those who brew traditional drinks in Mexico rely on many different points of control to coax out the right flavors and properties from a variety of microbes, including yeasts, molds, and bacteria. These invisible organisms transform the sugars in juices and saps and the starches in grains into alcohol, alongside other organic and flavorful compounds.

Fermentation, though, is a notoriously finicky process. Brewers in Mexico employ a toolkit of techniques that isolate environmental variables by intentionally selecting containers, ingredients, additives, temperatures, timeframes, exposures to sunlight, locations, and even superstitions. Combining these techniques to produce a consistent and desirable fermented beverage is an art that takes generations to develop and a lifetime to master. As a result of this, many of Mexico's traditional fermented beverages exist in only small pockets of rural society.

Speaking with practitioners of fermentation around Mexico, it becomes apparent that the labor of creating certain drinks is not always worth the financial reward. Such drinks are being pushed out of the sphere of viable economic activity and being relegated only to seasonal celebrations. It is not necessarily a bad thing for a drink to be prepared only for non-commercial ends, but it makes many of these beverages elusive and appear to be on the edge of extinction. To make things worse, modern food science has helped to popularize drinks like beer and soda while discrediting homemade ferments as supposedly unsanitary.

Another challenge which limits the distribution of fermented beverages is shelf life. Nearly all the traditional fermented drinks of Mexico are consumed with live microbial populations still in their contents. This factor makes these drinks extraordinary, but ephemeral by nature. They cannot be removed from their immediate surroundings without changing their character. Any effort to pasteurize such a fermented drink automatically compromises the true nature of that drink to begin with. Live yeast and bacteria have both positive and negative effects on the human body (particularly the gastrointestinal tract), so consumption of these ferments can be medicinal. Often, these beverages can only be prepared during a certain season when their primary material is ripening and must be consumed before they putrefy or turn into vinegar.

One comprehensive study on the topic of traditional Mexican fermented beverages, led by the ethnomicrobiologist César Ojeda-Linares, summarizes the modern problem:

> The traditional ecological knowledge involved in the preparation of fermented products appears to be at risk because of the overreliance on the massive campaigns of commercially produced beverages, which reach rural regions where the traditional products are prepared. This fact, as well as

> the decline of knowledge transfer and gaps in documenting the traditional know-how of local practices to manage the microbiota, ingredients, and fermentation process have favored the marginalization and disappearance of homemade fermented products.[1]

Indeed, for some beverages explored in this chapter, it is not immediately obvious if they still exist in Mexico today.

Inside the Fermentation

Only one factor unites all the drinks in this chapter—that they are fermented. Yet within this one process there is remarkable diversity that we are only just beginning to understand.

There are different kinds of yeasts, molds, and bacteria that contribute to fermentations by producing different flavor and nutritional compounds as they digest starches and sugars. Microbiologists are recently coming around to the fact that traditional processes in indigenous contexts might contain unique microbes that do not exist in fermentations elsewhere. That means these drinks could be one of a kind at a microscopic level. Of course, it has been 500 years since the Spanish brought their fermentation knowledge to the New World. Who knows to what degree a microbial Columbian Exchange has occurred in that time.

Mexico, in fact, has been at the vanguard of the field of microbiology, especially when it comes to research into fermented drinks. One of the forefathers of microbiology, Paul Lindner, came to Mexico to study fermented agave sap, called *pulque*, which will be covered later in this chapter, in the 1920s. Lindner's early efforts led to the identification of the bacterium *Zymomonas mobilis* (once called *Pseudomonas lindneri* after the researcher) in pulque and its ability to produce alcohol at a higher rate than some yeasts.

The German scientist had been contracted by the Secretaría de Industria to study *aguamiel*, or agave sap, and ultimately brought his research back to Europe where it was used in the beer industry.[2] Prior to Lindner's research in South Africa and Mexico, the world thought that alcohol was only generated by yeast.

The many fermentations of Mexican beverages contain bacteria like *Lactobacillus*, *Streptococcus*, and *Bacillus*, yeast like *Saccharomyces*, *Candida*, and *Brettanomyces*, and fungi like *Penicillium*, *Aspergillus*, and *Cladosporium*, among a long list of lesser-known names. The reality is that science does not yet have the bandwidth to appreciate the potential diversity that could exist even within one kind of drink prepared in different environments (i.e., pulque from one producer could contain different microbes than another). Still, there are exciting things happening in Mexican drinks that cannot be seen with the naked eye. Thankfully, the human tongue can sometimes taste these differences!

Fermenters in Mexico have codified cultural knowledge that helps them control these invisible populations for desired effects like flavor, strength, and stability. The many fermentation strategies employed in fermenting pulque elucidate just how resourceful Mexican brewers are.

Tlachiqueros, the men who make pulque, know how to create fermentation starters from scratch, sometimes called a *pie* ("foot") or *xinachtli*, by enclosing agave sap in a dried gourd to be rested in the sun for some time. Alternatively, pulque fermentation is facilitated using a *madre* ("mother") or *semilla* ("seed")—a more mature fermentation containing an existing and vibrant community of microbes. These fermenting dregs are natively called *xayotl*. Again, the *tinacales*, or brewhouses, in which pulque is traditionally fermented also store strains of the necessary microbes on their surfaces and, if we are to believe winemakers, in their atmospheric air. The vessels in which pulque ferments also contain microbes. Traditionally, animal hide containers, sometimes called *toros*, were used for fresh sap and finished pulque was transported in *odres* ("goatskins"). Finally, agave sap itself contains naturally occurring yeasts and bacteria. The quality of a finished pulque depends on the original qualities of the sap, but also on the tlachiquero's ability to curate the optimal microbial population across all these potential moments of inoculation.

The Origins of Mesoamerican Fermented Drinks

Controlling fermentation is difficult and transmitting knowledge of fermentation between producers is challenging. But acquiring that knowledge in the first place is somewhat up to fate. That is, alcoholic fermentation is not a given part of human society. Mexico, of all places, is a perfect demonstration of this point. While most of Asia, Europe, and Africa practiced some form of alcoholic fermentation since ancient times, other regions of the world never independently developed that form of food biotechnology. North America, adjacent to the fermentation-frenzied land of the Uto-Aztecan realm, is one such region where alcohol did not find a place in transmitted cultural knowledge.

Little pre-Columbian evidence of alcoholic fermentation exists northwest of the Gila River in present-day Arizona or northeast of the mountains of New Mexico. Some nineteenth-century anthropological reports detail indigenous North American alcohols like persimmon wine for the Cherokee, berry wine for the Creek, maple and sassafras brews for the Iroquois, corn beer for the Huron, manzanita berry wine for the tribes of California, and a drink made from the sweet excretions of aphids which feed on the *Phragmites communis* reeds for the Northern Paiute.[3] But some of these examples are more likely the result of the diffusion of knowledge after contact with Europeans and Mesoamerican peoples. Ultimately, we find a dearth of mythologies of native North American alcoholic beverages like those that exist in much of the rest of the world (e.g., Du Kang in China, Dionysos in the Mediterranean, and Mayahuel in Mesoamerica).

Why did alcoholic fermentation stop at the northern edge of Mexico's deserts? Several theories have been put forward. Some suggest that the foundational use of hallucinogens or tobacco in North American religion would have devalued alcohol as a potential entheogen. Looking at how Mesoamericans happily mixed alcohol with both hallucinogens and tobacco in drinks like pulque with psilocybin mushrooms, this is unfounded. Others note that corn cultivation came to North America rather late, several hundred years after tobacco, giving the smoked herb cultural precedent over fermented drinks.[4] An alternate explanation points to the Pueblo communities that straddled the Mesoamerican and North American worlds and their cultural penchant for temperance and sobriety—a sort of dry wall between realms.[5] A more likely explanation is that Mesoamerica was home to a more sedentary, agricultural, and hierarchical society. Generally, there is a correlation between farming and fermenting. Calendars, harvest cycles, and institutionalized religion found use in alcoholic beverages. Most North American peoples practiced foraging, hunter-gathering, seasonal migration, and otherwise nomadic ways of life. Sure, alcoholic fermentation almost definitely occurred in North America, but the paucity of evidence suggests that it would have been isolated and rarely codified in tradition as it was in Mesoamerica.

Given its relative absence to the north, we should not take widespread alcoholic fermentation in Mesoamerica and South America for granted. Humans arrived in the Americas well over 10,000 years ago, perhaps before alcoholic fermentation existed in any global culture. The absence of fermentation in the north (whence humans migrated from the Bering Strait down to Patagonia) confirms that alcoholic fermentation was developed independently in the New World. This independent and local innovation is reflected in Mesoamerican culture. Myths abound between different ethnic groups as to how their ancestors first learned to transform daily food crops into inebriating and healing beverages.

Pulque, for one, is associated with an entire pantheon of Aztec gods who are sometimes termed the "pulque cult" (cult, in this context, indicates a religious grouping or sect with dedicated priests). The goddess Mayahuel is synonymous with the agave, and her breast milk is often identified with the plant's fermentable sap. The pre-Columbian addition of a root that supposedly made pulque stronger was attributed to the ingenuity of a god named Pátecatl whose name meant "the One from the Land of Medicine," as these roots were *octpatli* ("pulque medicine"). Other myths recount the sudden invention of pulque by certain individuals like Lord Papantzin for the Toltec. The Mixtec attributed its discovery to the *Tlacuache* (Possum) who stole the blood of the dismembered goddess 11 Serpent, which became pulque.

It is not just pulque. The Wixárika of Mexico's Sierra Madre Occidental attribute the origin of their entire culture to the gift of the fermented corn drink, *naawá* (also called *tejuino*) from the deity Blue Deer or Kauyumari.[6] Even natives in the highlands of Chiapas have stories about how Jesus Christ brought the post-contact sugarcane beer known as *chicha* into the world.[7] Fermentation, passed on by ancestors and unexplained by science, was often attributed to divine intervention.

Healthy and Diverse Drinks

In addition to its cultural significance, fermentation enriches the nutritional value of the foods it touches. Yeast, bacteria, and molds add protein, probiotics, and vitamins to otherwise starchy foods. Many colonial commentators believed that pure pulque was a healthy part of the Mexican diet, helping with diarrhea among other things. In 1896, a Poblano physician named Francisco Martínez

Baca discovered that pulque could cure scurvy in prisoners. At the time, the world did not even know what vitamin C was. Other fermented drinks like tepache and huapilla are well established hangover cures and help to rehydrate in hot climates.

Not all of Mexico's traditional fermented beverages are alcoholic. Some, in fact, have only trace amounts of alcohol and are widely consumed by all members of society, including children. This is because fermentations are facilitated by a variety of different microbes in a variety of different settings. For some beverages in Mexico, fermentation occurs in a liquid. For others, it occurs in a solid (like corn-dough pozol). Many fermentations are alcoholic, with sugars being converted into alcohol molecules. Still, other fermentations focus on the creation of lactic acid, as well as other aromatic and biologically useful compounds.

Yet, as the world has come to understand fermentation at a more scientific level, we have begun to lose the art of fermentation as a cultural practice. Our understanding of microbes has driven us to a blanket policy of pasteurization. These last two centuries have witnessed what is perhaps the greatest contraction in fermented products in history. Mexican fermented drinks are also on the retreat. We must appreciate where these beverages came from, where they are today, and where they might be headed in the future.

* * *

Balché

Balché is a traditional Maya mead produced from the honey of stingless bees, pure cenote water, and the bark of the balché tree (*Lonchocarpus longistylus*). Each of these ingredients is unique to the Yucatán Peninsula.

The Maya and other peoples of the Yucatán have been devout beekeepers for thousands of years. The pre-Columbian Codex Tro-Cortesianus contains several folio pages depicting bees, apiculture, and honey. While the Yucatán is home to over a dozen varieties of native bee species, the Maya rely on the *Melipona beecheii*, locally known as *X unáan kàab* or *X ko'olel kàab*, meaning "Fine Lady of the Honey" or "Woman of the Honey," respectively. Beekeepers today also endearingly refer to their bees as *abejitas* ("little bees"). According to one contemporary beekeeper in Maní, Yucatán, keepers do not own the bees but simply care for them. The bees are free to leave at any time. While stingless, the bees can bite, though it is not particularly painful.

These bees do not produce combs; rather, they construct storage sacs for honey. Fray Diego de Landa, bishop of Yucatán, observed the strange hives in the sixteenth century, writing, "They do not make honeycomb as ours do, but a kind of small blisters like walnuts of wax all joined one to the other and full of honey. To cut them away they do nothing more than to open the hives and to break away these blisters with a small stick, and thus the honey runs out and they take the wax when they please."[8] The Maya call the bubbles of honey *lek*.

The production and consumption of balché is tied up in the spiritual processes of beekeeping. In the Maya pantheon, Ah-Muzen-Cab is the god of apiculture. Pivotal steps in beekeeping, including the splitting of colonies between two new hollow log hives (called *hobones*) or the harvesting of honey, mandate religious rituals. For example, in Maní, beekeepers offer sacred corn atole, called *saká* or *sakab*, in *jícara* ("gourd") cups, sweetened with the year's first harvest of honey to ensure a bountiful collection in April. They also prepare twelve tamales from wild meat, like venison, turtle, or iguana. The last Saturday in October, they offer balché to ward off predators, ensure good rain, and pray that the bees find the blooming flowers that they seek. Often, they present jícaras of balché and saká in the four cardinal directions or along the flight path of bees to their food.

Both the Maya palate and language are finely attuned to the flavors of honeys produced by bees feeding on certain plants. In fact, to feed their bees, the Maya planted gardens of flowers, while corn served as food during the dry season.[9] *Chakàah*, for example, is the specific word for honey of the *Bursera simaruba* tree which has a caramelized, herbal, and spicy flavor.[10] *Xa'an* honey is from the *Sabal yapa* palm and has an acidic fermented taste and a clear yellow color.[11] Nowadays, true Melipona honey is extremely expensive (costing up to $100 USD per liter) and has largely been replaced by honey from the more productive European bee, *Apis mellifera*, which arrived in the Yucatán in the 1910s, facilitated by biologist Dr. Geoffrey Gaumer. Still, melipona honey has unique properties that make it special.

Next to honey, the water used in fermenting balché is equally unique to the land, coming from subterranean cenotes. Maya men collected, *Zuhuy Ha*, or Virgin Water, from the many natural pristine wells of the peninsula. One modern balché producer insisted that any filtered water would do.

Finally, the bark of the balché tree acted as a flavoring agent and, perhaps, a fermentation inoculator. The balché is the *Lonchocarpus longistylus* tree. The tree must have a trunk of a reasonable size before the bark can be peeled. Nowadays, some versions of balché may contain powdered anise, cinnamon, and even cane liquor.

The mead is a highly ritualistic beverage. Thus, the production of the drink is also a ritual. Traditionally, Maya men took turns fermenting balché in canoe-like troughs called *chem*. Following colonization, women were increasingly involved in the production ritual as well.[12] The Maya still consume balché at milestone life events, offer it to idols, and employ it as a sort of medicine. When breaking ground on a new plot of farmland, or *milpa*, workers brew balché to appease the *aluxo'ob* or *aluxes* (invisible sprites that live on the farm and in nature) who would otherwise cause them mischief.

Consumption is also steeped in superstition. Drinking balché may seduce the object of one's desire.[13] When preparing balché, a folk belief suggests that the brewer balance kernels of corn on a censer to ward off the negative effects of a balché hangover.[14] For a more medicinal brew, the *propolis* ("bee resin") is added, giving it an opaque color and a more bitter flavor. The Maya believe that drinking balché kills intestinal worms.[15]

Due to the importance of balché to Maya culture and religion, the Spanish Inquisition outlawed the production of the beverage, punishing anyone found with shavings of the balché tree bark. They went so far as to systematically cut all balché trees indiscriminately. Still consumed today, balché is no longer made from the purely indigenous substances it once was.

Cebadina

Cebadina is a refreshing beverage best known in the city of León, Guanajuato. It is a lightly fermented mix of barley (whence it gets its name), pineapple tepache, tamarind, and hibiscus. Traditionally, it is fermented in wooden barrels and served with a spoonful of baking soda dumped into the drink at the time of service for an added explosion of effervescence.

The drink is new and has a definitive origin story. According to the Guanajuato Secretariat of Tourism, a man named Ramón Arrieta moved from Guadalajara to León in 1945 and introduced the beverage in a stall on the plaza. He later opened another shop in the city of Irapuato. The people of Guanajuato enjoy the quenching drink on hot days.

This story is true, but there is a long-standing tradition dating back to the eighteenth century of fermenting barley and pineapple into a drink sometimes called *zambumbia.*[16] Historical recipes for both chicha and beer in New Spain included the same ingredients of barley, pineapple, and tamarind, with the additions of lime and corn. Modern cebadina is not necessarily an isolated or novel recipe.

It is possible to find versions of cebadina outside of Guanajuato, but these are derivatives of the original 1945 recipe.

Chicha

Chicha is a generic term for fermented alcoholic beverages that exist across Latin America, ranging from indigenous Patagonian brews made from Chilean strawberries to the northernmost uses of the term, which coincide with fermented sugarcane or corn drinks in southern Mexico. In Latin America, the distribution of the term "chicha" was facilitated by Spanish colonization.

As early as the 1520s, the Spanish may have described beverages in modern-day Mexico as "chicha." A sixteenth-century author, the so-called Anonymous Conquistador, wrote, "Another is called Chicha, and this is made from the grain which they eat, and is of different kinds, red and white."[17] This early reference likely describes atole, a corn-based beverage. However, the text of this account was only preserved in an Italian manuscript from the second half of the sixteenth century, perhaps superimposing a slightly later use of the word "chicha" into the earlier context of the original Conquest of Tenochtitlán.

In Chiapas, chicha has been associated with Tzotzil indigenous communities in the highlands who distill a corn-and-sugarcane spirit called *pox*. Chicha is the undistilled base alcohol for this spirit. It is made of sugarcane juice, *piloncillo* (the solid form of pure boiled sugarcane and molasses), or corn.

A late eighteenth-century report described chicha in New Spain as being prepared from barley water, pineapple, honey, and corn left to ferment for 4 days, then sweetened and spiced, and fermented for 4 more days.[18]

Chamuco

Chamuco is a multifaceted term that refers to a few different beverages based on unrefined, solid sugar. The most basic definition of the word is that of "Satan," "devil," or "evil spirit" in Spanish. In Mexico, "Chamuco" is also the name of a sweet pastry from Aguascalientes.

In a historical context, chamuco was a fermented beverage made from red plum mixed with piloncillo. The fermentation of the native plums, or *ciruelas*, is indigenous, and Hernán Cortés noted the plums' presence at the Market of Tlatelolco in his *Segunda Carta de Relación*. In Jalisco, red hog plums are also called *ciruelas borracheras*, meaning "drunken plums," suggesting they were once commonly fermented into a wine.[19]

Chanuco with an "n" is also listed as a beverage in the annals of Mexican history. Typically, chanuco is defined as a type of cider with piloncillo added, which is a suitable, if not slightly broader, description for chamuco as well. In eighteenth-century New Spain, there existed two interchangeable names for a drink, "*chuámico*" and "*chuanuco*," that was made with plums or any other sweet fruit and the addition of *panocha* (another word for piloncillo).[20]

Chancuco with an added "c" is also the name of a local aguardiente made from *panela* (still another word for piloncillo) in Aldana, Nariño, in Colombia. Based on the varied spellings of chamuco through time and across space, we take the common denominator of alcohol made with some type of piloncillo and make an educated guess as to the etymology of these similar drink names. *Chancaca*, in fact, is yet another word for piloncillo, which the *Diccionario de la Real Academia Española* suggests could derive from a Nahuatl term for sugar—*chiancaca*. This is likely the ultimate root word, referencing the defining sweetener of all these drinks. The Castilian introduction of the devilish Chamuco has simply overlaid on these different sugar-based alcohols.

To add a final level of complication, some Mexican bars have co-opted the word chamuco in recent years as a name for a cocktail that mixes mezcal or tequila with chile liqueur and tamarind. This is simply a hellish, fiery, red drink referencing the devil.

Colonche

Colonche is the fermented wine of the prickly pear cactus, primarily from the *Opuntia cardona* and *Opuntia streptacantha* species, though there are dozens of varieties that vary in color from green to red and flavor from sour to sweet. The *tuna cardona* is the most popular variety of prickly pear fruit due to its high sugar content. In the Altiplano region, where wild prickly pears dominate the landscape, both the fruit and plant are a key part of the diet. For centuries, people have harvested the *tunas* ("cactus fruits"), mashed them, and fermented them into a kind of wine.

The season for colonche starts in August and peaks in September. This is when the prickly pears are most ripe, though the harvest is highly dependent on annual rainfall. Producers go to the wild-growing *tunales* ("tuna fields") in the morning to harvest fruit. Instead of picking individual fruits, a section of the green cactus paddle is cut off for convenience. Once in hand, *coloncheros* or *coloncheras* remove the fruits and use wild-growing herbs to clean the spines. These herbs include *escoba*, meaning "broom" (name recorded in Mezquitic de Carmona, San Luis Potosí), *limpiatuna*, meaning "prickly-pear-cleaner" (name recorded in Tepotzotlán, Mexico), or *pirul* of the *Schinus molle* tree (usage recorded in Laguna de Guadalupa, Guanajuato).

To remove the pulp, the top of the fruit is sliced off, lateral slices are cut, and the pulp is squeezed or scooped out. From this point, different regions and producers follow different processes to instigate fermentation. In Mezquitic de Carmona, for example, coloncheras boil their fruit pulp and strain it, at times using special clay colanders that prevent seeds from going through. In Guanajuato, on the other hand, it is the cactus seeds themselves that are used to transfer microbes from one fermentation to another—even being exchanged between producers. Some producers just add pulque. Still other fermentations are spontaneous from microbes on the fruit.

The juice is left to ferment for a short period of time, usually 1 to 2 days. With each day, it increases in alcohol content. The wine of colonche is usually red or pink in color. It is slightly effervescent, lightly sweet, mildly tart, and refreshing. There is also *colonche blanco* ("white colonche") made from green tunas. One producer in Guanajuato confirmed that *xoconostle*, a tart variety of prickly pear used in salsas and stews, could also be used to make a sour wine.

In Guanajuato, producers age their colonche as if it were grape wine. Bottles keep for several years. The flavor deepens with time and develops a port-like brown color. Some modern producers age the wine in wooden barrels.

Colonche is not the only term that has been used to refer to a fermented prickly pear beverage. In the eighteenth century, *chiquito* apparently referred to fermented tuna juice, as did *revoltijo*.[21] While some modern coloncheras do add pulque to begin fermentation, there has historically been the drink *sangre de conejo*, meaning "rabbit's blood." This brew was a mixture of pulque, prickly pears, plantains, guava, cinnamon, and cloves.

Colonche production is at risk of disappearing due to a lack of interest in learning the fermentation process from younger generations.[22] The drink still exists throughout the Altiplano in rural communities where cacti grow wild. The state of San Luis Potosí, specifically, has long been associated with colonche. The cactus wine is available for sale on Sundays in late August or early September across the dam in Mexquitic de Carmona, outside of the capital city, San Luis Potosí. There is also an annual festival, the Feria del Colonche, in Laguna de Guadalupe, Guanajuato.

Guarapo

Guarapo is both the sweet, pressed juice of sugarcane and, more often, the fermented juice of sugarcane. It is common around Mexico for street vendors to sell *jugo de caña* ("cane juice") made on the spot from cane squeezed with motorized presses on portable carts. When boiled and left to ferment for several days, that juice becomes guarapo.

The term "guarapo" arrived in Mexico from the Caribbean islands. The linguistic origins of the word are African.[23] Sugarcane crossed the Atlantic, first arriving in the Canary Islands, where the term "guarapo" is also used to refer to the fermented juice. While sugarcane guarapo is far more common in South American countries like Colombia or Venezuela, Mexican usages of the word include more than just sugarcane. In Tabasco, the Chontales, a specific group of Maya, are known for making *guarapo de maiz* with roasted corn. At times, fermented pineapple, usually called tepache, is called *guarapo de piña*. *Chilote* is a kind of corn, pulque, chile, and sugarcane guarapo drunk in Guerrero and Oaxaca.

Huapilla

Huapilla is a lightly fermented beverage made from the fruit of the *Bromelia pinguin* plant, locally called huapilla or *guapilla*. It could be considered a *tepache* of this specific fruit in certain contexts, although it is usually consumed as an *agua fresca* and is produced in a similar manner to *lechuguilla*. It is extremely common in the coastal city of Tampico and is also consumed in neighboring regions of Veracruz, where it is known as *cardón*. A drink called *timbirichi* is prepared similarly from other species of the *Bromelia* genus. Huapilla tastes like a light cider of pineapple or apple. Proud locals also compare the drink to champagne. It is both effervescent and semi-dry most of the time.

The huapilla plant is native to Mexico and is a close relative to the pineapple as both are in the *Bromeliaceae* family. The plant resembles the pineapple with a stem in the middle from which a bundle of lime-sized, yellow-orange fruits grows. In the region where the beverage is known, mainly in the tropical, culturally Huasteca area of Tamaulipas and Veracruz, the fruit is mature from August until December. Most of the plants that are harvested are wild, although the plants are also intentionally cultivated as fences and boundary markers. There is evidence that indigenous peoples also used the plant as food in times of scarcity in certain areas of the Huasteca region.[24] The flower of the plant is eaten in rural communities in Veracruz.

To prepare huapilla, Tampiqueños ferment the fruits for 3 to 6 months. The resulting fermentation is referred to as a *concentrado* ("concentrate") and is mixed with water and sugar (to taste) in a ratio of about 1 liter concentrate to

4 liters of water. The resulting mixture is the commonly consumed huapilla. The alcoholic content of the beverage is negligible, although fermentation will continue until the beverage degrades into vinegar.

It is a common daily refreshment and must be sold cold. Vendors sell the drink roaming the streets of Tampico with carts and at corner stands. The drink is typically consumed in bags with straws. At least one commercial bottled brand of the drink also exists. Many vendors in the city of Tampico attribute curative properties to the drink, particularly associating it with the cleansing of the kidneys. Humorously, one Tampiqueño brand uses the term *huapillosa* to refer to the models who promote the drink.

Lapo

Lapo is a regional variety of pulque fermented with piloncillo or sugarcane juice, though other recipes call for a mix of pulque, piloncillo, and mezcal. Lapo is embedded in local Poblano culture and is predominantly consumed during celebrations and festivities. Today, it is closely associated with the tradition of La Matanza, or the slaughter of goats that occurs each year in October and November. During the slaughter, locals cook *mole de caderas*, a goat dish, which is traditionally paired with lapo. The drink is served in a red jícara or hollow cane tubes.

The native Popoloca people have used lapo in marriage ceremonies, specifically the rite of Tetlahuantis, which is the presentation of a courting suitor to the family of his future bride. Two to three weeks before the ceremony, the suitor's father begins preparing lapo, and his bachelor friends spend each night pressing more sugarcane into wooden vessels to ferment.[25] They mix the fermented juice with pulque and present it to the young woman's family alongside rum and cigarettes.

There are barely any traditional producers of the drink left, but modern production exists in both San José Miahuatlán and San Gabriel Chilac.[26]

One informant noted that the drink existed in nearby Ajalpan. Nevertheless, production of lapo is extremely isolated, and it competes with other regional fermented beverages like *nochocle*, pure pulque, and *licor de garambullo*.

Lechuguilla

In the state of Jalisco, especially in the town of Autlán, lechuguilla is a nonalcoholic fermented beverage made by soaking chunks of a species of *Agave* locally called lechuguilla in water for several days. The drink is unique in that the agave is uncooked. The *piña* ("core") of the agave is chopped up and covered in water. Sugar is added to the fermentation. As the liquid ferments, the drink is removed each day and the volume replaced with fresh water. In this way, the piña of one agave can give lechuguilla for several months.

The drink is considered refreshing and medicinal. Autlán, Jalisco has a significant artisanal market for the beverage, but it is also found on the streets of Guadalajara. This kind of lechuguilla in Jalisco should not be confused with the Sonoran agave spirit by the same name.

Miztli

Historically, a fermented drink has been produced from fermented mesquite pods in the Altiplano region of Mexico where the mesquite tree has been a source of food for indigenous peoples. Miztli is the only name that is found in the scholarship discussing this drink.

Even in the 1930s, researchers did not report any existing mesquite fermentations, though the Cocopah, Akimel O'odham, Tohono O'odham, and Tepehuan have all once produced such a drink.[27] The sixteenth-century priest Sahagún described a fermented drink made from the inner bark of the mesquite tree. Finally, some reports indicate that communal vats of fermenting mesquite pods existed, but for chewing not necessarily drinking.

American botanist Edmund Jaeger described the process: "From this [crushed mesquite seeds] a cake was made and either dried in the sun or baked. Sometimes the Indians soaked the flour in water to make atole, a gruel-like sweet drink. If the infusion was allowed to ferment it resulted in an intoxicating drink of considerable alcohol content."[28] Some modern ethnography suggests that mesquite fermentations predated those of corn in the American Southwest.[29] Finally, a modern researcher reported a personal conversation with the chronicler of Jalpa, Zacatecas, named Héctor Pascual Gómez Soto, saying that the community used a fermented mesquite drink during festivities in the not so distant past.[30] It is from this source that we get the name miztli, which is some derivative of the Nahuatl *mizquitl* for mesquite.

Vino tepemé was a drink reportedly produced by indigenous groups at the end of the 1700s made from wild agave leaf juice boiled with mesquite twigs.[31] No version of a fermented mesquite drink could be located today. There is, however, still atole and agua fresca made from mesquite pods in both Mexico and the southwestern United States.

Nawait

Nawait is the fermented wine of several species of columnar cacti in the Sonoran Desert of both the United States and Mexico. The drink was traditionally produced by the Tohono O'odham, Akimel O'odham, Maricopa, and Seri (Comcáac) peoples. The drink is also called *haren*.

The Sonoran Desert is home to two massive species of columnar cacti, the saguaro, *Carnegiea gigantea*, and the organ pipe cactus, *Lemaireocereus thurberi*. Indigenous people have made wine from both. However, due to the height of these cacti, harvesting poles are required to pick the ripe fruits. The best harvesting poles are the dried vertical ribs of the deceased cacti themselves. The saguaro fruits come into season during June and July.

Traditionally, the fruits are peeled, crushed, fermented in vats kept warm by fire, sun, or blankets, and then strained into a clay vessel.

Outside observers have taken note of the region's penchant for making cactus wine since at least the Coronado expedition of July 1540 to April 1542. The Tohono O'odham still consume the wine ritualistically as part of a rain-bringing ceremony. Their traditional yearly calendar starts with the ripening of the saguaro fruit.[32]

Nochocle

Nochocle, also *nochoctli*, is a cactus wine fermented from the fruit of columnar cacti in the Tehuacán-Cuicatlán Valley of Puebla and Oaxaca. There is some overlap in the usage of the two terms *colonche* and *nochocle*, but they are distinct beverages due to the varieties of cacti used. Colonche, generally, is fermented from prickly pear varieties, while nochocle is made from columnar varieties. This is significant, given that the world of cacti is divided into two main sub-families: *opuntias* that include prickly pears and *cactoids* that include columnar species. Specifically, in southern Puebla, columnar fruits of a species known as *cardón* are used for fermenting. This common name is confusing, as colonche makers in San Luis Potosí prefer to use tuna cardona, a kind of prickly pear. The different fruits are likely called the same thing simply because they are both red in color. Poblano producers use the term "cardón" to describe *Neobuxbaumia macrocephala* or other columnar species in the same genus.

These fruits come into season in mid-April and last until early May. Those who make nochocle must harvest the ripe fruit early in the morning before the sun makes them burst. The fruits are cleaned, their pulp is filtered of seeds, and pulque is added to kickstart a fermentation. A locally renowned vendor of nochocle in Coxcatlán, Puebla, suggested that the addition of too much pulque changes the drink into a variety of tepache. It ferments for one day and is consumed as a non-inebriating refreshment. Today, nochocle production is largely a household activity with very little commercial production. In Coxcatlán, local belief suggests that the drink was once reserved for royalty.

Ostoche

Ostoche, also written *oztótzi*, is made from fermented corn stalk juice. While some sources claim it still exists in Puebla today, modern evidence is nearly nonexistent.

However, as a drink, ostoche highlights a little-discussed legacy in traditional fermented drinks in Mexico—the use of corn stalk juice. Sugarcane did not arrive in Mexico until the Spanish did, but Mesoamericans have been pressing the sweet stalks of maize since the distant past. In fact, Cortés wrote in his *Segunda Carta de Relación* that a kind of honey pressed from corn stalks was sold alongside real honey in Tenochtitlán's massive Tlatelolco marketplace. There is even a theory (dubbed the Sweet Stalk Theory) that suggests corn may have been domesticated and propagated over such a broad range of the Americas, not for its ears of corn, but for its sweet stalks (not only to make alcohol, but also to chew).[33]

Ostoche was known as the fermented mix of cornstalk juice and water nearly three centuries ago.[34] Moreover, the infamous *quebrantahuesos*, or "bone-breaker," was a sort of fermented cocktail found in the Central Valley concocted of cornstalk juice, toasted corn, and the red peppercorns of the *Schinus molle* tree. Another Poblano cornstalk drink, called *cuaruapa*, included the bark of *palo de timbre* and piloncillo. One version recorded in Veracruz in the eighteenth century was called *tazlcóm* by the Totonac people.[35]

Cornstalk juice was still commonly fermented in the early twentieth century, including by the Rarámuri who sometimes made their tesgüiño out of a mix of germinated corn and cornstalk juice, or out of cornstalk juice alone. The cornstalk version was known as *patcili* and involved pounding clean stalks, wringing them out in a net made from yucca that was strung between two poles, boiling the juice, adding a root, and fermenting for 5 days.[36] There are likely still isolated uses of fermented cornstalk juice, but the drink was decidedly more prominent in the past than it is today.

Pulque

Pulque is the fermented sap of several species of *Agave*, collectively known as *magueyes pulqueros*. These are most often the larger species including *Agave atrovirens*, *mapsiaga*, *americana*, and *salmiana* (also called *manso*). The Central Valley of Mexico, particularly the states of Hidalgo, Tlaxcala, and Mexico, is most specialized for pulque production. Pulque, known in Nahuatl as *octli*, was the most noteworthy beverage in pre-Columbian Mexica culture due to its associations with class, religion, and festival. It remained the most popular alcoholic beverage during both the viceregal and independence eras until its relatively recent decline following the Mexican Revolution of the 1910s.

With agave as the foundational foodstuff of many Mesoamerican cultures, pulque is the prototypical alcoholic beverage for the region.

How is pulque produced? Pulque is produced at the end of an agave's lifecycle because the plant has stored significant energy in the form of sugar to reproduce. Agaves are monocarpic, meaning they flower only once during their life cycle just before dying. As the massive *quiote* ("central flower stalk") of the agave sprouts after 8 to 12 years of growth, a *tlachiquero* ("pulque producer") will chop the stem off at its base, a process aptly referred to as castration. Some producers brand the agave after castration to mark the date of cutting.

The tlachiquero will wait for anywhere from 10 days to about 6 months and begin to scrape the center of the agave where the stem was cut. A special metal spoon with a wide blade is used to hollow out a bowl in the navel of the agave and scrape the surface of the wound twice daily. The process of scraping, called *raspando*, is the origin of the name of the profession tlachiquero, which is derived from the term "to scrape" in Nahuatl. Pulque is sometimes even called *tlachique* (or *tlapehue*), which might translate as "scrapings." When unattended, the carved-out hollow is covered with a stone, a dried agave *penca* ("leaf"), or a piece of plastic to protect it from the environment, precipitation, and insects.

After scraping the center of the agave, the wound will ooze a sweet sap called *aguamiel*. The tlachiquero will suck the aguamiel out of the center of the agave two times a day. During rainy periods, they perform a third extraction so that the pooling sap is not watered down. Traditionally, the siphoning of sap was performed with a gourd called an *acocote* operated with the mouth. Now, it is common for tlachiqueros to use two-liter Coca-Cola bottles with a tube inserted into them. They use their armpits to crush and expand the bottle, generating a vacuum. Aguamiel, unfermented, is also a common beverage and has a silky texture and herbaceous and sweet flavor.

Once they remove the pooled sap, they scrape the wound again for the next harvest and bring the aguamiel back to the *tinacal* ("fermentation room"), where it is mixed with already fermented sap to begin fermentation. Most tinacales rely on plastic barrels for fermentation, but traditional ones used animal skin vats, or *toros*. Once a tlachiquero begins extracting sap from a plant, a single healthy agave can produce up to 7 liters of aguamiel a day for anywhere from three to six months. Once exhausted, the agave shrivels and dies. The wizened agave hearts, called *ñonfis*, and the exhausted leaves, called *mezote*, were once harvested and used as firewood or to produce *ixtle* fiber to be woven into *ayate* agave fabric.[37]

Octli in Mesoamerica. Pulque, originally called *octli* in the Aztec Nahuatl, has been produced for thousands of years. However, the Tale of the Mexica Migration told in the Codex Boturini explains how the drink was first invented around the year 5-Técpatl, which is humorously recent—about 1276 CE.[38]

Aztec religion would enshrine the agave in the fertility goddess Mayahuel. A cult, or smaller religious following, was led by the priests of Mayahuel and subordinate pulque gods known as the Centzontotochtin, or 400 Rabbits.

These rabbits represented the infinite emotions one feels when drunk (the number 400 represented the uncountable in Aztec culture). These pulque gods had their own building in the central Aztec Temple Mayor, called the Centzontotochtininteopan. If an individual was born on the calendar day Ome Tochtli, or 2-Rabbit, they would be astrologically destined to be an alcoholic.

More than a dozen named gods were part of the extensive pulque cult, including the gods Tepoztecatl, Papaztac, Yauhtecatl, Toltecatl, Pátecatl, Tezcatzoncatl, Tlaltecayoua, Colhuatzincatl, Totoltecatl, Tlilhua, Acolhua, Izquitecatl, Chimalpanecatl, Tomixauh, Quatlapanqui, Nappatecutli, Naualpilli, and two goddesses, Mayahuel and Atlacoaya. Atlacoaya was the goddess of the drought—hinting at the utility of desert-tolerant agave sap as a source of hydration when and where water was scarce. When depicted in the codices and in pre-Columbian art, the pulque gods are identified by their crescent moon nose rings (called *yacametztli*), black and red mantles, distinctive shields, and obsidian hatchets.

The famous German Mesoamericanist Eduard Seler wrote of the pulque gods, "that these gods were, in their nature and essence, harvest gods. For when the harvest was brought in, when there was once again an abundance of food, then it was time to prepare pulque or other intoxicating drinks and to celebrate the new harvest blessing with wild feasts."[39] During the Aztec period, only the elderly, priestly, and warrior classes were allowed to drink pulque, except on festival days when the entire population could indulge. The Codex Borgia depicts a jaguar (a symbol of the warrior and courageous souls) in front of a pulque god. Elsewhere, the bellicose relationship is depicted with both an eagle and a jaguar in reference to the title of *cuauhtlocelotl* (Eagle-Jaguar Warrior) earned by the bravest Mexica warriors. Victims of human sacrifice would generally consume pulque on the eve of their ritual death to fill them with divine euphoria.

Pulque in New Spain. As the first wave of Spanish conquistadors moved inland from Veracruz, Bernal Díaz del Castillo described vats of "wine of the country" stored underground in the conquered Huastec communities of Chila along the Panuco River. When Cortés described the Aztec capital's vast and organized marketplace, he noted the presence of wine made from agave sap. After the fall of Tenochtitlán, pulque became an increasingly secular beverage and bars, called *pulquerías*, sold the drink to the masses. At first, pulque remained mostly an indigenous commodity, but nearly all sects of colonial New Spain came to drink the sap. Still, the drink retained some of its former holiness. As late as Jacinto de la Serna's 1656 account, pulque was still being poured into fire as a libation, offering, or sacrifice.

Where the Crown outlawed virtually all alcohol production in New Spain, pulque was consistently viewed as an exception. In 1529, the first Spanish legislation was passed on pulque which did not ban the drink itself but outlawed the addition of a medicinal root into the fermentation of the drink. The law would then vacillate between banning pulque and taxing its sale. In both 1545 and 1607, pulque was prohibited entirely by royal decrees. In 1608, the Justicias y Ministros de Doctrina formally authorized the sale of pulque again. A second illegalization of pulque occurred from 1692 to 1697 following an uprising that supposedly arose from discontent sown in pulquerías.[40]

Throughout the colonial period, the viceregal government pitted its sober, Christianizing mission against pulque's drunken-but-lucrative tax haul. For nearly 300 years, bans on pulque resulting from perceived sinful or uncivilized behavior were dismissed by new tax initiatives. But the August 1608 Ordinance of the eleventh (and previously also ninth) viceroy, Luis de Velasco, kicked off the official regulation of commercial pulque sales, empowering *justicias* in each pueblo to grant licenses to indigenous vendors.[41] The viceroyalty went on to develop the *Asiento de Pulque* in 1668 and 1669 to tax pulque and the agaves from which it was produced.

Pulque production had remained in the hands of indigenous peoples for the first two centuries of conquest. But, by the second half of the 1700s, haciendas in Apan, Hidalgo began to replace cattle with agave. Pulque first came to Apan, which would later become synonymous with mass-produced pulque in the nineteenth century, in 1730 when Jesuits and the Count of Xala, Manuel Rodríguez de Pedroso, began to produce it.[42] Pulque was an attractive investment. One of New Spain's richest men, the silver-mining mogulPedro Romero de Terreros, Conde de Regla, bought five previously Jesuit-owned haciendas around Ciudad de México to produce the drink.[43] Toward the turn of the nineteenth century, more than 215,000 mules entered Ciudad de México carrying an estimated 24 million liters of pulque annually.[44]

As the viceroyalty reached its final years, the fiscal importance of pulque came to light. As the Bourbon Reforms sought to restore taxing authority into the hands of the Crown, the 1754 *administración directa* ("direct administration") tax regime led to the creation of the Dirección General de Alcabalas y Pulques in the 1770s. As Spain wrangled in entrenched private tax collectors who had long managed New Spain's *alcabalas* ("sales taxes"), pulque was deemed a titular part of the colonial tax bureau.

Pulque in Independent Mexico. Pulque's popularity would increase as modernization helped drive a pulque frenzy. In the nineteenth century, houses selling pulque would advertise their wares by hanging agave pencas outside their doors as a sort of sign.[45] By the 1860s, trains were built between the population center of Ciudad de México and pulque producing regions like Apizaco, Mexico, or Apan, Hidalgo. Around this time, Countess Paula Kolonitz, a friend of Empress Carlota, the wife of the short-lived Maximilian I of Mexico, wrote, "wine and beer are drunk little, but the pulque is never missing from the table of the rich."[46]

Tight control on the number of pulquerías licensed to operate that had been in place for a century was dissolved in 1871, establishing free trade of pulque as a commodity which drove a proliferation in drinking establishments. Wealthy men in Ciudad de México came to control the haciendas and pulquerías and have been dubbed the "Pulque Aristocracy" of the Porfiriato era.

Consumption grew steadily and this golden age of the pulquería occurred under the Porfiriato regime at the turn of the twentieth century. In 1864, it is estimated that each resident of Ciudad de México drank 175 liters of pulque per year.[47] By 1896 that number was 333 liters per person, and in 1916, 342 liters per person. Suddenly, in 1939 that number dropped to only 107 liters and was a mere 56 liters by 1949.[48] Pulque consumption had come to its zenith and quickly disappeared.

The modernization policies of Porfirio Díaz that helped pulque to boom also brought in global trends that would de-popularize the beverage. Modern food science, anti-alcohol sentiment, and industrialized brewing converged on Mexico in the first half of the twentieth century. Pulque lost its position at the pinnacle of Mexican drinking.

During the Mexican Revolution, the Carranza government actively espoused anti-pulque rhetoric to such a degree that the industry lobby group, *Compañía Pulquera*, met in 1916 and chose to dissolve itself.[49] Brewers launched slander campaigns calling the drink unhygienic and even claiming pulque contained feces (there was a popular rumor that pulque fermentation was started by feces wrapped up in cloth, called a *muñeca* ["doll."]). In 1905, the newspaper *El Tiempo* railed against alleged unsanitary practices in pulquerías, "There is a custom to which we assume that the Consejo Superior de Salubridad has drawn its attention, and that is, that of mixing the pulque left in each glass by the consumers who go to the tavern, with those in charge pouring it back into the barrels to sell it again to the public."[50]

Land reforms following the Revolution also broke up pulque haciendas which would never be reconstructed at such a scale again. The drink has only recently begun to make a modest recovery from the revolutionary blow in the last 30 years. Now, pulque is a trendy alternative to mass-market beers. Civil society organizations sponsor competitions for films and other media productions focused on pulque culture. For-profit endeavors hold yearly pulque festivals (some pulque festivals are venerable religious observations that have been celebrated consistently for over a century. One such ritual is the conquest-era *Tlahuanca* or *Embriaguez Espiritual*, meaning "Sacred Drunkenness," of Cholula that occurs every year during Lent). One man from Puebla, the late Javier Gómez Marín, even amassed a vast library of thousands of pulque texts, drinking cups, and paraphernalia.

The Taste of Pulque. Pulque has a thick, gooey texture and a sweet and sour flavor. The drink is also prepared as *pulque curado*, or flavored pulque. Flavors can be sweet or savory and popular options include mango, guava, celery, and oats. Mexican history brings us a wide array of intriguing beverages that include pulque as their base. Some of these archaic pulque cocktails include *charángua*, made with starch, chiles, and toasted corn husks; *ojo de gallo*, made with honey, anise, and ancho chiles; *tecolio*, made with agave worms; *sangre de conejo*, made with prickly pear fruit; and *mantequilla*, made with sugar and rum.

While many of these complicated mixtures are no longer around, some regions of Mexico still produce traditional pulque-based drinks. *Chilocle* is still prepared with ancho chiles and epazote in states like Mexico and Puebla. In Querétaro, *menjengue* (also *mejenje*) is made with piloncillo, pineapples, plantains, cinnamon, and corn. In Ixmiquilpan, Hidalgo, a festival in honor of San Nicolás de Tolentino involves mass production of *charápe*, made from pulque, honey, cloves, cinnamon, and flavors like piñon nut, guava, and walnut.

While pulque is readily available in major cities, the freshest, highest-quality pulque is best sought out in Hidalgo or Tlaxcala in tinacales, where it is produced. There is always the risk of consuming adulterated pulque that has been cut with *higuerilla* ("castor oil") or *baba de nopal* ("prickly pear mucilage") for thickening and with cane alcohol for strength. Like wine, pulque can be of fine or ordinary qualities. While formal connoisseurship was lost during the twentieth century, there is a resurgence in interest in finding quality pulque in Mexico today, with professional *catadores* ("tasters") and a wide range of institutions dedicated to disseminating accurate information about the drink. Pulques differ in their viscosity, ranging from thin and translucent to *espeso* ("thick") and opaque. Flavor, too, depends on the variety of agave, the maturity at which the pulque is harvested, and the soil and climate of the region from which the aguamiel came. A nineteenth-century Poblano cookbook, *Formulario de la cocina mexicana*, argues that high altitude, cold climate pulques are the finest, while those from low, hot areas are inferior. The tax regime of the late colonial era also differentiated between *pulque fino* ("fine pulque") and *tlachique*, of the worst quality, made from wild agaves, and taxed at a lower rate.

Finally, a common belief among pulque drinkers stipulates that if the last drops of pulque in the cup are flung onto the ground and form the shape of an *alacrán* ("scorpion"), the pulque is good quality. Many drinkers practice this test even today, spilling long strings of pulque dregs onto the ground from which little perpendicular splatters spread, as if the legs of an arachnid.

Pulque, in all its complexities, stands as the single most significant beverage across several thousand years of Mesoamerican, New Spanish, and Mexican history.

Roasted Agave Wines

Before distillation arrived in Mexico, roasted agave sugars were fermented into a sort of wine. The fermented liquid that modern distillers transform into mezcal and tequila was once consumed on its own.

The practice would have been adjacent to food preparation, as agave hearts have been roasted in stone pits and eaten or chewed for at least 10,000 years. Agave and its many preparations have been dietary staples throughout Mesoamerica for longer than sedentary agriculture has existed. According to Henry J Bruman, author of *Alcohol in Ancient Mexico*, "Mescal [i.e. agave] for food, and possibly for drink, was so widespread a complex that it cannot be treated adequately in terms of the other drink areas. It was the universal understory upon which the later food resources were superimposed, and it was apparently basic to all regions except the tropical lowlands."[51] As far north as present-day Arizona, the Apache fermented drinks from agave. The agave is foundational, and Mesoamericans exploited wild agaves as food before they even domesticated corn.

These roasted agave wines were the clear precursor to mezcal and tequila, but they are almost extinct in terms of consumption today. Of course, distillers are still fermenting roasted agave into a must, but they do not consume it at this stage. During the colonial period, drinks called *charángua*, *maguees*, or *mexcalli* were made in this way. The only extant version of agave wine is usually a special preparation of *tesgüiño* in the state of Chihuahua in northern Mexico that uses roasted agave in conjunction with or in place of the usual germinated corn.

Sendechó

Sendechó is a pre-Columbian fermented beverage made from corn, butterfly bush, and chiles. The beverage is also called *zendechó*, *sendithe*, or *sende*. It is still produced in the states of Mexico and Michoacán, as well as by certain indigenous groups, principally the Jñatrjo and the Hñähñu.

The name Sendechó likely derives from the Otomi (Hñähñu) language compound of *zey* ("pulque") and *detha* ("corn"), only to have *Zayhthá* bastardized to Sendechó.[52] Legend has it that Moctezuma Ilhuicamina, Aztec emperor from 1440 to 1469, had a child who married an Otomi. When the emperor was presented with a drink of sendechó from his Otomi in-laws, he liked it and approved of its use among the Aztecs.

Like other fermented corn beverages, sendechó depends on germination of corn prior to milling to assist with fermentation. *Buddleja americana*, commonly called butterfly bush, is mixed with corn during the germination process. After the sprouted kernels are sun-dried and ground, chiles can be added. Often, pulque is used to seed the fermentation process.

Hñähñu groups in Querétaro use the term *sendithä* to describe pulque mixed with germinated corn.[53] Sendechó has long been a nutritious staple in the area around Toluca as well. Other similar fermented corn beverages with limited distribution include *tokere*, fermented by the Purépecha in Michoacán from corn cooked in salt water, and *chilote*, fermented from corn mixed with honey and sugarcane.

Taberna

Taberna is the fermented sap of the *Acrocomia aculeata* palm, commonly known as the coyol. It is produced in the southern part of Mexico in the regions of Frailesca, Centro, and Soconusco in Chiapas, and in the neighboring Isthmus of Tehuantepec in Oaxaca.[54] The palm is native to Central America and the fermented sap has roots in pre-Columbian gastronomy. In fact, ancient palm tapping may have been the model upon which pulque production was based, though it was not common north of present-day Nicaragua.

To produce taberna, producers cut down a mature palm tree and create an incision in its side. Sap pools in the cut and is collected to ferment. The fermented sap is consumed pure, without additives, but is also watered down and sweetened to make *agua de coyol*. Coyol wine is much more common in Central America than in Mexico, and it is particularly well-known in Guanacaste Province of Costa Rica.

The name of the drink itself, taberna, translates to "tavern" or, more correctly, "taproom." The term arrived with the Spanish who called the tapped palms of the Canary Islands tabernas. The coyol is not the only palm exploited in Mexico. The Xi'ui people of San Luis Potosí and Querétaro have been known to rely on the *palma real* or *palma barreta* for water when out in the countryside. They would create a deep incision and drink the sap fresh, but they would also let it ferment for a day and then drink it. Alternatively, if they left the incision for a couple of weeks, worms would invade the wound in the palm which could be eaten.[55]

Tepache

Tepache is a light fermentation of sweet fruit with added sugar, whether it be piloncillo or white cane sugar. The roots of this drink date prior to the Conquest, and tepache currently exists throughout Mexico. It is widely produced at both a commercial and a household level. While it is fermented, the drink does not contain much alcohol. It can be compared to kombucha or water kefir. Sometimes, water kefir grains, known as *Tibicos*, are used to produce tepache, including a drink known literally as *tepache de tibicos*. It is sometimes theorized that water kefir grains originated in Mexico, although the scholarship is inconclusive.

Many Mexican families will ferment a version of tepache at home. It is almost always made from pineapple, although domestic recipes vary. Some recipes call for only the rind of the pineapple. Others also use the flesh of the fruit. The pieces are sliced, soaked in water, and left to ferment for up to 5 days. The fermentation is spontaneous with no active yeast added. After about 4 days, the liquid is racked off and refrigerated to be served with sugar to taste as a refreshment.

Tepache is also commonly sold by street vendors, at markets, and on bicycle carts. Often, it comes in large wooden barrels, called *tepacheras*, which allegedly help with fermentation. These versions of tepache have a much broader array of ingredients. Other fruits, like tamarind, apple, orange, prickly pear, and guava, can be added to the mix to change the flavor. Spices, like cinnamon, cloves, and anise, are also added according to recipe.

There exist hyperlocal variants of tepache which use special ingredients as their base fermentable. In Veracruz, the fruit of the huapilla plant is fermented into a tepache. According to a man in Tlaxcala, the community in San Francisco Ixtacamaxtitlán, Puebla brews a tepache from the quiote of agave during Lent from February to April. There is also hog plum tepache in the Huasteca region. In Tzeltal communities around Ocosingo, Chiapas, unfermented pineapple with piloncillo is called "*chilha*'."[56]

Historically, tepache has referred to a variety of beverages. The term itself comes from the Nahuatl language. One theory suggests that the name comes from the word *tepachoa* which means "to grind something with a stone."[57] Another etymology suggests that the name comes from a combination of *tepitl* ("a kind of corn") and *atl* ("water"). Tepache would have originally been made from fermented corn, but early colonial recipes called for pulque agave. For example, in 1791, Don Antonio Pineda, Chief of Natural History on a royal expedition, reported that tepache was a white pulque boiled with brown sugar and anise. He describes a recipe for a common tepache: "From the sediment which the Pulque Tlachique deposits daily, a quantity is collected, which is dissolved in water. To this is added dark honey, pepper, and a corn leaf; with little diligence it ferments."[58] A kinship with pulque makes sense—after the Spanish Crown authorized the sale of pulque in 1608, the administrative positions of *Juez del Pulque* and *Juez del Tepache* were put in place—though treated separately both fermented drinks were regulated.

Today, tepache is common throughout Central and Coastal Mexico. There is also tepache in Chiapas, Yucatán, and Sonora. In Toluca, a similar drink is called *garapiña*. Increasingly, tepache is being commercialized and has been bottled for sale outside of Mexico.

Tesgüiño

Tesgüiño is the Rarámuri ritual beverage fermented most often from germinated corn. It holds nutritional, religious, and cultural significance for the peoples of arid northern Mexico. There are also instances of tesgüiño made from other sugars, including roasted agave and corn stalk juice. While the Rarámuri are especially known for brewing this drink, the Yaquis, Warihío, Tepehuáns, and Wixárika all have records of producing and consuming a corn drink called by a similar name.

Tesgüiño is the closest thing to true beer that the New World produced prior to European contact, particularly because it relied on the germination of corn, a process akin to malting barley. To produce the drink, corn kernels are germinated (often in the dark to concentrate sugars), ground on a metate, cooked for several hours into an atole, cooled, and left to ferment for a week in designated vessels. It ferments to less than 5 percent alcohol by volume.

The Rarámuri mix a wide variety of foraged herbs into the brew to add curative properties including the stems of *Usneaceae usnea* (called *deté powará*), the fronds of *Polypodium erythrolepsis* (called *muchavetana*), and the sap of *Lophophora williamsii* (called *jíkuli wamamé*).[59] Some nursing mothers will mix tesgüiño into milk for infants.[60]

The Rarámuri hold gatherings called *bajíachi* or *tesgüiñadas*, which are institutionalized drinking occasions where communities from different *ranchos* come together to meet, hold rituals, make payments, perform collective labor, or celebrate momentous occasions. Bajíachi literally means "place or time to drink."[61] Players of the multi-day, long-distance kickball game of the Rarámuri, called *Rarajípari*, also drink tesgüiño or *batari* during gameplay. The drink is still consumed today, mostly in Chihuahua state, in indigenous contexts.

Tolonche

Tolonche is a variety of pulque curado flavored by the seed of the *Schinus molle* tree, which is called *arbol de Peru* or *pirul*. The beverage, though, is only extant in a circumscribed region, even though its ingredients are available throughout central Mexico. Popoloca communities in the biodiverse Tehuacán Valley produce the drink in San Gabriel Chilac, Reyes Metzontla, Santiago

Chazumba, and Zapotitlán Salinas. According to one informant in Zapotitlán, drinking too much of the fermented beverage can cause headaches. Tolonche may follow several recipes, but the red pepper-like seed of *Schinus molle* is always present. Pulque, piloncillo, water, and spirits are other ingredients. Once mixed, the slurry is left to ferment.

Tolonche is not a common beverage and is associated with festivities and weddings. It is increasingly rare today and local knowledge of production is limited to a few individuals.[62] Moreover, the *Schinus molle* tree is a non-native implant from Peru, where indigenous Andean groups have long made a fermented beer out of the same seeds sometimes called *huigan* and *chicha de molle*. After the tree's introduction to Mexico in the 1500s, Mesoamerican groups also learned to use the seeds in fermentation. New Spanish records discuss drinks fermented from pirul including tolonche, *copalotle*, *quauchan-vino*, and *cuauchán*. Finally, a historic beverage was known as *quebrantahuesos* and was brewed from sweet corn stalk juice and toasted pirul seeds.

A March 18, 1899, article in *El Chisme* uses the term "tolonche" to describe a medicine made from *Datura stramonium*, the hallucinogenic jimsonweed.[63] Based on this usage, a possible etymology of tolonche is that of *toloache* or *toloatzin*, both indigenous names for the *Datura* species that are also used in certain medicinal and alcoholic beverages. Perhaps the prototypical version of tolonche contained jimsonweed.

Tuba

Tuba is a beverage derived from the sap of the coconut palm along the west coast of Mexico. It is common in Jalisco, Nayarit, Guerrero (especially the town of Chichihualco), and, above all else, Colima. Tuba is the most iconic refreshment in the state of Colima. While tuba is a fermented beverage, a considerable amount of daily consumption of the tuba sap is fresh. In fact, *tuberos* boil, refrigerate, and sweeten the sap because the fermented flavor is unsavory. Still, Colimense food does incorporate vinegars produced by fermenting palm sap, and some people allow tuba to ferment at home.

Tuba is produced by tuberos, men whose job it is to scale palm trees up to 20 meters in height twice a day. The tuba production process is surprisingly analogous to that of pulque. When a palm tree is ready to flower, it grows a woody efflorescence known as a *vástago* ("offshoot"). At this point, the tubero must climb the tree and slice the tip of the vástago to promote sap flow. They then tie a bucket beneath the sliced area to collect the drops of sap during the day. At one time, the collection vessel would have been a bulbous *balsa* gourd, but is generally made of plastic today. Each time they climb the tree, they empty the collection bucket into a secondary vessel, called a *bajador*, to bring the tuba back down. If they neglect to slice the tree daily, the tree will give sap less reliably. In many ways, the tubero is just a tlachiquero who isn't afraid of heights.

Often, modern tuberos do not own the land where palm trees grow. They must enter into an agreement with landowners to harvest the sap, or, in the case of the city of Colima, must get a permit to tap trees on public land from the Ayuntamiento. Generally, tuberos learn the craft from a young age from their families. While coconut palms have a wide distribution in Mexico, the fact that tuba is geographically limited proves that its production hinges on knowledge and skill. Some tuberos in Colima wonder about the future of the trade as young people are not learning the dangerous and time-consuming skill.

In the morning, tuberos sell their tuba raw because it has not had the chance to heat up and turn sour. The typical breakfast in Colima city is *bolillo* bread and a cup of tuba, sometimes sprinkled with peanuts. Afternoon tuba must be refrigerated and sweetened to ward off spontaneous fermentation. It is enriched with fruit like apples, strawberries, mangos, prickly pears, and lime. It is also common to blend tuba with almonds or walnuts.

Tuba is not a pre-Columbian beverage. There is some debate as to when the coconut palm arrived on the west coast of Mexico, but plantations first appeared in the late 1500s. The technique used to extract tuba was taught to Mexicans by Filipino sailors operating the Manila Galleon, or *Nao de China*, sailing between 1565 and 1815, who also brought the drink to Guam and the Mariana Islands. The journey across the Pacific was the most grueling ocean passage in history, covering over 15,000 kilometers and lasting, on average, 6 months.[64] When Filipino sailors arrived in Acapulco, they could hardly be convinced to get back on board to sail back across the Pacific. One galleon, *Espíritu Santo*, arrived in 1618 to Acapulco. Records indicate seventy out of seventy-five Filipino sailors fled to work on tuba plantations in nearby Colima.[65] Tuba, in fact, is a Tagalog word.

Inexplicably, the 1784 Navarro report on drinks in New Spain lists "tuba o pincharro" for the *alcabalatorios*, or tax regions, of Chautla and Tehuacán, both in present-day Puebla.[66] Tuba must have had broader distribution previously, but the drink called *pincharro* appears in no other known texts.

Zambumbia

Zambumbia, also spelled *sambumbia*, is a loosely defined group of fermented beverages that consists of a fermentation of sundry ingredients that can include piloncillo, pulque, cloves, pepper, pineapple, and sometimes a source of starch, such as corn, barley, or rice. The isolated examples of modern zambumbia do not necessarily relate to older versions, except that they are fermented.

The drink was common during the nineteenth century, often being sold from a *ventorillo*, a kind of portable cantina that sold cheese, rum, and other drinks. One recipe from an 1844 text about the traditional lifestyle of the Jarocho, or cowherd of Veracruz, defines zambumbia as "pineapple fermented with spices, and sweetened with piloncillo."[67] In the late 1700s, a report to the

Spanish Crown stated that zambumbia was made of fermented barley. Modern versions invariably contain piloncillo and pulque.

The name is likely of Nigerian origin, which makes sense as Cubans also consume a group of drinks called zambumbia, especially water with sugarcane juice.[68] Moreover, the Veracruzano El Jarocho culture has historical African influences. The term likely arrived with enslaved Africans to Mexico's east coast and simply referred to fermented beverages. Extant versions exist in specific communities in the state of Mexico and are associated with celebrations.

* * *

A deep mastery of the microbial world has been a hallmark of drinking culture in the region since Mesoamerican times. Nearly every major foodstuff, whether indigenous or introduced, has been subjected to the process. From the autochthonous fermentations of ancient staples like prickly pear and corn to the innovative adaptations of introduced products like coconut palms and barley, the peoples of Mexico have demonstrated a penchant for fermenting all kinds of alcoholic and nonalcoholic beverages.

Today, traditional fermented beverages like tepache are making their way into global bar culture. You can find pineapple tepache fermented in-house at critically acclaimed bars in Mexico, the United States, and Japan. Brands are beginning to sell tepache in shelf-stable, canned formats. But many of Mexico's ancestral ferments are increasingly relegated to circumscribed pockets of rural society, inaccessible to most Mexicans, never mind the world.

In the Yucatán, a balché producer noted that it is not feasible to teach others how to make the ancient honey drink because true melipona honey is unobtainably expensive. In Colima, a family of tuberos discussed the occupational dangers in teaching their children to climb palm trees every day to make a living from fermented sap. In Guanajuato, coloncheros point to inconsistent rains as a threat to harvesting wild prickly pears, and regional insecurity makes the prospect of venturing far into the countryside for fruit collection risky.

More and more, young Mexicans look to formal education, internal migration to cities, salaried careers, and modern professions as clear paths to a stable livelihood. Agrarian living tied to ancestral foodways is increasingly neglected. Producers of these fascinating fermented drinks are disappearing with each generation. With a highly saturated market of industrialized beverages like beer and soda, consumers are also losing interest.

In many ways, the fermented beverages discussed in this chapter are antithetical to a modern capitalistic society and contrary to the exigencies that economic efficiency puts on mechanized food systems. Many fruits are highly seasonal. Many ingredients are harvested wild and have not been subject to monoculture in the modern era. The ferments are alive and have short shelf lives, preventing transportation over long distances. The knowledge required to master their production takes patience and apprenticeship to learn. Many of the drinks are derided as unsanitary by urbane consumers.

But, as the twenty-first century begins to show signs of pushback against the highly processed food systems of the twentieth century, the healthful benefits of probiotic, natural drinks are increasingly praised. There is hope for a resurgence of interest in Mexico's traditional fermented beverages. Still, the particular culture of microbes that make each of these drinks unique must be shepherded carefully between generations. If we do not learn to value the artistry of these drinks now, we may lose their true character in the decades to come.

3

Beer

It is no coincidence that Mexico is so closely associated with beer; the country has been the world's largest exporter of the malt beverage since 2011. The drink has become one of Mexico's most outspoken cultural currencies around the world. Homegrown, Mexican brands like Corona, Modelo, Dos Equis, and Tecate enjoy name recognition nearly everywhere. Corona has been served at bars on all seven continents (yes, even *that* one). Many who don't speak Spanish will proudly utter the word "*cerveza*," even squeezing a lime into their beer without knowing what a *michelada* is.

The brewing industry has matured into one of the most profitable sectors of the Mexican economy. Mexico's Instituto Nacional de Estadística y Geografía (INEGI) reports that the beer sector is the largest of any alcoholic beverage space in Mexico, employing 49.3 percent of personnel and accounting for 65 percent of gross alcohol production.[1] Annually, the country produces around 120,000,000 hectoliters of beer, about a third of which is for export (production is concentrated in the north near the US border). As a manufacturing industry, brewing is the nineteenth most economically consequential to Mexico of 288 sectors that INEGI measured in 2019.

Still, it is anomalous that Mexico has achieved such prowess in the brewing space. Beer culture was virtually nonexistent in the country until after its independence from Spain. Spain, which brought wine and liqueur to the country, was not a beer-drinking culture itself. In fact, Mexico's history with

European-style beer only dates back a bit over a century, making its global dominance even more impressive.

Beer Before Mexican Independence

The history of malt alcoholic beverages in Mexico, though, is pre-Columbian in origin. Tesgüiño, the corn beer of northern Mexico, involves germinating kernels of corn in a similar manner to barley in the European tradition. The indigenous groups who brew the drink also add herbs to their tesgüiño, which contribute to flavor and help to prevent bacterial growth, not unlike hops. Sendechó is an indigenous germinated corn drink that is "hopped" with *tepozan*, or butterfly bush of the species *Buddleja americana*. Deveined chiles were also used in some corn beer recipes, about which the author of *La cerveza entre los antiguos mexicanos y en la actualidad* comments, "The chile, due to its principle resinoid called capsaicin helps to preserve the alcohol from rapid acidification, like hops in beer."[2] True *bier* produced from northern European ingredients, though, would not be possible until both barley and hops arrived in the New World.

Barley was introduced during the first decades of the Conquest. It was cultivated in present-day Mexico as early as 1514.[3] The historian Juan Bautista Pomar, writing in 1582, noted the European bias in exploiting indigenous labor to raise Old World grains in New Spain, "Wheat, many varieties, and barley yield wonderfully on Spanish farms and estates, because very few Indians dedicated themselves to it because they have no space, even just for their own crops, because they are usually occupied in the service of the Spanish."[4]

Imported beer, particularly from areas in present-day Germany and Belgium, would remain an expensive and limited commodity in the upper echelons of New Spanish society over the centuries. Spain's King, Charles V, who ruled over the early years of the Conquest from 1516 to 1556, was raised in northern Europe where he must have developed a taste for beer himself. In June of 1542, Charles V granted the first license to brew beer in New Spain to Alfonso de Herrera, who established his *cervecería* ("brewery") at the hacienda El Portal, between volcanoes which provided good, clean water for his wort. The king permitted the use of 200 slaves in the endeavor and expected one-third of the profit in tax.[5] In 1558, Herrera died and formal beer-making in New Spain disappeared with him for nearly three centuries.

Beer was not entirely unknown. Forty years before Mexican Independence, the viceroy of New Spain, Matías de Gálvez, issued note #840 on July 2, 1784, describing some contrived recipes for drinks that were being produced and considered to be "cerveza."[6] Barley water, lime, tamarind, and sugar were combined and fermented. Another version included pineapple rinds, clove, pepper, cumin, coriander, and sugar, fermented in a barrel which once held aguardiente. This eighteenth-century "cerveza" could be likened to a modern tepache or even Guanajuato's famous cebadina. When Mexico won independence from Spain in 1821, the floodgates were opened for an influx of immigrants from European countries that had previously been unrepresented in Mexico's demographics. Barley beer became more common.

Beer in Early Independent Mexico

As early as 1824, new "cervecerías" were appearing in Mexico. At la Calle del Refugio (now la Calle 16 de Septiembre), Juan Eduardo y Compañía announced the opening of a cervecería where a *vinatería*, or liquor store, had been.[7] 1825 saw the opening of Cervecería de San Cosme in the *portales* of the eponymous market.[8] Other newspapers in the 1820s list cervecerías occupying the stalls along the Zócalo as landmarks for meetings or points of sale for the purchase of tickets for passage to Veracruz.

Whether these early cervecerías brewed beer in addition to selling it is not clear. In this context, "cervecería" may have just indicated that they sold imported beer or other alcoholic beverages. What these new businesses likely demonstrate is that Spain no longer had a monopoly on imports into Mexico. Exciting new products from around the Atlantic were finally being unladen at the port of Veracruz. Around Latin America, it was the wars of independence that would open the doors to foreigners who would eventually lay the foundation of national brewing industries.

Reports from the mid-1800s are peppered with Germanic names in large Mexican cities opening small breweries, which would later go out of business. During the 1840s in Ciudad de México, for example, Swiss maltster Bernhard Bolgard opened La Pila Seca and Bavarian brewer Federico Herzog brewed at La Candelaria. Both produced pale ales. These two factories are the first examples of malting in Mexico during this era.[9] While this first wave of post-independence brewers swept across the nation, few stuck around as an American invasion and the Mexican Civil War from 1858 to 1861 ravaged the economy. This instability helped lead to another full-scale military intervention when Mexican monarchists and French troops helped to install Maximilian I of Austria as emperor.

It was the provenance of these early brewers, the increasing influence of northern Europeans in Mexico, and the eventual staying power of Mexico's earliest successful beer brands that solidified the style that the world today thinks of as Mexican lager. Generally, most of Mexico's mass-market beers today are either pilsners—think *claras*—or Vienna lagers—think *oscuras*. The brief empire of Austrian Maximilian I, which lasted from 1864 to 1867, may have shepherded in the preference for these dark and aromatic Vienna lagers. Other nineteenth-century brewers produced and sold a range of styles including beers known as *sencilla*, *standard*, *bock*, and *lager bier*. While most exports today are light and crisp lagers, darker Vienna-style beers are still popular in the Mexican domestic market.

The Birth of Mexican Industrial Brewing

The de facto dictatorship of Porfirio Díaz brought a degree of stability to Mexico. Díaz prized European values and focused on modernizing Mexico. It was during the Porfiriato that the seeds of Mexico's modern beer prowess would be sown.

Breweries of consequential industrial size began to open in the last three decades of the nineteenth century. Both supply and demand for the drink focused in the border states in the north. Compañía Cervecera de Chihuahua, S.A., la Cervecería Sonora, S.A., and Cervecería Cuauhtémoc, S.A. represented three of the five largest breweries in the country in 1900. The north had a higher demand for beer than other regions, partly due to American influence, partly due to the unavailability of pulque, and, perhaps, due to the desert.

The famous author Salvador Novo, who wrote a history of Cervecería Cuauhtémoc titled *Crónica regiomontana* (*Breve historia de un gran esfuerzo*) upon being invited by the brewery's owners on its seventy-fifth anniversary in 1965, reflected,

> It must have been thirst, a physical thirst, an organic need to quench it with refreshing and stimulating beverage, which towards the end of the 19th century induced a small group of neighboring Mexicans in little Monterrey to form a partnership to found what was to become the mother company and productive nucleus of many that, with time, would forge the greatness of Monterrey and of Mexico: The Cuauhtémoc Brewery.[10]

Outside of the north, the population centers of Ciudad de México and Veracruz also fostered large-scale breweries. Across the board, European and American brewers and investors featured prominently in the foundation of these enterprises. Many of the earliest breweries were built by ethnic German brewers from the United States who consulted on the design, construction, and operation of the facilities. Most of the machinery was American-made, and the bulk of the malt and hops came from Europe.

The 1890s saw nearly a dozen breweries open that would define the beer-making scene for the next century. With a burgeoning domestic supply, imports of beer into Mexico fell nearly 70 percent between 1890 and 1910.[11] While the Revolution in the 1910s threatened the survival of many breweries, the strong and proactive outlasted the tumult and would go on to integrate vertically, reshore capital and expertise within Mexico, and consolidate the market into the massive duopoly that accounts for a staggering majority of Mexican beer production today. As the industry took off, a new licensing entity, the cervecería, was established by the government—putting the sale of beer in its own "family-friendly" atmosphere outside of more disreputable watering holes like cantinas, pulquerías, and saloons.[12]

The Fall of Pulque

At odds with beer's development, Mexico's ancestral love affair with pulque was coming to an end. The country developed a taste for beer while losing its thirst for pulque. In the 1854 book, *Los mexicanos pintados por si mismos*, a characteristic pulque vendor describes the advancing enemy: "This individual is the brewer, whose damned beer has dislodged pulque from the aristocratic tables, competes with it in the middle class, and already has some followers among the lower classes."[13] Other observers later discussed the "education" of the palates of Mexico's Revolutionary Generals in Restaurante de Chapultepec where they ate lobster *a la americana* and paired certain meats with dark beer and certain others with light beer.[14] Finally, between 1943 and 1953, production and consumption of beer overtook that of pulque.[15] Within a century of the establishment of commercial brewing in Mexico, the ancestral Mesoamerican beverage had been bested by barley.

The remaining history of beer in Mexico is dominated by the stories of two breweries that slowly consolidated their hold on the market to become the foreign-owned duopoly that makes Mexico the largest beer exporter in the world. To understand Mexican beer through the 1900s, it is easiest to explore the growth of these behemoth breweries. We then turn our attention to the nascent birth of Mexican craft beer.

* * *

Cervecería Cuauhtémoc Moctezuma

Cervecería Cuauhtémoc Moctezuma, nicknamed "Sultan of the North," now Heineken México, is one of the two large beer conglomerates that defines the Mexican market. Cervecería Cuauhtémoc is based out of the northern city of Monterrey in the state of Nuevo León and brews famed brands like Dos Equis, Sol, Indio, and Tecate. The history of this brewery exemplifies the last 130 years of beer history in Mexico. Ultimately, it brings us to 2010, when FEMSA sold off a controlling share of its brewing business to the Dutch brewing giant.

The Founding of Cervecería Cuauhtémoc. In the late nineteenth century, one of Monterrey's largest general stores, Casa Calderón, owned by Don José Calderón Penilla, was regularly importing German-style, St. Louis-produced beer from Schnaider Brewery. Calderón saw firsthand that there was a foreign demand for the imported beverages in his city. In 1882, he acquired a local ice factory and went on to launch his first brewery, Cerveceria León, in 1886.[16] The project, however, lacked technical expertise.

Calderón still believed in the idea and brought in the son of the Missouri brewer that supplied his shop, in addition to some local Regiomontano business partners. In 1890, the men formed Cervecería Cuauhtémoc. The names of this original group of founders echo around Monterrey today like Carnegie and Rockefeller do in the United States. Alongside Schnaider, the men—Garza, Sada, and Muguerza—went into business.

The American, Schnaider, brought brewing operations know-how to the new endeavor, but the brewery also employed two German men, Thomas Radke and Charles Hasselbart (sometimes written Juan Radke and Carlos Hesselbart), who had already been brewing with little commercial success in Monterrey.[17]

The first beer that Cervecería Cuauhtémoc produced was Carta Blanca, a brand the brewery still makes today. Its second in-house brand, called Saturno, did not last. Its Cuauhtémoc brand debuted in 1893 as a draft beer and would later turn into the famous Indio, which is still in production. In 1904, Carta Blanca won Gold in a St. Louis World's Fair beer showcase. Bohemia was launched in 1905.

The brewery's first two decades witnessed exponential growth, but luck would soon run out. On October 22, 1914, Carrancista revolutionaries captured the brewery in Monterrey, only to abandon it 2 days later due to the arrival of Huerta's federal troops. Beer was reported stolen.[18] Again, on April 24, 1914, the Carranza government seized the brewery's assets and used the seizure as blackmail to ask for a 500,000-peso loan from its shareholders who were fleeing to Houston.[19] The brewery was returned by December of that year, but the Carranza government aimed to increase taxes on beer, which resulted in Mexico's brewers forming the *Asociación Nacional de Fabricantes de Cerveza*, which defeated the tax and heralded the birth of a strong beer lobby.[20]

The cost of the Revolution to the brewery was high, halting production entirely, but new challenges were just around the corner. The First World War meant that brewing materials, mostly imported from the United States and Europe, would be in short supply. Only Cervecería de Toluca and La Perla were producing their own malt within Mexican borders during these decades.

Vertical and Horizontal Integration in the Beer Market. The instability that killed brewing's potential in the mid-1800s had returned, but the Monterrey shareholders were quick to pivot. Cervecería Cuauhtémoc began an aggressive policy of vertical integration, bringing production of nearly all its inputs under its own ownership. Within two decades, hops, malt, carbon dioxide, bottles, boxes, caps, and transportation, which had previously been contracted from outside, were all internalized. Once launched, each product line was quickly scaled to outpace the brewery's own needs. They became new lines of business in their own rights.

The brewery acquired their own rolling stock in 1918 to service their internal transportation needs.[21] In 1923, the business opened a carbonic gas plant which helped to thicken the beer's foam and facilitated the sale of draft beer (which had been available as early as 1893).[22] In 1926, it opened a box factory. In 1928, the brewery opened a facility to manufacture its own crown corks. In 1929, they went into the business of producing their own malt.

The vertical integration of their supply chain was followed by decades of horizontal expansion across Mexico to broaden distribution, absorb regional brands, and compete with national challengers. In the 1920s, Cervecería Cuauhtémoc tried to purchase its main rival, the recently founded Cervecería Modelo, and they attempted the same with Cervecería Moctezuma in the 1930s.[23] They bought Ciudad de México's Cervecería Central in 1928 and built factories in Veracruz and Jalisco between 1933 and 1935. In April of 1933, Cervecería Cuauhtémoc began exporting to the United States.

Through all of this, Cervecería Cuauhtémoc began to create separate legal entities to manage their new holdings. It was Manuel Gómez Morín, a key figure in the Bank of Mexico and an eventual founder of the PAN political party (in 1939), who would advise the shareholders of the brewery to develop a holding company in 1936, called Valores Industriales, also known as VISA.[24] VISA went on to become the business known today as FEMSA, which operates Latin America's largest convenience store chain, Oxxo, privately bottles the most Coca-Cola in the world, and still holds a valuable share in the original brewing business. Curiously, Vicente Fox, the PAN's first candidate to win the presidency, had been a key leader in Coca-Cola's Mexico business in the 1970s, and FEMSA's Coca-Cola distribution would flourish under his early-aughts presidency.[25]

VISA and Cuauhtémoc continued to consolidate the market through the latter half of the twentieth century with innovations on bottles (like the 1964 introduction of the famed 1-liter *caguama*) and openers (such as the pull tab or *quitapón*). Tecate was acquired in 1954. They acquired the Hermosillo-based Cervecería de Sonora in 1961. In 1979, they launched Brisa, dubbing it Mexico's first "light beer."

The Modern Brewing Giant. Finally, in 1985, Monterrey-based Cuauhtémoc merged with Orizaba-based Moctezuma in what was called "the Union of the Monarchs." Moctezuma had been founded by a group of French Swiss investors in 1896 and brought legacy brands like Sol, XX Lager, Noche Buena, and Superior with them. With this merger, Mexico's beer duopoly was born. Only Grupo Modelo remained as a legitimate competitor.

At home, Cervecería Cuauhtémoc was one of Monterrey's earliest manufacturing businesses. Today, Monterrey is Mexico's most industrialized city. The brewery was a key driver behind the development of the manufacturing hub of Mexico's north. The city grew alongside its favorite beer.

Grupo Modelo

Cervecería Modelo stands as a contrast to the early years of industrial brewing in Mexico. It was founded much later (after the hardships of both the Mexican Revolution and the First World War), and it was founded by a group of Spanish men rather than Germans or Americans. Ultimately, it would become Mexico's largest brewery by focusing on selling beer to the domestic market and leaning on its signature marketing.

The brewery's key early figure was Braulio Iriarte Goyeneche, a Basque man from Navarre who made his early fortune in Mexico selling bread. When the Mexican Revolution restricted access to yeast, he opened a compressed yeast factory in 1912 called Leviatán y Flor followed by a bread factory he named El Pan Ideal.[26] Pablo Díez Fernández, the man who would transform Modelo in the 1930s, was Iriarte's partner in these early baking endeavors.

Iriarte's success during the unstable years of the Revolution allowed him to purchase a variety of depreciated assets in and around Ciudad de México.[27] He owned several mills and haciendas which grew grains in the Central Valley of Mexico. In 1922, Iriarte moved to open a brewery with capital from a group of well-to-do Spanish living and doing business in Ciudad de México. Three years later, at Tacuba, the Cervecería Modelo was born. It still stands there today.

The new brewery was state-of-the-art. A 1922 article reported that Fernandez de la Reguera, a shareholder in the enterprise, had returned from New York, where he was purchasing equipment for the factory. Even before opening, the article boasted, "The 'Gran Cervecería Modelo' will include elements of such a nature and with machinery of such importance, that it could be considered as the second brewery in America."[28] When the brewery launched, their head brewer, Schemedtje, was from Anheuser-Busch, and their malt was imported from Germany.[29]

Since its inception, the brewery produced Corona Extra and Modelo in clear bottles. In 1930, Negra Modelo launched, followed by Moravia in 1935. That same year, Modelo acquired Compañía Cervecera de Toluca y México, which had not weathered the years of the Revolution well. The Toluca and Mexico Brewery had been founded in 1865, and later sold to the Swiss entrepreneur Santiago Graf in 1875. Their hallmark beer, Victoria, was registered as a brand in 1906. At the time, it had a regional monopoly on beer around the capital city.

With the Toluca y México merger, Modelo acquired the rights to Victoria (as well as the brands Pilsner, Marzen Bock, and Toluca). The year after the acquisition, Modelo profited 54,000 pesos from Victoria alone.[30] They openly boasted in newspapers, "La Victoria es nuestra" (Victory is ours)![31] The acquisition had been favored by Pablo Díez, the bread-maker and business partner of Iriarte. Following Iriarte's death in 1932, Díez would become a majority stockholder and would shepherd the brewery through the next decades with great success.

In the 1940s, Modelo focused on the domestic market, where other breweries were looking to export. They became "Mexico's Beer." Their marketing strategy quickly became inextricably tied up with entertainment—concerts, fútbol, celebrities. They even owned Toluca's fútbol team until the late 1990s. From 1956 until 1982, Cervecería Modelo sponsored an event called the Caravana de Estrellas Corona, a circuit of concerts that traveled around Mexico giving shows and building brand identity. Mexican stars as big as Pedro Infante were associated with the brewery.

Of course, Modelo also moved to acquire other prominent brands. In the 1950s, they acquired the regional brands of Estrella in Guadalajara and Pacífico in Mazatlán. Later, in 1980, they took over the Cervecería Yucateca. In the late 1990s, Anheuser-Busch took a 50.2 percent stake in Modelo. In 2012, the multinational (by then AB-InBev) purchased the remaining half of the Mexican brewery.

Cerveza Artesanal

Since around 1995, craft beer has found a home in specific regions of Mexico and is continuing to grow. As the two large macro breweries have been sold off to international conglomerates, craft beer stands as a promising Mexican-owned future for brewing in the country.

By the 1990s, the growing popularity of craft beer and homebrewing in the United States was making headway in Mexico. In 1995, Gustavo González, who credits his inspiration to British supermarket beer, began homebrewing when he registered Cosaco as a brand, later to launch in 2000.[32] Beer Factory (a *restaurante-bar* or brewpub) opened its doors in 1997 in Ciudad de México. In

Guadalajara, Cervecería Minerva launched in 2003, and Calavera later opened in 2008. Cervecería Primus opened in 2006 in Ciudad de México.

As the industry has expanded, the bulk of Mexican craft beer has been produced in the north of the country, where Mexican brewing began 130 years ago. The major Baja California cities of Mexicali, Tijuana, and Ensenada produce more craft beer than any other region in Mexico today, around 18 percent of the total.[33] The Baja California border region has enjoyed a boom since 2015, but the region was also a hotbed of brewing during US Prohibition in the 1920s, when Americans would cross the border to drink beer from Aztec Brewing Co., De Anza, Cerveza Mexicali, Cerveza Tijuana, and Cerveza Tecate.

Craft beer presents a range of flavors that have been previously unknown in Mexico. Any style you might imagine an American craft brewer to make, Mexicans are also producing. They also focus on introducing distinctly Mexican ingredients to beers such as chile, cacao, corn, and even insects.

Michelada

The michelada is a popular Mexican form of preparing beer with other ingredients to enhance its flavor and refreshing qualities. The most basic preparation of a michelada involves beer, lime juice, and chili powder or salt—but there are unending riffs and takes on the beloved Mexican concept. The michelada is also a modern concept, with most histories giving it an antiquity no earlier than the 1960s. The term *cerveza preparada* ("prepared beer") is synonymous.

We can summarize the historical evidence by saying that the michelada emerged during the 1960s and may have been a take on a *curacruda*, or "hangover cure." Popularly, there are two origin stories for the michelada and its name. One theory suggests that michelada is an abbreviation of *mi chela helada*, meaning "my cold beer." Alternatively, a story goes that a man named

Michel Ésper drank beer with salt, lime, and ice out of a *chabela* cup in a San Luis Potosí club.

To complicate the story, Bar Acueducto in Hotel Lucerna of Mexicali, Baja California, lays a claim to inventing Clamato juice (a popular addition to micheladas) by combining tomato juice with red abalone broth in the 1960s. A bit later in 1972, in the same city, Pepe Angulo, owner of La Conga Bar, added beer to the clam and tomato juice and mixed in lime, salt, and dried chili powder, giving birth to the drink that they still call *chabela* (also *chavela*). Elsewhere in Mexico, this concoction is known as an *Ojo Rojo*, *Clamacheve*, *Gringa*, or *michelada con Clamato*. The tomato juice version of the michelada preparada is likely as old as the michelada itself.

Today, the michelada enjoys international recognition, and there is significant innovation in the michelada space. The beer cocktails can contain ingredients including Worcestershire sauce, tabasco, powdered instant noodle broth, salsa, tomato juice, Clamato juice, chili powder, salt, pepper, chamoy, and other sweet pastes. Among the riffs on micheladas are the *Cubana* (with salsa), the *gomichela* (with gummy candies), and the *licuachela* (served in a blender-shaped cup). Regionally, in Colima, there exist the *tejuichela* (beer with corn masa tejuino), and, recently in Xico, Veracruz, the *morichela* (a mix of *morita*, a local raspberry wine, with beer).

It is worth mentioning that Mexicans commonly call beers *chelas* or *cheves*.

Sidra

In Jalacingo, Veracruz, a cottage apple industry existed as early as the seventeenth century.[34] Similarly, the eighteenth century knew a drink called *zagardúa* or *yagardiza*, a kind of punch composed of cider, citrus, and sugar water. But cider enjoyed a moment in Mexico in the early 1900s thanks to the influx of immigrants from northern Spain, principally Asturias and Basque country where cider is a beloved tipple.

Cider was regularly imported to Veracruz from Spain, but by the 1920s, it became a significant commodity. Between 1926 and 1935, cider was one of the top nine most imported products from Spain.[35] Of all the cider imported into Mexico during these years, an overwhelming 98.61 percent of it came from Spain.[36]

In 1902, the Catalan businessman, Arturo Mundet Carbó, moved to Mexico from northeast Spain and went into business selling soda bottles and crown corks. Shortly after, he was producing sodas, vinegars, and ciders. While many sources suggest he launched into his soda business immediately, a Catalan biography suggests that the transition to apple soda occurred sometime between 1915 and 1918.[37] Either way, Mexico's favorite cider-inspired soda, Sidral Mundet, was off to the races. Sidra Pino, which also produced sodas, was opened in Mérida in the 1880s.

Today, the areas around Huejotzingo and Zacatlán in Puebla continue to be famed for their locally grown ciders. Acaxochitlán in Hidalgo is also known for cider (in addition to acachul wine).

* * *

In June 2023, Modelo Especial became the highest-selling beer in the United States. Imported from breweries in northern Mexico that exclusively brew for the US market, it temporarily overtook the domestic macro lite beers that have dominated the market since their introduction in the 1970s. The moment represented the culmination of over a century of intense industrialization in the Mexican brewing industry that began in the 1880s. Beer in Mexico has always been a professionalized industrial endeavor. Only recently has small-scale, craft beer-making caught on.

Not only is Mexico's brewing industry a case study in the country's entrepreneurial knack for selling abroad, but beer has become a cornerstone of vibrant social life at home. A carne asada is invariably accompanied by a box of Coronitas or a shared caguama. The meat on the grill is often marinated in beer and lime juice. Breakfast at a market stall may involve a morning swig of beer alongside a tlayuda or gordita, depending on the region. More than any other drink, beer is the persistent accompaniment to the many edible pleasures of Mexican gastronomy.

From the refrigerated shelves of the local Oxxo to the Tajín peppered rim of a towering michelada, beer has become a ubiquitous presence in Mexican life in only 150 years. It arrived just as pulque had reached its peak moment of mass consumption in Porfirian Ciudad de México and went on to subsume pulque's status in popular taste. Today, rattling crates of empty bottles crisscross the country from Modeloramas to vast, mechanized cervecerías for reuse. But as Mexico's two homegrown duopolistic breweries have been sold off to foreign conglomerates in the last two decades, who stands to benefit from Mexico's love affair with beer?

4

Wine

Vino, in the vernacular of generations of Mexicans, has less often meant grape wine than a number of other alcoholic beverages including pulque, fruit wine, liqueur, tequila, mezcal, and other types of strong spirits. Drinks like *vino de cocos*, *vino de mezcal*, and *vino de membrillo* have taken the European word and applied it to traditional and novel beverages. Sahagún, among others, referred to pulque as "*vino de la tierra*," or "wine of the land." Alexander von Humboldt would go on to call the agave the "vine of the Aztecs" in his *Political Essay on the Kingdom of New Spain*. Yet, true wine, produced from the fermentation of the fruit of the *Vitis* genus, also has a history of consequence in Mexico, even if its consumption is not as popular today as other drinks.

Native Mexican Grapes

Writers who comment on viticulture in the Americas regularly boast that more species of *Vitis* vines grow natively in North America than the rest of the world combined. This fact, paired with the Mesoamerican penchant for fermenting local fruits, poses the question: did indigenous people make grape wine before the Spanish arrived? Mexico, after all, is home to a wide array of native species.

There is an impressive list of autochthonous species of *Vitis* in the country: *V. arizonica* in the northwest, *V. berlandieri* in Chihuahua and Coahuila, *V.*

candicans in Nuevo León and Tamaulipas, *V. cinerea* in Guerrero, Michoacán, Nuevo León, Puebla, Sonora, and San Luis Potosí, *V. tillifolia* (sometimes written *V. caribaea*) in Tabasco, Campeche, Chiapas, Guerrero, Hidalgo, Jalisco, Mexico, Michoacán, Morelos, Nayarit, Oaxaca, Puebla, San Luis Potosí, Veracruz, and Yucatán, and *V. champini* in Coahuila, where Mexico's wine industry is centered at Parras de la Fuente (*parras* in the place name means "vines," and originally referenced the bountiful *V. champini* species in the region).[1]

Before a critical number of European vines had taken root in New Spain, Spanish settlers were known to use some of these native species to produce wines for self-consumption. In some regions of Mexico, this could have been the case as late as 1769.[2] Early settlers in Coahuila would have used the wild *champini* grapes that grew so abundantly there. Motolinía's sixteenth-century account, *Historia de los indios de la Nueva España*, recorded that there were "very thick, wild vines . . . And some Spaniards make vinegar out of them, and some have made wine, although it was very little."[3]

For indigenous groups, prior to the definitive arrival of *Vitis vinifera* vines, most scholars agree that native grapes were not used to produce fermented drinks. Modern winemakers discuss how native Mexican grape varieties lack sugar content and acidity, and sometimes never reach peak maturity, making them unsuitable for vinification.

Yet some evidence points to indigenous groups in the Americas drying the fruits of the native vines into raisins, which not only had nutritional value, but also medical and religious uses.[4] Archaeological research has discovered evidence of use of seeds of *Vitis tiliifolia* dating back to the Classic Period at Chinikihá in present-day Chiapas.[5] This is the same species which is used in winemaking in Naolinco, Veracruz today.

Wine Arrives in New Spain

In Mexico, and much of the New World, the arrival of wine preceded the arrival of the *Vitis vinifera* grapevine, but not by much. Columbus brought stores of wine on his second voyage to the New World in 1493, landing in the Antilles. In Mexico, wine would have arrived on the shores of Veracruz as rations for the conquistadors who were making their way to Tenochtitlán. In April 1518, Juan de Grijalva sailed from Cuba with wine on board and landed on Mexico's Caribbean Coast a month later. The account of conquistador Bernal Díaz del Castillo tells us that indigenous emissaries came aboard the ships of Cortés outside of Veracruz on Holy Thursday of 1519 and were served grape wine.

Hernán Cortés himself enjoyed wine. Various reports suggest that the conquistador drank his wine with water and had large earthen jugs of wine buried in the floor of his house in Veracruz. His contemporary historian Francisco López de Gómara noted, though, that Cortés was temperate in his drinking.[6] When Tenochtitlán fell to Spanish troops, wine was brought in from the coast and a drunken banquet ensued.

Once the viceroyalty of New Spain was established, wine was regularly shipped from Spanish wine regions like Jerez de la Frontera, Puerto Real, Chiclana, Sevilla, and Sanlúcar to the port of Veracruz.[7] During the early years of the Conquest, between 50 and 100 casks of Spanish wine were arriving in New Spain annually. Later in the 1500s, even fifty large transatlantic vessels laden in part with wine (alongside commodities like cloth and flour) could not satisfy the new domain's thirst.[8] In addition to scarcity, some of the imported wine was spoiled or *mareado* by the less than temperate conditions encountered in a ship's hold during an Atlantic crossing. It would have been prohibitively expensive for most people living in New Spain.

To meet Spanish (read: Catholic) demands for wine, in 1521, Cortés began facilitating the importation of grapevines. That same year, the ruling conquistador began to tax imported wine. Cortés ordered in 1524 that any Spaniard granted a *repartimiento* had to plant 1,000 grapevines for every 100 indigenous workers tied to the land for a duration of 5 years.[9] On August 31, 1531, the Crown issued a decree stipulating that anyone who crossed the Atlantic destined for New Spain would be required to bring grapevines and olive plantings.[10] They sought to Iberianize the landscape, to terraform this New World with the comforts and constants of life whence they came. Wine, wheat, and olives were to the Spanish what agave, corn, and prickly pears were to Mesoamericans. Wine was sorely missed. It was also necessary in the celebration of the Catholic mass.

Ironically, the mission-oriented Church was generally not keen on promoting grape wine as a sacramental substance among converted natives during the sixteenth century.[11] Reports differ, but friars frugally meted out the scarce wine during masses (and provided it in tending to the sick). Besides this, there was a concerted effort by the Spanish to keep grape wine from the indigenous peoples.

By 1525, some Spanish had already begun to criticize native consumption of wine. Rodrigo de Albornoz, royal auditor to Cortés's New Spain, wrote in December 1525, "And since the land is in the domain of Your Majesty, with the conversation and dealings of the Christians . . . they [the indigenous peoples] drink wine from Spain with better will than the pulque that they have as wine, which seems a bit like beer, although it is not."[12] In 1545, a royal decree prohibited the sale of grape wine to non-Spanish populations in New Spain, including indigenous and African peoples. The decree had been based on a recommendation made by friars working in New Spain who met with Bishop Zumarraga in the *Segunda Junta Eclesiástica* of 1539. The prohibition would be reaffirmed in 1594, 1637, and 1640. In May of 1609, King Philip III outlawed the payment of native day laborers with wine, threatening a fine of twenty pesos per infraction.[13]

In the face of this prohibition, opportunistic and unscrupulous Spaniards continued selling wine to native populations. Fray Gerónimo de Mendieta wrote in the late 1500s that some Spaniards resided in native communities only to work as tavern keepers where they sold wine for clothing, sex, labor, land, and more. In the words of the priest, "And so the ordinary entrance of a Spaniard as a neighbor to the Indians is with a pipe of wine in front of him."[14] Motolinía, for his part, suggests that Spaniards made counterfeit wines from sugar and agave sap. Boiled-down grape juice, called *arrope* or *jarabe*, was also mixed into low-quality wines. In Guatemala, as well, evidence suggests that Spaniards cut wine with honey and water to sell in indigenous communities.[15]

Even in Ciudad de México, the sale of wine was restricted, closely regulated, and taxed. Pedro Hernández Paniagua received an early permit to sell bread and wine in the city on June 5, 1528.[16] Later, wine sales were prohibited in the vicinity of the city's largest markets.

Vineyards in New Spain

Through the sixteenth century, the conquest of the vine continued aggressively across New Spain. Querétaro, Guanajuato, Aguascalientes, Oaxaca, Puebla, and Michoacán all had vines planted in the 1500s.[17] In 1555, a Ciudad de México delegation was sent to Spain to petition the Crown for land to plant vineyards. Apparently, winemaking in New Spain was consequential enough that in 1571 a law was passed indicating that vendors of wine had to hang handkerchiefs outside of their Ciudad de México shops to demonstrate the provenance of their product: white handkerchiefs meant the wine was Spanish, black handkerchiefs meant the wine was from the New World.[18] Finally, in 1593, the first true commercial vineyard and *bodega* ("winery") were established at the hacienda Santa María de las Parras (now Parras de la Fuente) in Coahuila by Capitán Francisco de Urdiñola. The property would become the largest legitimate winery and distillery in New Spain, acclaimed for the quality of its wine.

Vintners in Cadiz had been complaining to King Philip II that colonial demand for their peninsular wines was in decline, presumably due to local production in New Spain. So, in 1595, the king outlawed the planting of new vines, the replacement of established vineyards, and in some cases required that vines be uprooted in the viceroyalty. The law was ratified again by Philip III in 1610 and again by Philip IV in both 1628 and 1631. What's strange—if the vineyard at Santa María de las Parras was the first commercial endeavor in 1593, the Cadiz winemakers would not have become so frustrated in only 2 years—it was not even enough time for a first vintage. Production existed unsanctioned by the Crown.

The year 1595 also represents an intriguing duplicity in the history of wine in New Spain. While the total prohibition on the expansion of vineyards and maintenance of healthy vines would continue for two more centuries, so would the domestic production of wine! In 1597, for example, Don Lorenzo García founded Bodegas San Lorenzo in Parras, which has become Casa Madero, S.A. today. This underscores a central issue in telling the history of colonial Mexico through Spanish regulations. The Crown had limited influence in the New World, and the colony was largely ruled by Mexican-born elite who could buy their way into the Audiencia.[19] If they wanted local wine, they would have it.

A century later, viticulture was expanding into the northwest of Mexico as Father Juan de Ugarte brought vines to Baja California at the Mission of San Francisco Javier in 1697. These vines would be moved up the Pacific Coast and become the early basis for California's wine industry. In the 1760s, Fray Junípero Serra founded missions in San Diego with adjacent vineyards. A belt of missionary vineyards flowed from Sonora to San Diego by the end of the eighteenth century.

Yet grapes grown on missions did not produce wine of distinguished qualities. Invariably, these vines were of the Criolla or Mission Grape varietal, which likely came to the New World with the Conquistadors, but were generally not known in Europe. The grape has poor color and low acidity for vinification.

For the entirety of the colonial period, importation of Spanish wine continued. A wide array of wines would have been consumed by New Spain's elites including Aranda, Bordeaux, Cabezon, Claret, Graves, Guadalcanal, sherry from Jerez, Malaga, Malvasia, Manzanilla, Moscatel, Pajarete, Pedro Ximenez, Peralta, Tenerife, Tintilla, Valdepeñas, and Vidueño.[20]

Wine in Independent Mexico

Padre Miguel Hidalgo, the Father of Mexican Independence, openly defied Spanish law as he planted vineyards and taught indigenous communities in his parish to produce grapes for winemaking. When Hidalgo defied an order from the Real Audiencia that all vineyards be burned, the first battles of the war for independence began in Guanajuato.

The early governments of independent Mexico attempted to foment a domestic wine industry. The Provisional Government Junta moved to tax imported wine in 1822, while the Mexican Congress gave domestic vineyards a decade-long tax break the following year.[21] But after independence, Mexican viticulture would largely lay fallow until the Porfiriato encouraged California winemakers to invest in northern Mexico.

Before Díaz came to power in 1876, only one new winery had been established in independent Mexico—Bodegas Ferriño at Cuatrociénegas in Coahuila, founded in 1860. Mexican viticulture was on the verge of extinction. During the Porfiriato, however, investment was made in the wine space. Díaz assigned the son of the Hungarian ambassador to oversee that each Mexican state had at least one vineyard.[22] Cuttings were brought in from France and placed around Hacienda Roque near Celaya. An Irishman named James

Concannon had gotten concessions from Díaz, importing several million cuttings from California's Livermore Valley, moving Mexican viticulture away from a monoculture of mission grapes between 1889 and 1904.[23] In 1892 alone, 1,053,450 vines were imported from California, of which 500,000 were planted at Parras.[24] Another California winemaker, Antonio Perelli-Minetti, planted Zinfandel, Petit Sirah, Malaga, and Flame Tokay around Torreón, Coahuila. Ultimately, when Díaz fell and a decade of Revolution embroiled Mexico in the 1910s, winemakers returned to California and the vineyards fell into disarray.

Now, since the 1950s, Mexico has reestablished its viticultural industry that has braved nearly 500 years of hardship. Between 1939 and 1972, the area planted with vines grew by a factor of fifteen.[25] From 1940 to 1942 alone, the planted area increased by over 400 percent.[26] Between the 1950s and 1973, around fifty wineries had begun operating.[27] During the 1970s, production volume boomed, but most regions still lacked knowledge of the grape varietals that were best suited to the local geography and climate. Mexico produced 4,260,000 liters of wine in 1970, 6,300,000 liters of wine in 1974, and 11,669,500 liters of wine in 1976.[28] Since the 1980s, the industry has really taken off in terms of quality, but international trade liberalization hurt the young industry following its 1983 peak.

One figure rises above the rest in the reignition of Mexico's modern wine industry. Don Nazario Ortiz Garza, who served as governor of Coahuila and later Secretary of Agriculture, would become the largest producer of wine and brandy in Mexico as he built vineyards at Saltillo, Coahuila, and later Aguascalientes in 1952. He was the first president of what would become today's *Consejo Mexicano Vitivinícola*. The overall domestic industry was buoyed when import tariffs on European wines were quadrupled following the Second World War. In Baja California, one-time president of Mexico, Abelardo L. Rodríguez, owned and operated Santo Tomás winery, which helped to develop world-class viticulture in Baja California's five wine growing valleys.

During the twenty-first century, a robust wine ecosystem has come to life in Mexico with universities, government agencies, and private entities working to improve the quality of wines and educate both Mexicans and the world on the quality of Mexican wines.

The largest wine growing regions today are Zacatecas (primarily around Fresnillo) and Baja California (near Ensenada). Together, they produce 71 percent of Mexico's processed grapes.[29] In total, the Consejo Mexicano Vitivinícola counts fifteen wine producing states, including Aguascalientes, Baja California Sur, Baja California, Chihuahua, Coahuila, Durango, Guanajuato, Jalisco, Nuevo León, Querétaro, Puebla, San Luis Potosí, Sonora, and Zacatecas. In addition to grapes, other fruit wines have been produced in Mexico over the centuries, including those made from figs, oranges, peaches, quinces, pineapples, and raspberries.

* * *

La Polla

La polla is a wine-based breakfast pick-me-up made from milk, raw eggs, vanilla, and *vino tipo Jerez* (i.e., imitation sherry). The egg is either floated in the drink to be consumed whole and raw or beaten into the liquid. The drink is a hangover cure and a fortifying breakfast drink. It is also rumored to help with male virility, which explains its suggestive name, which we might translate as "Cock." Some versions call for sugar, cinnamon, chocolate powder, and orange juice. It has its origins in Guadalajara, but is common in other large cities as well. Orange juice street vendors often offer pollas for sale and will add fresh juice into the wine.

Sangría

Sangría is at home in Mexico. The drink emerged in Spain around the end of the 1700s and may have been consumed in Mexico shortly after. During the viceroyalty of Matías de Gálvez y Gallardo between 1783 and 1784, it has been noted that consumption of limonadas was popular in New Spain.[30] Early sangrías were essentially wine-lemonades, mixing red wine, citrus juice, and sugar. Even in Spain, there is great diversity in how a sangría is prepared, but spices, liquors, fruits, and juices can all be added.

In cantinas in mid-nineteenth-century Mexico, sangría was a common drink and was also consumed in the morning as a hangover cure. It must have been popular, because Sangría Señorial, a nonalcoholic, sangría-flavored soda, was launched in 1960 and is still widely consumed today.

Wild Grape Wine

While there is no compelling evidence that Mesoamericans vinified native grape varieties before European Conquest, there are clear examples of native wines in Mexico today. Drinks referred to as *Sangre de Baco* ("Blood of Bacchus") in Guerrero, *Sangre de Pichón* ("Pigeon's Blood," generally a descriptor of the color ruby red) in Veracruz, and, at times, simply *vino de uva silvestre* are all wines or liqueurs of native grapes.

In both Huitzuco, Guerrero, and Naolinco, Veracruz, *Vitis tiliifolia* is used in both wines and liqueurs. A thriving native wine market exists in Naolinco. In the hills around the shoe-making town, the *bejucos*, or vines, grow wild on the shade trees of coffee farms. The season for the wild grape, which Naolinqueños simply call *uvita*, is from September to November. The bunches of grapes are made up of fruits which each contain one small seed. Their flesh is very acidic. The wine is produced by soaking the fruit in water until a foam begins to form. The pulp is then filtered out, and it is left to ferment (with sugar added). Some producers attest that the practice is generations old, with one winemaker noting he had been producing it for at least 40 years and that his grandmother had a massive *uvita* vine in her garden with which she made wine. The availability of wine is highly seasonal, but bottles may be available at Restaurante Pilatos near the town center.

In Coahuila, it has been widely reported that a drink called *vino de acachul* is produced from wild grapes, although the plant may be of the genus *Ardisia* or coralberry. The word acachul, though, refers to different, small native fruit depending on local usage. The *Ampelocissus acapulcensis*, not technically a grape but in the same family as the genus *Vitis*, is used to produce a liqueur called *petaquilla* in Guerrero. Sea grapes (also not true grapes), from the species *Coccoloba uvifera*, are used along the Pacific Coast to prepare jams and wine-like alcoholic drinks.[31] There is also a tradition of producing wines from wild raspberries in Xico, Veracruz. The sweet, raspberry wine is simply called *la mora* or *la morita*.

* * *

Mexico is home to one of the largest populations of Catholics in the world. The religious groundwork that the early Conquest and its missionaries laid has created a five-century tradition of a distinctively Mexican approach to the faith. Perhaps no other image has been adopted more widely in the modern Roman Catholic Church than Mexico's own Our Lady of Guadalupe. Where there are Catholics, there must be wine.

Wine was the first European beverage to reach the shores of Mesoamerica in the holds of Cortés's ships, and it continued to be a constant colonial presence through the expansionary ambition of Catholic missions. Production of wine became entrenched in the northern reaches of the colony and eventually spread along the Pacific Coast into the Baja Peninsula and up into modern-day California. But production of wine has faced challenges for centuries. From peninsular antagonism during the viceroyalty to economic and regional instability during the pre-Revolution Independence Era, Mexico's potential as a wine growing region has been stunted. Today, its full potential is still not realized.

But consumer demand is beginning to tell a different story. Domestic demand outpaces production. In 2018, the Mexican government stepped in to pass the Ley de Fomento Vitivinícola to expand winemaking within the country. Imports of wine have skyrocketed since 2000, favoring wines from Spain, Chile, France, and Italy. As more sophisticated viticulture and vinification come to regions like Zacatecas and the Baja Peninsula, Mexico could soon be producing wines that turn heads in the most discerning circles.

5

Spirits

Mexico has one of the most vibrant and diverse distilled spirits landscapes in the world. It ranks among the top global exporters of spirits, buoyed by tequila's meteoric rise in global consumption over the past several decades. Thanks to the limited geographical distribution of agave spirits, the country basically has a monopoly on a whole category of liquor used in modern mixology.

More than business, though, distillation is a hallmark of regional identity in Mexico, with some spirits only existing in extremely circumscribed areas. Clandestine distillation, what Americans would call moonshining, informs much of the history of Mexican spirit making and is still extant in remote regions today. To understand the landscape of Mexican spirits, it is necessary to delve into history, technology, agriculture, language, geography, and a bit of law.

The Global Spread of Distillation

Globally speaking, commercial distillation of beverage alcohol came of age around the same time that Europeans arrived in the Americas. When Columbus landed in the New World in 1492, the average European would have been drinking almost exclusively beer and wine, with the occasional shot of medicinal gin from the doctor. In China, sorghum-based *baijiu* distillation was maturing along a similar timeline under the Ming Dynasty. The world's first book dedicated to the topic of distillation, *Liber de arte distillandi de simplicibus* (The Book of the Art of Distillation out of Simple Ingredients), was published after the Old and New World first made contact in 1500. The Americas were initiated into the modern global system of transoceanic exchange just as humans began drinking spirits for fun.

Before the Spanish conquered Mexico, though, Mesoamericans had no knowledge of distillation that we can prove definitively today. Indigenous peoples were drinking traditional fermented beverages containing alcohol, but did not fortify them via evaporation and subsequent condensation. This statement comes with a disclaimer—starting in 1980, there has been considerable academic interest within Mexico in proving that Mesoamericans independently developed the technology to distill. Some scholars suggest that the archaeological record contains ceramics such as figure-eight or gourd-shaped pots and ovens like conical kilns that could have been used for distillation. They have even recreated systems based on pottery recovered from Colima's Capacha Period (1500–1000 BCE) and successfully employed modern mezcal distillers to use the pottery to produce liquor.[1] But the complete set of pieces required to produce a distillate has never been found in one place in any archaeological dig, and chemical analysis of pottery does not support the use. These academics discuss the potential, not the reality.

For our purposes, distillation came to the New World after European contact. But it is not straightforward where it came from. Most modern theories suggest that it crossed both the Atlantic Ocean and the Pacific Ocean in different forms. Researchers look at the design and construction of stills, the boilers used to extract alcohol from a liquid, to determine where the knowledge required to build and operate the equipment could have originated. Agave spirits, therefore, have existed for less than 500 years.

The earliest mezcal stills that existed in much of western Mexico—upon which the modern agave spirit industry was founded—are related to

Asiatic designs rather than Mediterranean ones. The postulation is that this technology was transmitted by Filipino sailors operating *La Nao de China*, or the Manila Galleon, from the Spanish colony in the Philippines to port cities along the west coast, usually Acapulco. This transpacific exchange began when the Manila Galleon started connecting the two colonies in 1565.

Historical records discuss how Filipino sailors would often arrive in Mexico and stick around. The eastward journey from the Filipino port of Cavite covered over 15,000 kilometers and lasted a grueling average of 6 months. Sailors and passengers alike suffered from starvation, disease, and exposure to the elements. One galleon, the *Espíritu Santo*, arrived in Acapulco in 1618. Seventy out of seventy-five Filipino *grumetes*, or ordinary sailors, on board fled to Colima to avoid a return voyage where they found employment climbing coconut palms to extract sap that was fermented into *tuba* and distilled into *vino de cocos*.[2] Writing in 1619, Captain Sebastián de Pineda discussed how extensive plantations of coconut palm trees were fueling a cottage industry of coconut brandy distillation. By the 1640s, a group of "chinos," namely Miguel Pano, Sebastián de la Cruz, Juan de Triana, Francisco Ramos, and Nicolás Mananquel, owned and operated their own plantations for brandy production.[3]

In the states adjacent to Colima, many of the indigenous groups who now distill mezcal for local consumption have had their unique styles of still construction documented by anthropologists. For over a century now, academics have been discussing Cora stills, Huichol stills (of the Wixárika), *tachica* stills (of the Nahua), Tepehuano stills, Zapoteco stills, and Tarasco stills (of the Purépecha).[4] Each of these forms of distillation is unique and nuanced, and not all of them are still in use today. All these indigenous stills, however, rely on the design principles of the technology traditionally used in the Philippines. Tequila and mezcal, it turns out, have Asian roots.

Generally, this style of still heats a fermented liquid in a column, pot, or cone that is capped with a bowl containing cold water. The alcoholic vapor will boil off and encounter the inverse side of the water bowl. The vapor condenses on the cool, convex dome and runs down the surface to the lowest point on the bottom of the bowl where it drips into a funnel, a ceramic gutter, a wooden spoon, or an agave leaf. The liquid then runs out of the still in a spout. Finally, the spout funnels the condensed spirits into a collecting bottle for consumption. Variations exist, but the basic concept is that of a still from Asia.

Compared to the indigenous renditions of the Asiatic still, it is surprising how little academic attention has been directed toward the arrival of the Arab still in Mexico. Sugar production came to Europe via the Islamic world (consider that both the words sugar and *azúcar* derive from the Arabic *al-sukar*). The Arabs had taken rudimentary sugar production methods from India and made advancements in processing, improving both the clarity of syrups and the crystal quality of solid sugar.

This is particularly salient in the Spanish context. The Moors had only recently been expelled from *al-Andalus*, that is, Spain, prior to the Conquest of Mesoamerica. The same year Columbus arrived in the New World, the Muslim Emirate of Granada was finally defeated in southern Spain. Under Moorish rule, the southern coastal city of Motril had been a sugar-producing hub.

It was the Arab-style metal still, or alembic (in Spanish *alembique*), that arrived on the eastern shores of the Gulf of Mexico along with sugarcane production. The marriage of the alembic with sugar gave birth to the New Spanish scourge of *chinguirito*. The use of the word *vino* to refer to both wine and spirits obfuscates the history, but one of the first mentions of cane spirits in the New World came from the mining community of Taxco, Guerrero, in 1600, where miners apparently bought and sold an aguardiente called "*vino de azúcar*."[5]

On the other coast, the Filipinos, who introduced wooden still designs to the indigenous peoples of western Mexico (who would also build them out of clay), settled into an existing agave culture and built a nascent coconut palm industry. Only later would Arab stills be adopted for agave spirits, while the Asiatic stills have not been adopted outside of their historical context of mezcal and coconut brandy production in the western states (with the small exception of some cane-based charanda produced using a Filipino still).

In terms of function, the Arab still consists of a pot in which fermented liquid is boiled until its vapor passes through a curved neck into a snake or coiled pipe that is cooled with water from the outside. The underlying concept of the Arab still is popular around the world, and this technique is used in making whiskey, gin, and certain mezcals.

So why does all this regional historical conjecture about the style of distillation matter? Ultimately, Mexico has two distinct historical traditions that are producing spirits that go by the same name. These traditions derive from opposite sides of the Old World. There is the sugarcane-alembic tradition and the coconut-Filipino one. They mingle together at will among the agave. Yet, mezcal will be called mezcal, whether it is distilled in an Arab still or a Filipino still. Certain producers in states like Colima, Nayarit, and Jalisco, for example, continue to produce mezcal commercially using Asiatic-style stills. The rest of the producers generally use some version of the Arab alembic. In this sense, Mexico represents an incredible hybrid of the Mediterranean and the Asiatic traditions of distillation found nowhere else in the world.

Centuries of Bootlegging

After the technology of distillation was firmly established in Mexico, it ran up against a major problem in the Spanish Crown. As the conquering power, Spain wanted to hold a monopoly on the production and sale of alcoholic beverages in the New World. Distilled spirits were a particularly sore point for the viceroyalty in Mexico. As early as 1615, the Spanish Crown had prohibited the use of sugarcane to make distilled spirits.[6] It was not until 1796 that Spain legalized the production of *chinguirito*, or sugarcane spirits, on Mexican soil. Grape brandy, which would have been the main type of liquor in Spain, was illegal too, because the Crown prohibited the planting of vineyards. Still, at Santa María de las Parras, grape brandy was produced as early as 1659.[7]

Vino de cocos, the distillate that Filipino sailors brought to Colima from their homeland, was legally produced for around 80 years during the 1600s. While the Crown had tried to chop down all the coconut palms in Colima in the 1610s to stymie its production, the viceroyalty issued a permit for its distillation following a hurricane in 1627 that decimated the region's cacao crop and its economy along with it.[8] Colimenses managed to renew that permit throughout the seventeenth century, but eventually had it revoked toward the year 1700.

Elsewhere, though, distillation was not permitted. Over the centuries, a culture of clandestine spirit making was born. Spirit makers were forced into the geographical backcountry and the legal backwaters. Remote, indigenous distilling flourished in local contexts, building the deep, local, and varied tradition of mezcal we know today.

The nineteenth century saw a loosening of laws regarding spirits, but during American Prohibition an eager post-Revolution Mexican government once again clamped down on spirits. When we see diversity in Mexican spirits—hyperlocal still designs and nearly a dozen different names for agave spirits—we see the isolation in which they have flourished.

Legal Spirits and Denominations

Today, the modern Mexican state is drawing on the rich heritage that isolation has created. In the last 50 years, the Mexican government has registered six denominations of origin for distilled spirits, four of which apply to agave spirits alone. Unlike wine denominations, which typically justify themselves based on terroir and microclimates, Mexico leans more on legacy and tradition.

Only now are local spirits being consumed outside of their traditional context. Tequila has found its way into bars on all seven continents. Oaxacan mezcal is now exported on an industrial scale. Regional drinks like *raicilla*, *sotol*, and *bacanora* appear in specialty bars abroad. Mexican whiskey gets featured in magazines.

Mexico now has 500 years of experience distilling. The modern footprint of the Mexican spirit is increasingly complex as more legal definitions enter the space of the back bar. Ultimately, though, the landscape of distilled spirits has its roots in local history.

* * *

Agave

Agave spirits are the largest category of distillates that derive from an indigenous ingredient in Mexico. Throughout its natural range, there are over 200 species of *Agave*, and several dozen varieties are commonly used in the commercial production of spirits. Many other wild species are harvested for artisanal spirit making. The overwhelming majority of agave spirits, though, are produced from only two species: *Agave tequilana* and *Agave angustifolia*.

Mexico is the birthplace of the agave spirit, but it is not the exclusive producer of them. In the plant's native range, Venezuela produces *cocuy*, and Ecuador has *miske*. Agave has also been introduced to arid regions in Australia, South Africa, Madagascar, Israel, and California where farmers are betting on a market for non-Mexican agave spirits.

Due to the genetic diversity of agave and the regional differences in how the plants are transformed into spirits, there are many different classifications and naming conventions. Four of these have been formalized into Mexican law: mezcal, tequila, raicilla, and bacanora. Still others are the informal or colloquial names for spirits produced locally. The many different categories of agave spirits are outlined below.

Bacanora

Bacanora is an agave spirit distilled from *Agave angustifolia* and *Agave rhodacantha*. It is made exclusively in the state of Sonora. Sonorans have made the spirit for over 300 years, but it has had its own denomination of origin since the year 2000. The spirit is named after a municipality in Sonora, and the term "bacanora" has been used since the late nineteenth century to refer to spirits.[9]

For a significant part of the 1900s, bacanora was illegal in Sonora and had a national reputation as a kind of clandestinely manufactured spirit. It is now protected, celebrated, and available internationally.

Destilado de Agave

Destilado de agave is a legal category of spirits that are distilled from agave and resemble mezcal, but do not, in one way or another, fit into Mexico's legal definition of the mezcal name and label. These beverages highlight both the advantages and shortcomings of Denominations of Origin.

For many producers of destilado de mezcal, they cannot label their spirits as mezcal because they exist outside of the geographic region that is authorized to use the name. One example of agave spirit producers who lay claim to at least a century of tradition is that of Zumpahuacán in the state of Mexico. These distillers could not use the term "mezcal" starting in 1995 when the new government standards excluded them from the denomination. The law was later expanded in 2018 when specified municipalities in the states of Aguascalientes, Mexico (including Zumpahuacán mentioned above), Morelos, and Puebla were all added to the list.

Even producers within the geographic designation will produce spirits from agave that cannot be called mezcal. Because the law also dictates that mezcal be produced, bottled, and labeled in a certain way, any practices outside of the norm result in destilado de agave. Some wild agave mezcals use the destilado de agave label, perhaps because the law requires the percent of each species to be displayed on the bottle, which may not be known. Other producers simply do not want to work with industry regulators to register their products as compliant. In other words, destilado de agave might be called mezcal informally, but has no legal right to the name.

Comiteco

Comiteco is a specific variety of agave spirit distilled in the city of Comitán, Chiapas. It is most often produced from *Agave americana* or *Agave atrovirens*. Comitán has a strong tradition of distillation which includes sugarcane aguardiente, Chiapaneco *pox*, and comiteco. The spirit can be the distillate of fermented agave syrup, rather than just the juice of the ground hearts. It is sometimes associated with low-quality spirits and illegal distillation.

The area has been producing agave spirits since at least the 1800s. Comiteco's reputation used to be known much more widely. Central American countries would import Comiteco from Chiapas instead of paying for pricier options from Guadalajara.[10] The Mexican Consul to Guatemala reported to Mexico's House of Commerce in 1905 saying, "The 'comiteco' and the 'tequila' are well known and well appreciated here; and in general, the names of all alcoholic beverages that are made in Mexico, are shown conspicuously in advertisements at bars and liquor stores, and are well sought after by consumers."[11]

Lechuguilla

Lechuguilla is the spirit distilled from various agave species including *Agave palmeri*, *Bovicornuta*, *shrevei*, and *deserti*.[12] This spirit should not be confused with *Agave lechuguilla*, a common agave used for fiber, nor should it be confused with the lightly fermented beverage produced in Autlán, Jalisco, called by the same name. In the northwestern state of Sonora, lechuguilla is a regional term for locally produced agave spirits. Generally, the term "lechuguilla" is used for any agave spirit that is not bacanora. Because it is distilled in Sonora, lechuguilla does not legally qualify as mezcal.

Sisal, Destilado de Henequén

Sisal is the distilled spirit of the *henequén* plant, or *Agave fourcroydes*, produced in the Yucatán Peninsula. This species of *Agave* has long been used as a source of fiber for weaving and manufacturing textiles at both a homespun and industrial level. Yucatán enjoyed a period of wealth during the 1800s due to demand for sisal fiber from US industry and agriculture. The conversion of the fibrous agave into a distilled spirit is a novel, modern occurrence, perhaps due to the popularization of mezcal and tequila. Yucatán, after all, is isolated from traditional mezcal areas.

In 2005, a group of researchers at Centro de Investigación Científica de Yucatán A.C. successfully filed a patent with the Instituto Mexicano de la Propiedad Industrial for a process of producing alcohol from the henequén plant. There are now commercial producers of the spirit. To find a bottle, visit the Pueblo Mágico of Izamal near the Yucateco city of Mérida.

Tuxca

Tuxca is a name for agave spirits produced in the area surrounding the Nevado de Colima volcano in both Jalisco and Colima. The name of the spirit derives from the city of Tuxcacuesco, Jalisco. The area has been distilling liquor since the sixteenth century out of its native species *A. angustifolia Haw* and *A. rhodacantha.*[13] The same local name for the spirit exists in communities like Zapotitlán de Vadillo and Tolimán in Jalisco as well as Comala in Colima. While distillation in this region relies on the Filipino still more than in other regions of Mexico, tuxca is not exclusively defined by production methods. Bottles of tuxca are easily purchased in shops in Comala and are consumed with coffee to stay up at night in the town. The distillate is also common in Tuxpan, Jalisco.

Destilado de Pulque

Destilado de pulque, sometimes called *vino de maguey* or *mezcal de pulque*, is a spirit that is derived from the distillation of fermented agave sap. While this is technically a spirit derived from pure agave, it is distinct from the predominant methods of creating agave spirits which rely on baking the hearts of the plant to obtain fermentable sugars. Pulque agaves, like the *A. atrovirens*, *A. mapsiaga*, and *A. salmiana* species, are some of the largest in size and are distributed around the Central Valley.

Pulque has been distilled since at least the eighteenth century in central Mexico where the agave sap is most common. The 1784 Navarro report calls aguardiente de pulque "*sisíque*" and notes that it existed in Tampico. It was also called *bingarrote*, distilled from a pulque called *binguí* and was common in the area around Querétaro. Where some mezcal (called *mezcal de pechuga*) is produced with a chicken breast cooked along with the fermented agave wine in the still, there exists historical evidence to suggest that bingarrote in Querétaro also included chicken or rooster meat.[14] It was alternatively called *pachuca* and *mesquital.*

If pulque was Mexico's favorite alcohol in the pre-distillation era, why is destilado de pulque less common than mezcal? The answer likely has to do with the high intensity of labor required to extract even moderate quantities of pulque. Distillation cuts the volume of the fermented liquid to a fourth or fifth of its original amount. A significant quantity of pulque would be required to support the industry. Another distillate, *vino de cocos*, which also relies on a fermented sap and a similar extraction process, likely also fell out of favor due to the relatively high cost of extraction. Moreover, pulque is quick to ferment into vinegar, creating supply chain headaches for aspiring bulk distillers. The spirit is most common in the central states that produce pulque, mainly Mexico and Hidalgo. Some versions of destilado de pulque are even available internationally.

Mezcal

Mezcal is a denomination of origin protected spirit made from agave. Agave distillation developed throughout much of western Mexico over the past 300 years. Local techniques, diverse *Agave* species, and linguistic idiosyncrasies have all carried down into the modern mezcal marketplace, which offers consumers a variety of flavor profiles. As the Mexican government tries to protect these traditions by drawing borders and delineating definitions, we can better describe what mezcal is, as well as what it is not.

Mezcal is made from a broad array of *Agave* species for which regional distillers often have affinities. The most common of all is *espadín*, or *Agave angustifolia Haw*. Other popular mezcals are distilled from *barril* (*Agave rodacantha*), *tobalá* (*Agave potatorum*), *mexicano* (*Agave macroacantha*), and *Agave karwinskii*. Mezcal can be made from "other species of agave, as long as they are not used as raw material for other beverages with designations of origin within the same State."[15] Indeed, the list of mezcals generally includes fourteen core varieties of agave, including several wild species.

What this means, though, is that other denominations of origin protected agave spirits linked to specific *Agave* species are not technically types of mezcal. Many people, for example, describe tequila as a type of mezcal, qualifying that not all mezcal is tequila—a sort of square-is-a-rectangle situation. Legally speaking, much of tequila is made in Jalisco, which is not included in modern mezcal's denomination of origin. Moreover, the regulations for commercial mezcal exclude beverages made from specific agaves that are classified with another existing designation within a state. Tequila, which is only made from *Agave tequilana*, therefore, is not technically a mezcal, even if it is distilled in the mezcal-protected states of Michoacán, Guanajuato, or Tamaulipas.

How Mezcal is Made. There are three tiers of mezcal production, each of which has a slightly different production process. Mezcals can be *ancestral*, *artesanal*, or labeled only with the word "Mezcal." All of these follow the general process of harvesting, cooking, milling, fermenting, distilling, and bottling, but the differences within each production step determine the classification of the resulting liquor.

Both mezcal ancestral and artesanal reference more traditional, less scalable methods of production. Both methods rely on stone pits for the *cocción* ("baking") of the agave. Humans have been baking agave to convert their starches into edible sugars in subterranean pits for thousands of years within the Mesoamerican world.

To cook the agave hearts, distillers first take an ax and split them into quarters. They then heat up a pile of large volcanic stones using firewood. When the stones are glowing red, sections of the agave are placed in a pile on top of the stones. The pile is then covered with tarps, leaves, branches, and soil to keep out oxygen and prevent a fire from forming. This method slowly cooks the agave over several days. While the mound smolders, much of the smoke is trapped inside. This imparts the final mezcal with its signature smoky quality.

From the oven, the cooked agaves are ground up to extract their sweet juices. Non-industrial milling occurs in circular milling grounds that rely on large stone wheels, called *tahonas*, that pivot around a central pole. Producers of mezcal ancestral and artisanal use horses, mules, and tractors to move the grinding wheel over the cooked agave, crushing the hearts. Most milling grounds are built with drainage that directs the pressed juice off into a collecting container.

The juice of mezcal is then fermented using yeasts. Traditional mezcal factories usually maintain mother yeast batches foaming perpetually in well-fed barrels, but industrial processes rely on measured quantities of standardized, lab-grown yeast. As the must ferments, a thick head of solids will form, protecting the bubbling liquid below. After several days, the alcoholic must is ready for distillation.

Mezcal ancestral is generally milled manually with animals, fermented in animal hide containers, and then distilled in traditional clay stills. Mezcal artesanal is fermented in cement, wood, or plastic, and distilled in copper stills. Industrial mezcal will use gas ovens in place of firewood for cooking and will use mechanized milling and highly efficient continuous distillation.

These production factors contribute to the final organoleptic properties of mezcal. Each step of the process will have a marked effect on the resulting product. Most of the finest commercial bottles on the market today will list the most salient aspects of production, including *Agave* species, production region, distiller name, still type, aging method, and so on.

With industrial mezcal, stainless steel machinery means that the resulting product is devoid of production flavor. Contact with animal hides, wood, concrete, stone, clay, copper, and a bit of hard labor all add to traditional mezcal's distinctiveness.

One last note should be added—only mezcal labeled "100% Agave" contains no additives. Producers can legally add sugars from non-agave sources to assist in their process and to produce a smoother product.

The Producers of Mezcal. Today, mezcal is mostly produced in nine of Mexico's states that have a long tradition of making the agave distillate. These nine states are Oaxaca, Puebla, Durango, Zacatecas, Guerrero, San Luis Potosí, Michoacán, Guanajuato, and Tamaulipas. This number is slightly inaccurate, though, as Aguascalientes and Mexico have had small municipalities protected under the mezcal name since 2018.

Each of these states has a cultural, historical, and legal claim to the name mezcal, and there are quality mezcals produced in all of them. Nevertheless, due to the ubiquity of production in the state of Oaxaca, it represents over 90 percent of commercial output. Mezcals on the global market almost exclusively come from Oaxaca.

Mezcal Potosino, at one time, was once a common name around Mexico. Alternatively, the place of production sometimes becomes synonymous with the mezcal it produces, as is the case with Chichihualco Mezcal produced in

Chichihualco de los Bravos, Guerrero. Producers of mezcal are called *maestros, mezcaleros, palenqueros*, or *vinateros* depending on local usage.

Tepe

Tepe is a specific market name for mezcal produced by the native Tepehuano communities in Jalisco (especially in Huejuquilla), Zacatecas, and Durango (especially in Canoas). It is distilled from *A. durangensis*, which is known as *ji ja* in the Tepehuano language, but is protected by mezcal's denomination of origin when produced in Zacatecas and Durango.[16] Commonly, tepe is made into a medicinal infusion that is macerated with herbs.

The term "tepe" sometimes also refers to a Wixárika ceremonial agave distillate from *A. bovicornuta* also called *tuchi*.[17] Distillers in Durango will also sell this spirit under the name *cenizo*, in reference to the agave's common name.

Raicilla

Raicilla is an agave spirit distilled in Jalisco and Nayarit from the species *A. maximiliana Baker, A. inaequidens Koch, A. valenciana, A. angustifolia Haw*, and *A. rhodacantha*. In 2019, it became the sixth distilled spirit in Mexico to receive a denomination of origin. Sixteen municipalities in Jalisco and one in Nayarit can produce the spirit. Within the world of raicilla, there are two distinct regions of production. Coastal raicilla is distilled from *Agave angustifolia Haw.* and *rhodacantha*, while Sierra raicilla is distilled from *Agave maximiliana Baker, inaequidens Koch*, and *valenciana*. Raicilla is available internationally.

Tequila

Tequila is the denomination of origin protected spirit distilled from blue Weber agave, or *Agave tequilana*. It is the most commercially consequential spirit produced in Mexico and has wide-reaching global popularity.

Tequila is produced using a similar process as mezcal, just with a different *Agave* species and in a different group of states. The denomination of origin for tequila was Mexico's first, established in 1974. The states of Jalisco, Michoacán, Tamaulipas, Nayarit, and Guanajuato legally produce tequila. Jalisco, however, represents over 90 percent of annual production. Internationally available tequila generally comes from Jalisco.

Historically, the spirit was called *vino de tequila*, in reference to the name of a town outside of the state capital of Guadalajara, where tequila is made. The town of Tequila is still home to large distilleries and vast blue agave plantations. A luxury alcohol tourism industry has developed in the area.

Tequila also has its own vocabulary, largely distinct from other agave spirits. The *jimador* is the harvester of the blue agave. The shot glass that is used to consume tequila is typically called a *caballito*. Traditional tequila bottles are referred to as *pachitas* or *pachoncitas*.

Like mezcal, only tequila labeled "100% Agave" includes no added sugars. Tequila is generally sold based on how long it is aged. It can be classified as *Blanco* (Silver), *Oro* (Gold), *Reposado*, *Añejo*, and *Extra Añejo*.

Grape Brandy

Destilado de uva, or grape brandy, has an underappreciated role in the recent history of Mexican distillates. Spirits produced from Mexican-grown grapes eclipsed other popular spirits like tequila and aguardiente to become the most consumed by volume in the mid-twentieth century.[18] As late as the 1990s, it was preferred to wine. An attestation to this is that Casa Madero, Mexico's largest winery at Parras, Coahuila, promoted the cocktail "Cubamadero" as an alternative to the rum-based Cuba Libre.[19]

The history of grape brandy production, though, stretches back to 1659 when *aguardiente de uva* was first produced in the wine growing region of Santa María de las Parras. There is even evidence of wild, native grape species being used to produce "*aguardiente de uva silvestre*" in Huauchinango, Puebla, in the late eighteenth century.[20]

The Secretaría de Agricultura y Desarrollo Rural states that the majority of grapes grown at Parras, Coahuila, in 1885 (then the largest producer in the country) were destined for distillation rather than vinification. When Mexican viticulture picked up steam after the 1950s, grapes continued to be distilled into brandy rather than vinified. An estimated nine out of every ten grapes grown in Mexico were transformed into brandy in 1972.[21] Later in 1980, estimates suggest that 95 percent of grape musts were distilled, and sometimes aged in American oak barrels.[22] At this time, 40 percent of all distilled spirits sold in Mexico were brandy, while tequila only amounted to around 24 percent of market share.[23]

Pox

Pox (pronounced "posh") is the local designation for the clear spirits distilled in Chiapas from either corn, sugarcane, or wheat. Some versions are a combination of all three. Pox, in the Tzotzil language, means "medicine," and was previously a term used to refer to several forms of tobacco consumption, one of which involved smearing a paste of the leaf on the skin.[24]

In the indigenous regions of highlands Chiapas, pox has been produced for over a century. The first commercial pox factory opened in the 1920s in Chanal and became a regional monopoly. When that monopoly crumbled in the 1950s, the vacuum in the market drove widespread clandestine moonshining that became synonymous with the term "pox."[25] The spirit is still commonly produced in the Naranjal neighborhood of Chanal.

Pox has enjoyed high status in Chiapaneco culture, being involved in religious rituals of indigenous groups. The monopoly which distributed pox co-opted its power and infrastructure after it fell to distribute Coca-Cola instead, which has achieved similar religious prominence.

Sugarcane

The twentieth-century geographer Henry J Bruman wrote, "sugarcane, entirely unknown in aboriginal America, was one of the first economic plants to be introduced by the Spaniards. However, a sweet cane in the broader sense was not only known but widely utilized prior to the Conquest."[26] The implications of his observation meant that sugarcane would become one of the greatest sources of distilled alcohol for most of modern Mexican history.

Sugarcane fit perfectly into an existing culinary niche on the Gulf Coast of Mexico. Mesoamericans already knew how to make sugar, syrup, and alcohol from the sweet stalks of corn. They also produced both raw sugar and alcohol from agave sap. When Columbus brought sugarcane to the New World on his second voyage in 1493, it was a foreign plant, but its sweet potential was already well-known. The Nahuatl term for green cornstalks, *ohuatl*, was eventually used for sugarcane.[27] The burgeoning accessibility to sugarcane on early Spanish plantations presented a ready opportunity.

Aguardiente

Aguardiente was a name that arrived in the New World from Spain. Europeans called the nascent class of distilled spirits "burning water," "water of life," or "burnt wine" in their many languages. The Dutch word for burnt wine, "*brandewijn*," for example, gives us brandy. Aguardiente would have described any distilled spirit, particularly grape brandy in Spain, but in the context of

New Spain (and the rest of Spanish-colonized Central and South America), it was largely synonymous with cane spirits or *aguardiente de caña*. More emblematic of colonial Mexican sugarcane distillation, though, was the notorious term for cane liquor, *chinguirito*. The related name *chínguere* is still used to refer to cheap aguardiente in the country today.

Juan Navarro's February 29, 1784, report to Viceroy Don Matías de Gálvez described chinguirito alongside a drink called "*zlizitle*" in Huayacocotla, Veracruz, which was cane juice fermented with herbs in bark containers, but was likely once produced from corn stalks.[28] In modern Veracruz and Tabasco, we still find a drink called *lliztle* (sometimes written as *iliztle*), which is a contemporary local term for aguardiente. Most references note that today's lliztle also contains peaches, grapes, or pears. Linguistically, along the east coast, we see the evolution of corn stalk beer into sugarcane beer into distilled cane spirit.

Early aguardiente production established itself around elite-owned haciendas that specialized in sugar production. Sugar and liquor coexisted around Cuernavaca, on plantations in southeast Puebla, in the states of Michoacán and Veracruz, and along the west coast from Sinaloa to Colima. It is no coincidence that many of these regions today have strong local traditions focused on cane spirit production.

In the state of Morelos—one of the most suitable areas to grow sugarcane in Mexico—aguardiente is known by its place of origin, the town of Zacualpan de Amilpas. The town exports its eponymous distillate to other cities in Morelos, as well as the nearby states of Guerrero, Puebla, and Oaxaca. In Guanajuato, San Luis de la Paz also produced an eponymous aguardiente. The state of Michoacán also has several site-specific designations for aguardiente, including *charanda*, which is addressed below, *cuitzonco*, which has herbs in it, and *la excomunión*, so called because the Bishopric of Michoacán had prohibited it under the threat of excommunication.[29] Alternatively, Tonaya,

Jalisco, produces extremely cheap cane liquor, and the name Tonaya has come to mean cheap liquor in general.

Further south, sugarcane cultivation had begun on the Yucatán Peninsula under the Montejo family in the 1540s. They were later stripped of their lands due to egregious abuses of the native workers.[30] The Yucatecan rum industry would really take off during the heyday of sisal fiber production in the nineteenth century. It was then that rum became both a currency and a means of indenture. Workers were paid with rum on sisal haciendas, particularly unpleasant jobs such as clubbing rats were rewarded with bonuses of rum, and cantineros would tell landowners which workers had high bar tabs so that the debt could be transferred to the exploitative employer.[31] Children, too, were provided aguardiente for free until they were old enough to be indentured to the hacendados.[32]

Sugarcane spirits have also been distinguished by different levels of refinement. A French traveler in the late 1800s recorded that aguardiente in Tabasco fit into three categories: *tafia*—the worst, *aguardiente*—normal, and *ron* or *habanero*—the best.[33] Indeed, as late as the 1940s, the Departamento del Impuesto sobre Bebidas Alcohólicas considered habanero to be a variety of rum.[34] As far north as Louisiana, low-quality rum produced from impure molasses was also called tafia. The term "habanero" must refer to aguardiente of the quality of rum produced in Cuba.

And Mexico has another Cuban rum connection! Bacardi opened one of its first two distilleries outside of Cuba in Mexico in the 1930s. After the company's assets were seized in Cuba in 1960 by the new Castro government, production would continue in other countries, one of which was Mexico. It is no surprise that the Cuba Libre cocktail would become one of Mexico's favorite cantina drinks during the mid to late 1900s.

Charanda

Charanda is a denomination of origin protected variety of sugarcane distillate made in any one of sixteen municipalities around Uruapan, Michoacán. The spirit can be distilled from any fermented derivative of sugarcane grown in the region including guarapo, *melaza* ("molasses"), or piloncillo. This means that charanda spans categories of traditional rum production, from molasses to cane juice. Charanda also uses both alembic- and Filipino-style stills.

Charanda is a Purépecha word meaning "red soil," which is common in the *tierra caliente* zone where the sugarcane is grown. The soil and climate of the region, in addition to Purépecha distilling tradition, are common explanations for charanda's unique denomination of origin. It is common to macerate *changungas*, or wild nances, in the liquor as well as *nurite*, which is Purépecha for calamint or *Clinopodium macrostemum*. Charanda is traditionally consumed at community events, but is also a key commercial product in modern Uruapan.

Today, Casa Tarasco is the only large-scale charanda producer in Uruapan and is the only company to export the spirit. The family-owned company traces its history back to 1907 when Don Cleofas Murgia began distilling sugarcane spirits in the town of Ziracuaretiro, later moving operations to Uruapan. The brand-name "Charanda" emerged in the 1930s, distilled by Fidel A. Contreras.

"Charanda Yuco" was a kind of cheap cane spirit for the Pame or Xi'ui people further to the east.[35] Alcabala tax records from colonial Valladolid, now Morelia, Michoacán, show a vibrant aguardiente de caña industry in the region as early as the late eighteenth century.[36]

Sotol

Sotol is a distilled spirit made from a fermentation of the sotol plant of the genus *Dasylirion*. While the sotol plant is in the same family as agave, they differ at the genus level. Mexican law protects the spirit as a unique product of origin grown and distilled in one of three northern states: Durango, Coahuila, or Chihuahua. Around 70 percent of the annual production of about 500,000 liters of sotol comes from Chihuahua.[37] Sonoran distillers make a spirit from the same plant, but refer to it as *palmilla*.

The process of manufacturing sotol is like that of agave spirits. The sotol harvest occurs in autumn months due to the high sugar content of the plant at this time. The *piña* is cooked to caramelize sugars, then ground. The sweet juice is fermented and distilled, usually twice.

Modern commercial production of sotol spirits began in 1908 when the first *vinata de sotol* was built at Parras de la Fuente in the state of Coahuila.[38] As the United States entered Prohibition in the 1920s, the federal government of Mexico began prosecuting the owners of vinatas de sotol as well. The state of Chihuahua was particularly keen to stop sotol production, perhaps because elite families in the state were profiting by distilling corn whiskey to smuggle across the border into the United States.[39] The spirit developed a reputation as backward and clandestine because it would remain illegal to produce until 1994. The category is still largely artisanal, but more investment has been made in the spirit in the last two decades. There are now sotol brands available internationally.

Both the plant and beverage are also known informally as *sereque* or *zotol*. There is evidence that *Dasylirion* was consumed as a food by natives along New Mexico's Pecos River as early as 7,000 years ago.12 In the context of fermentation, Tarahumara people have used the sotol plant in the production of tesgüiño, in place of, or in tandem with, corn. While the sotol plant grows south of the region of its traditional use in distillation, sotol is generally secondary to mezcal wherever agave grows.

Tuna Brandy

There is evidence of historic distillation of cactus fruit wines, namely colonche. In the 1907 book, *The Tuna as Food for Man*, the authors write,

> Sometimes, but not so often as formerly, old colonche is distilled into an alcoholic beverage. It was a common practice a few years ago to distill the fermented peelings of the tuna, but the practice has not been successful because of the ill effects which the product is said to have. The natives say it produces violent headaches, and for this reason it has been almost entirely supplanted by mescal, tequila, and other maguey (agave) products which produce less deleterious effects.[40]

While this historic report is probable, most texts that mention *aguardiente de tuna*, *vino de tuna*, or *licor de tuna* from the late 1800s lean toward discussing novel uses of underutilized agricultural goods—meaning that it was not a traditional craft but a thrifty way to use waste material. Many of these references complain of the empyreumatic smells given off by the tuna brandy if not distilled to a high enough proof.

Modern craft distillers have also turned their eyes to the sweet fruit of the nopal that is so bountiful in arid Mexico. Tuna brandy is a promising new category of spirits in Mexico, as craft distillers look to combine legacy and innovation. There are several distillers now commercially producing the spirit, and some bottles are available internationally.

Vino de Cocos

Vino de cocos is the distillation of fermented coconut palm sap, called tuba. A convincing argument can be made that vino de cocos was the first distilled spirit in North America.[41] The coconut palm, though, is not native to Mexico.

It arrived in one of two manners: on ocean currents from Panama or on the Manila Galleon from the Philippines.[42]

In the late sixteenth century, Filipino sailors who manned the Manila Galleon arrived on the west coast of Mexico and taught locals how to gather tuba, or palm sap, ferment it, and distill it. It was the Filipino introduction of distillation that sparked the development of mezcal culture. To this day, that culture is stronger in Mexico's western states. Moreover, some distillers in Colima, Nayarit, and Jalisco still use the Filipino-style still that the sailors introduced over 400 years ago.

The palm liquor was one of Colima's main exports during the seventeenth century. It was sold in nearby cities like Guadalajara. Starting in 1627, the Spanish Crown even permitted the region to distill vino de cocos because their economy was so dependent on it, particularly after a hurricane decimated the region's cacao industry. Otherwise, no distillation was permitted in the viceroyalty. Vino de cocos was then illegalized around 1700, and the spirit disappeared through the eighteenth century as other coconut derivatives became more profitable.

In 1672, Queen Regent Mariana of Austria emancipated all "indios" in the Spanish colonies including "chinos," which referred to any Asiatic people disembarking at Acapulco.[43] While some traders continued illicitly trafficking in humans, the transpacific slave trade contracted at the end of the seventeenth century. Moreover, free sailors conscripted to sail round trip could no longer abandon the Galleon so easily at Acapulco. A law passed in 1757 threatened 10 years in the galleys if a sailor was caught abandoning.[44] Perhaps, restrictions in both the enslaved Asian labor supply and the free Asian labor from runaway sailors contributed to the disappearance of vino de cocos through the 1700s. Tuba production is highly labor-intensive. Sugarcane and agave were ultimately more bountiful and easier to transform into spirits.

Today, Jorge Velasco Rocha, a native of Colima, is trying to revive the spirit by recruiting tuberos to collect large volumes of the sap and distilling the fermented stuff into a spirit. He calls his brand *La China Mestiza* in reference to the drink's Asiatic history. There are some other commercial products called vino de cocos, but they are not authentic versions of distilled tuba.

* * *

Within 500 years of the introduction of distillation to the region, Mexico has become a distinct participant in the human endeavor of spirits production. Existing traditions of distillation in the Old World have relied on substrates like sorghum, rice, palm sap, wheat, rye, grapes, and other fruits, but the introduction of agave into this mix is a uniquely Mexican trait.

With the exception of American corn-based whiskeys, no other New World nation has developed such a robust business around the distillation of an indigenous ingredient as Mexico. Yes, Brazil has its still-obscure cassava *tiquira*, but sugarcane cachaça overpowers the market. The Québécois have innovated with their niche maple syrup acerum. Producers in different European countries make vodka from the Andean potato. Meanwhile, Peru and Chile rely mostly on European grapes to produce pisco. Bolivia also favors Mediterranean Muscat of Alexandria grapes for its *singani*. Sugarcane aguardiente has spread everywhere in Latin America and the Caribbean. Agave spirits stand out as the greatest indigenous-ingredient category to emerge from the Western Hemisphere. Along with corn bourbon, annual sales measure in the tens of billions of dollars.

The historical pathway that distillation followed to bring us agave spirits is fascinating and underappreciated. It was an Asiatic still design that came to the Pacific Coast of Mexico that gave birth to the early mezcal and tequila traditions. Now, production has been industrialized to the point of abstracting tequila from its roots. Agaves, once baked slowly in subterranean, stone pit ovens following a 9,000-year-old culinary tradition, are now steamed in bulk in tanker-truck-like, metal autoclaves. Their fermented juices are distilled in highly efficient, modern column stills. Flavorings, coloring agents, and cane sugar are added to finished products.

Agave, the prototypical foodstuff of the Early Archaic peoples of this region, has emerged as a hyper-commercialized industrial commodity. A monoculture of the crop has claimed vast swathes of arable land in Jalisco. The home state of tequila is now fraught with overplanting of the blue agave.

While the industrialization of tequila has taken the humble agave spirit to new heights, lesser-known Mexican distillates are beginning to attract global interest. The complex, regional landscape of spirit making in Mexico holds great intrigue for sippers and mixers alike. As mezcal achieves global acclaim, it is only a matter of time before raicilla, baçanora, sotol, and tuna brandy come to bars around the world. Perhaps, vino de cocos, Mexico's first spirit, will even make a comeback.

6

Liqueurs

Modern Mexico has a widespread tradition of infusing spirits with fruits, nuts, barks, herbs, spices, dairy, and various sugars and sweets. The names and flavors of these drinks vary widely by region, but most are essentially local versions of liqueurs, cordials, or crèmes. Around Mexico, such liqueurs are called by common names like *licor*, *curado*, *compuesto*, *ponche*, *mistela*, *nectar*, *torito*, and *mosco*. In typical Mexican fashion, many of these liqueurs are endearingly referred to in the diminutive, with *-ito/a* indulgently added to the end: *torito*, *mosquito*, *curadito*, *pasita*, *carnavalito*.

To make these curados, flavorings are macerated in a base of strong spirits. Sugarcane aguardiente is the most common base spirit, but mezcal is also widespread. Fruits, roots, herbs, flowers, and more will soak in the liquor for anywhere from one month to a year or more. Sugar is generally added to taste in the form of syrup.

The practice of making liqueurs in Mexico necessarily followed the development of distillation in the region, especially the introduction of aguardiente. Many inherited traditions of liqueur making exist adjacent to historical centers of sugarcane and aguardiente production like in Michoacán, Veracruz, and the Huasteca region. Producing macerations from strong local aguardiente has served as a household and commercial strategy to improve the flavor and palatability of strong (and sometimes harsh) spirits.

The conceptual development of Mexican liqueurs has a more complicated trajectory. Some versions of liqueurs, like mistela and *resolí*, are directly inherited from Spain, where it's hard to ignore the many regional liqueurs and *anisados*. Others appear to be shortcuts taken to replicate pre-Columbian fruit wines, herbal medicines, and flavored pulques. Some result from a combination of influences and local ingenuity.

The Spanish brought with them from Europe the practice of making both flavored wines and brandy infusions—think citrus-spiked sangria and Basque, sloe berry *patxaran*. At the time of colonization, these preparations were popularly called by names like spirituous waters, wine ratafias, and mistelas. Resolí, also written *rosoli*, was one of New Spain's favorite liquid imports, ranking fourth after the perennial necessities of white wine, red wine, and aguardiente.[1] The term "resolí" was essentially synonymous with liqueur and could be flavored with things like anise, orange peel, cloves, or cinnamon.

Life in Mexico necessarily transformed some of these Iberian tipples into local North American digestifs. Traditional Spanish mistela, for example, was usually produced from grape juice mixed with wine. By the eighteenth century, records suggest that mistela was being produced in New Spain from aguardiente, water, sugar, star anise, lime, and cinnamon.[2] Today, "mistela" is still used as a generic term for a wide array of liqueurs in southern Mexico.

Native Origins of Modern Liqueurs

While Spain infused spirits with anise and other classic Iberian herbs, many of the flavors of modern Mexican liqueurs come from fruits native to the land. Among the most popular liqueurs in Mexico are flavorings which had been used in herbal teas, fruit wines, and flavored pulques before the Spanish Conquest. The addition of aguardiente is new, but the use of these flavorings in beverages is part of an ancestral tradition.

First, there is the use of foraged herbs. Strong spirits, absent in pre-Columbian Mesoamerica, make for excellent solvents that extract medicinal compounds found in leaves, barks, and roots. Where these compounds are not always uniformly distributed in vegetal matter, an alcoholic extraction also helps with consistent dosing. Europeans drank spirits as medicines before they drank them recreationally. When people in Mesoamerica who drank hot water infusions of native plants like *nurite*, *damiana*, and *prodigiosa* suddenly had access to high-proof aguardiente, they made tinctures with the same herbs. Some had an agreeable flavor and have become modern recreational drinks as well, if not consumed as aperitifs or digestifs.

Second, Mesoamericans had a strong tradition of fermenting native seasonal fruits into lightly alcoholic wines. Hog plums, nances, and tejocotes were all used in natural fermentations. With access to strong spirits, however, the labor and variability of fermentation could be reduced while still preserving the flavor and sweetness of seasonal fruit via maceration. The new process has other benefits too. Creating a fruity drink with a maceration would have required less fruit than a true wine. Where a fermentation of fruit and pulque might only last a week or so, a liqueur made of hog plums will last for months, if not years.

Finally, there is the influence of pulque curado. Pulque was the original base alcohol into which Mesoamericans mixed their entire spectrum of flavors. Flavorings like prickly pears, chiles, and peanuts—all of which are now used to produce crèmes or liqueurs—were used in the production of pulque curado. So, the concept of flavoring alcohol was not a new one, but the advent of distilled spirits certainly increased the potency of these curados.

If these three theories sound specious, it is useful to consider how regionally circumscribed some of these flavors are. We know that indigenous groups in the Baja Peninsula consumed damiana tea as medicine. Now the liqueur of damiana is a famous regional aphrodisiac. We know that the natives of the Huasteca made wine from hog plums. Now *jovito* is a beloved aguardiente-based liqueur in the mountainous forests of Tamazunchale. Lastly, it is no coincidence that both flavored liqueurs and flavored pulques share the term "curado." These local flavorings are part of a wider regional beverage tradition.

There exist modern commercial versions of some liqueurs, but the majority are made locally at a household or cantina level for sale. Among the common liqueurs that are not explicitly described in this chapter are lime, fig, apple, tamarind, passion fruit, sangria, guava, hibiscus, and quince. Cream liqueurs, which have a defining dairy component, include peanut, pecan, walnut, dulce de leche, coconut, rice, and *chorreado*, a kind of chocolate eggnog. *Amargos*, or bitters, are a class of liqueurs that feature rue and fruit rinds.[3]

The importance of liqueurs in Mexican drinking should not be discounted. Many regions have iconic, must-visit bars that have become emblematic over the last century for dispensing their homemade boozy infusions. Certain towns around Mexico, particularly the Pueblos Mágicos, often specialize in liqueur production. Comala in Colima, Tenancingo in Mexico, Tlahuelompa in Hidalgo, Arteaga in Coahuila, Xico in Veracruz, and Zacatlán in Puebla are just a few of these centers of artisanal liqueur production. It is a curiosity as to how these towns become specialized in the production of certain types and flavors of curados, but they help to drive tourism. In the small town of Comala, for example, over two dozen shops make and sell ponches, and the tradition has been around in the idyllic, white-washed pueblo for nearly a century.

Very few of Mexico's liqueurs make it outside of the regions in which they are produced, never mind the country, so a review of the country's macerations is an excellent way to get a sense of regional flavors and products.

* * *

Carnavalito

Carnavalito is a tequila or aguardiente-based liqueur that combines orange juice, sugar, and cinnamon typical of Huichapan, Hidalgo.

Chumiate

Chumiate is a fruit and herbal liqueur made with aguardiente. The term is common in the states of Mexico and Puebla. Chumiate combines various flavors and is often based on nance or wild cherries with other flavors added like tejocote and anise. In the 1900s, it was also called *chinchol*. In the state of Mexico, the towns of Jilotzingo, Xonacatlán, and Almoloya de Juárez produce chumiate.

Crucetillo

Crucetillo is a medicinal liqueur produced from the maceration of the fruits of crucetillo, or *Randia monantha Benth*, in aguardiente mixed with wine, especially *vino tipo jerez*, in the state of Veracruz. Above all else, the maceration is used in treating venomous snake bites by consuming the liqueur orally or by applying it topically to the bitten area. Among a long list of other things, it is also said to help arthritis, diabetes, cancer, and cholesterol. It can be found at traditional pharmacies that specialize in herbal cures around Veracruz. During the height of the COVID-19 pandemic, the demand for crucetillo skyrocketed because it was being used as a folk medicine for the disease.

Garañona

Garañona is a liqueur produced in the town of Metepec just outside of Toluca in the state of Mexico. One bar in particular, Bar 2 de Abril, has been producing the herbal infusion since 1932. The recipe is rumored to contain fourteen different herbs, but ultimately remains a trade secret. Ángel Herón Pineda created the recipe.

The name of the drink hints at the belief that it has aphrodisiac properties. *Garañon* translates to "stud" or "sire" (referring to horses or bulls used for breeding). While this name makes sense alone, it should be noted that there are at least two medicinal herbs native to Mexico that also sometimes bear the name garañona related to fertility. In Michoacán, it is reported that both *Castilleja canescens Benth* and *Castilleja tenuifolia* are called garañona and are used for fertility treatments and vaginal douches.[4] Also in Michoacán, the indigenous minty herb consumed in a tisane called nurite is known as garañona in the town of Quiroga. In both cases, they are used in traditional medicine to cure infertility.[5] Perhaps the secret recipe of Ángel Herón Pineda contains one of these native herbs—though we cannot be sure.

Holcatzín or Licor de Capulín

Holcatzín is an aguardiente-based spirit macerated with the *capulín* of the species *Prunus salicifolia*. The capulín, also known as the Mexican black cherry, is native throughout all of Mexico's latitudes. The 1571 Nahuatl-Spanish dictionary of Alonso de Molina defined *capoloctli* as "*vino de cerezas*" or cherry wine. Today, instead of producing wine, areas where aguardiente production is common take advantage of the fruit to macerate it into a liqueur. Sweet tamales are also made with the cherries.

While many states have home production of licor de capulín, the name Holcatzín is specific to the southeastern states of Campeche and Yucatán. The name likely derives from the place name of an old hacienda in Campeche state. An 1893 report by the Anuario Estadístico de la República Mexicana confirms that the hacienda Holcatzín had two sugarcane trapiches and was manufacturing aguardiente.

Elsewhere, the same capulín liqueur goes by another regional name, *huikimo*, in the states of Puebla and Chihuahua. *Acachul*, a term that may refer to the capulín in addition to other small fruits like the coralberry, is another popular flavoring agent in liqueurs in Puebla state. This liqueur is generally just called acachul and can be found in Xicotepec de Juárez, Puebla.

Licor de Café

Licor de café is a coffee liqueur and is common throughout Mexico. Coffee was introduced to Mexico at the end of the eighteenth century and was quickly combined with aguardiente. When Santa Anna and Gómez Pedraza arrived in Ciudad de México in 1833, the city's powerbrokers met at the famous Café de Águila de Oro and discussed politics while drinking *fósforos*, a concoction of equal parts coffee and aguardiente.[6] Many coffee-growing regions, like the cloud forests of Xalapa, Veracruz, support sugarcane production. In Chiapas, the early sowing of large-scale coffee plantations at the end of the 1800s involved planting sugarcane for piloncillo and aguardiente production to turn a profit while coffee bushes matured.[7]

Otherwise, licor de café is not particularly noteworthy except that Mexico produces it at the highest commercial level with the brand Kahlúa, now owned by Pernod Ricard. Kahlúa started in 1936 in Veracruz. In 1960, Jules Berman began importing the branded liqueur into the United States. Nearly 100 years later, it is synonymous with coffee liqueur at bars around the world.

Coffee liqueur is sold in most places that produce liqueurs or curados.

Licor de Changunga

Licor de changunga is common in Michoacán where aguardiente production and nance fruit exist in proximity. The small, yellow nance fruit is from the native tree *Byrsonima crassifolia*. During the harvest season, street vendors sell bags of the tart fruit out of pushcarts in the plazas of cities like Uruapan. Locals eat the fruit alone as an astringent snack, but many bars in Michoacán have jars of the fruit soaking in aguardiente or charanda year-round.

Several sources in Michoacán insisted that the term "changunga" only refers to wild nances, not domesticated plants (which are just *nances* in Spanish).

Licor de Damiana

Licor de Damiana is a Baja California product made from the maceration of the damiana flower of the *Turnera diffusa* plant. The flower is native to Mexico and is commercially harvested in the southernmost portion of the peninsula in Baja California Sur state to make tea, medicine, and liqueur. Modern harvesting continues to depend on foraging the flower from wild plants. There is some cocktail lore that suggests the original margarita might have contained this liqueur!

Chroniclers of the Spanish conquest noted indigenous use of the leaves of the plant, suggesting a long-standing herbal tradition. Damiana is generally believed to be an aphrodisiac in Baja California and is also said to cure cataracts and assist with conceiving a child.

There are several Baja California Sur producers of commercial brands of damiana liqueurs. Most are limited to sales in the region, although some, such as Damiana Guaycura with its iconically voluptuous, Venus-of-Willendorf-like bottle, can be found at bars around Mexico and internationally. Another version branded "el Jeque" (the Sheikh) in Baja California Sur combines red wine with licor de damiana.

Licor de Garambullo

Licor de garambullo is a cordial common in the arid Tehuacán-Cuicatlán biosphere. It is made from the cactus fruit of the *Myrtillocactus geometrizans* species. The fruit is harvested between April and May and is then macerated for at least a month in aguardiente or mezcal. The longer the maceration, the more potent the flavor—something like a wood-aged blueberry. Sometimes, *chiotilla*, the edible fruit from the *Escontria chiotilla* cactus, is used as a substitute. Locals in Zapotitlán Salinas, Puebla, consider this to be adulteration, noting that the purest licor de garambullo looks like coffee. Folklore suggests that licor de garambullo has hallucinogenic properties that derive from mezcaline in the cactus. There is no chemical evidence that this species of cactus contains mezcaline.[8]

Licor de Jobo

Licor de Jobo is a liqueur common to the Huasteca region of eastern Mexico. The drink is also called *jobito* or *jovito*. The jobo is the fruit of the native *Spondias purpura*. The name jobo likely came to Mexico from the Caribbean.[9] Meanwhile, the Nahuatl name for the fruit was *xocotl*. Even in Aztec times, the fruit was associated with alcohol due to the indigenous tradition of fermenting it into wine. The Nahuatl term *xocomictia*, meaning "to get drunk," likely derived from the name of the fruit. The geographer Bruman wrote, "The existence of a general word for drunkenness based on *xocotl* would point to an important early utilization of the acidulous fruits in the manufacture of fermented drinks."[10] Cities like Matlapa and Tamazunchale in the Huasteca Potosina are good places to find homemade jobito for sale today.

Licor de Prodigiosa

Licor de Prodigiosa is a mixed liqueur typical of Querétaro state that contains the namesake plant of the species *Brickellia cavanillesii*. The prodigiosa herb is the defining feature of this liqueur, but other flavors can be added according to the establishment's recipe, including wormwood and rue. The drink is known to be a bitter aperitivo.

The prodigiosa herb is an established native medicinal plant used for centuries to help with bile, colic, and stomach pain. The liqueur has been consumed for close to 100 years.[11] Most of Querétaro's truly traditional cantinas will have their own versions of this liqueur macerated in-house.

Licor de Tejocote

Licor de tejocote is a liqueur produced from the maceration of tejocote, or Mexican hawthorn, of the species *Crataegus mexicana*. The liqueur is common throughout much of Mexico. Notably, it is popular during Las Posadas, the observation of the 9 days leading up to Christmas.

Mistela

Mistela is a fruit liqueur common in Chiapas, sometimes made from dried fruits or preservatives rather than fresh fruit. Typically, Chiapanecos consume and produce mistela in December during the celebrations of Posadas and Christmas. The fruits are left to macerate in alcohol for a full year. Jocote and nance are a popular mistela combination, but many other local fruits are used.

Mistela in Europe is distinct from mistela in the Americas. European mistela is generally made by pressing overripe grapes and adding wine to prevent fermentation—a way of preserving the natural sweetness of the juice. It is then used as an ingredient in aperitifs and fortified wines, which is likely how it became conflated with liqueurs in the New World. In Latin America, mistela is always a spirit-based drink (in both Ecuador and Colombia, for example). At one point in time, mistela also referred to a mixture of mezcal, simple syrup, and anise in Jalisco.[12] Mistela in Mexico dates to the earliest days of Spanish conquest, when wine and viticultural products were being shipped across the Atlantic.

Moscos or Mosquitos

The names Moscos and Mosquitos ("flies" or "fruit flies") can be used interchangeably for a specific brand of orange liqueur produced in the city of Toluca in the state of Mexico. The name mosco allegedly comes from the idea that everyone is *buzzing* to drink the liqueur.

The shop "La Miniatura," which occupies one of the storefronts in Los Portales of Toluca's central plaza, has sold Moscos since 1933, when Jose Luis Almazán registered the brand. The Almazán family is now on their third generation selling the orange liqueur. They sell it at four different strengths, with 42 percent being the highest alcohol by volume. Moscos or mosquitos are consumed cold as a digestif or aperitif.

In the 1970s, a prominent historian, Alfonso Sánchez García, took interest in the city of Toluca's gastronomy and earned himself the name "Professor Mosquito." He showed that the practice of producing the orange beverage was isolated to modern commercial sales.[13] The brand is still a key part of Toluca's gastronomical identity. La Miniatura advertises itself as indispensable to the Toluca experience with the slogan "Visitar Toluca y no llevar una botella de moscos . . . equivale a ir a Acapulco y no bañarse en el mar," which means "To visit Toluca without bringing back a bottle of Moscos . . . is the same as going to Acapulco and not swimming in the ocean."

Pasita

Pasita is a raisin-flavored liqueur emblematic of drinking in the historical center of the city of Puebla. Pasita is sold by a bar with the same name, "La Pasita," which means "little raisin," that has been offering the liqueur since 1916. In fact, the bar takes credit for inventing it. Puebla has generally been known for its "muscat style raisin liqueur."[14] Traditionally, pasita is served in a tall shot glass with a toothpick-skewered cube of goat cheese and a raisin as garnish. The drink is sweet and becomes a sort of wine-and-cheese tasting experience.

Petaquilla

Petaquilla is a wild grape liqueur made with a base of mezcal typical of Guerrero. The wild grapes in Guerrero are of the *Ampelocissus acapulcensis* species, named for the state's famous port Acapulco. The name of the liqueur could derive from the Guerrero town of Petaquillas or from the Spanish word for flask, *petaca*.

Ponche

Ponche, or *ponche navideño*, is a hot punch prepared by Mexican families for Christmas. It is made by boiling water with cinnamon, piloncillo, lime juice, dried fruits like raisins, tamarinds, or prunes, and fresh fruit like guavas, apples, and pears. Rum is added to taste.

Outside of its festive context, ponche is also a kind of liqueur traditionally made in the small town of Comala, Colima. The most famous of these liqueurs is *ponche de granada* ("pomegranate liqueur"). The town also offers flavors like dulce de leche, pecan, red fruits, and sangria. Ponche de granada has made its way to Ciudad de México as well, and is the most popular drink at the century-old cantina Salón Tenampa on Plaza Garibaldi.

The origin of Comala's unique version of ponche dates to the 1950s, when *botaneros* ("snack vendors") opened up around the town's old Spanish plaza. They would serve locally distilled mezcal called tuxca to workers who were eating and drinking on their lunch break. The late Hermenegildo Salazar Torres, a botanero, is a seminal figure in bringing ponche to Comala. He was the mastermind behind mixing local tuxca with fruit to entice afternoon visitors to drink a bit. The term "ponche" has long been used in Mexican drinking contexts including a *ponche de pulque* from the eighteenth century.

Rompope

Rompope is an eggnog that is well-known throughout Mexico. Recipes differ, but the drink is generally a cream liqueur of egg yolk, whole milk, sugar, cinnamon, and cane alcohol or rum. Other ingredients could include vanilla, cloves, nutmeg, carnation milk, condensed milk, pecans, piñon nuts, almonds, or chocolate. Around holidays, many Mexican families will make their own rompope and allow it to rest a couple of weeks for consumption, but there are also many commercial brands of the drink, most prominently Santa Clara, owned by Casa Cuervo, the tequila giant. Rompope is a potable part of the Poblano tradition of *repostería*, or confectionery.

Mexican Rompope was invented in a convent of Clarisa nuns during the colonial period in the city of Puebla. Legend has it that a sister named Eduviges created the recipe and convinced the bishop to let her share it with the other sisters in the convent. The bishop agreed once she mollified him saying, "One cup a day doesn't hurt anyone." Nuns have historically baked and made crafts to fund convent life during the time in which they are not praying. Rompope has been a perennial source of funds that contribute to self-sufficiency and sustenance in the convents.

Today, in Puebla's La Calle de Los Dulces, a confectionery district built around the now-abandoned former convent of the Clarisas, many commercial bottles of rompope sport nun-themed branding. To buy rompope from actual nuns (and to support their convent), look for las Hermanas Clarisas Capuchinas next to the sacred Iglesia del Santo Niño Cieguito. They still sell church goods, baked goods, and rompope in downtown Puebla. One nun explained that sales support their mission to pray for the world.

Torito

The torito is a generic name for crèmes or dairy-based liqueurs produced in Veracruz from cane spirits. The name translates as "little bull" and has roots in the state's sugarcane producing history. Supposedly, workers would consume liqueurs made of cane spirits and local fruits while they worked in the fields to give them the vim and vigor of a bull. The inclusion of dairy in the drink must have helped to give it a bovine name.

Now, peanut torito, or *torito de cacahuate*, is emblematic of the Sotavento region of Veracruz. During the festival of Santa María Magdalena, Veracruzanos around Xico offer toritos to the celebrated saint.[15] Peanut torito consists of aguardiente, peanuts, water, sugar, condensed milk, and evaporated milk. Other popular flavors include coffee, soursop, coconut, hog plum, walnut, mango, and cajeta (a type of caramel). Toritos are commercially available within Veracruz, but are produced at a small scale.

Outside of Veracruz, the state of Guerrero uses the name torito for similar products. One recipe from Guerrero for a local torito lists garlic, pepper, cloves, and green chiles as the key flavoring agents, making for a decidedly spicier version of the drink.[16]

Verde or Verdín

Verde and Verdín are herbal liqueurs which have a vibrant green color due to maceration of fresh, chlorophyll-packed herbs. Verde is typical of Xico, Veracruz, where it is made with lemongrass and *hierba maestra*. Verdín, on the other hand, contains anise and hierbabuena, or peppermint, and is made in Tabasco. It is sometimes drunk with ginger.

Xtabentún

Xtabentún is a variety of liqueur typical of the Yucatán that combines aguardiente with honey and anise. Modern brands of xtabentún macerate spirits with the other ingredients, but the legacy of the drink is more complicated.

Xtabentún, for the Maya, is the name of *Ipomoea corymbosa*, or morning glory. Throughout the expanse of southern Mexico, indigenous groups exploited this plant for its psychotropic properties (called ololiuqui in Nahua-speaking communities). As far back as 2,000 years ago, archaeologists have found evidence that the Maya used the plant in rituals and perhaps in the manufacture of ritual drinks like balché.[17] The flower has also been canonized in Maya myth: When Xkeban, a promiscuous but kind-hearted girl, died, aromatic flowers sprouted from her grave, which became xtabentún.

The coincidence of the name of the morning glory with the liqueur is explained through honey. Maya beekeepers kept their hives close to xtabentún blooms so that the bees could feed off their nectar and produce a particular kind of honey. Likely, the fermented mead of this honey was the original xtabentún, but somewhere along the way, anise and aguardiente came to stand in for a fermentation process. As early as the 1930s, manufacturers in the Yucatán sold xtabentún commercially as an anise-flavored drink. Nowadays, xtabentún does not often contain Maya melipona honey due to high costs. Some brands are available in international markets.

Yolixpa

Yolixpa is an herbal liqueur produced in the Nahua community of Cuetzalan del Progreso, Puebla. The *yolixperos* who prepare the aguardiente macerations can use upward of two dozen different herbs, many of which are medicinal. The herbal tincture is sweetened with sugar or piloncillo. Among the known herbs are rue, Guatemalan skullcap, fennel, lemongrass, sweet wormwood, chamomile, and lime.[18] The tincture is a digestif.

The name yolixpa comes from the Nahuatl *yolix* for chest or heart. The name could mean "happy heart" or "heart medicine" or translate as "in the face of the heart."[19] The town has been deemed a Pueblo Mágico by the Mexican government and the liqueur has become a tourist draw bolstered by the Festival del Yolixpa since 2014. It is available for sale from various vendors at Mercado De Artesanías Matachiuj.

* * *

Often overlooked, the widespread practice of producing liqueurs from locally available spirits and flavorings is a homey invitation to regionality in Mexico. The tradition has a clear analogue in the context of the Iberian Peninsula, but has been transformed by the local character and flavors in different parts of Mexico.

For tourists in the country, liqueurs are a constant source of intrigue. Many of the Pueblos Mágicos designated by the Secretaría de Turismo have homegrown traditions of making infused spirits. Elsewhere, old-school bars that straddle the line between the pharmacy and watering hole have become multi-generational successes thanks to their proprietary cordials.

Above all else, tasting one's way through the many liqueurs of Mexico allows the drinker to experience local, seasonal produce in a new way. There are the jobo fruits of the Huasteca, the damiana flowers of the Baja Peninsula, the garambullo berries of the Tehuacán Valley, and the tart changungas of Michoacán. All offer up their rare flavors preserved in the great tradition of artisanal liqueur production.

7

Cocktails and Mixed Drinks

Mexico has one of the most vibrant, sophisticated, and distinct cocktail scenes in the world. Bars in urban centers like Ciudad de México, Guadalajara, and Oaxaca, as well as tourist areas like Quintana Roo and the US–Mexico border, have risen to international acclaim for their original recipes, often combining staples of Mexican flavor with spirits from around the world.

On top of this, some of the world's most beloved mixed drinks have Mexican origins. None is more famous than the margarita. The combination of tequila, orange liqueur, and lime juice is rightfully one of the most consumed cocktails in the world. It has also been tequila's Trojan Horse into the non-Mexican palate. The sight of a salted rim alone conjures up the magic of Mexican mixology.

Within Mexico, there exists an array of more traditional cocktails which rarely achieve international acclaim. Some of these drinks are only served at the bars where they were invented. Others are regional staples or home bar favorites. Before reviewing some of Mexico's lesser-known cocktails, it's necessary to understand where its cocktail culture originated.

Mixtures of flavors and alcoholic beverages have been a key feature of Mexican drinking culture through the centuries. Pulque, for starters, was the base of a variety of mixed curados. Historical records record dozens of elaborate pulque drinks which have names and ingredients that feel right at home in the world of mixology. Imagine a cocktail bar menu . . .

Rabbit's Blood: pulque, prickly pear, guava, plantain, cinnamon, and cloves

Cock's Eye: pulque, honey, chile, and pepper

The Butter: pulque, sugar, rum

These drinks from the late eighteenth century had the trappings of mixology but usually involved mixing ingredients and allowing for further fermentation.

Foreign Cocktails in Mexico

Mixology and the legacy of cocktails that we know today would have arrived in Mexico with the invasion of the US army in 1846. Shortly after the capture of Ciudad de México, opportunistic Americans established businesses and imported goods that their countrymen would want. The market was there; well over 5,000 American soldiers occupied the capital city from September 1847 until the signing of the Treaty of Guadalupe Hidalgo in February 1848. An English-language newspaper was established, called The American Star, which was printed wherever the US army encamped.[1] During the 5-month occupation, the newspaper advertised Sarah Foyle's Theatre Coffee House which had obtained Monongahela whiskey (from Pennsylvania) and intended to sell hot whiskey punches, eggnog, and the classic cocktail, the Tom and Jerry.[2] Mrs. Foyle was not the only purveyor of American drinks during these months—among others, there were the Eagle Coffee House, the United States Hotel, the Lone Star House, the Olive Branch Coffee House, and the Old Kentucky Restaurant.

Mexico's subsequent foreign invasion by the French military brought in European products and influence as well. It was during the rule of Emperor Maximilian I that advertisements emerged for "Licores Franceses," which included a "Brandy Cocktail," cognac, gin, "Marraschino superior" [*sic*],

English beer, French anisette, and Vermouth Noilly Prats, among many other familiar cocktail ingredients.[3]

Though foreign military incursion ended with the death of Maximilian I, foreign individuals living during the Restored Republic and the Porfiriato continued to develop a nascent cocktail scene in Ciudad de México. It was the foreign owners of cafés and cantinas in the capital who acted as purveyors of these tipples. The consumer of cocktails too was often foreign or was a well-to-do Mexican who valued the perceived prestige of European culture.

The theater district of Ciudad de México was a testing ground for cocktail culture in the last decades of the nineteenth century. A group of cafés and bars began selling cocktails that were inspired by the nearby Gran Teatro Nacional (before the legendary La Opera Bar even opened). Between 1872 and 1873, a couple of new cocktails were reported to be invented with operatic names. At Vinatería del Seminario, owner D. Simon Baexa drew inspiration from a Compañía de Opera Italiana staging of Pacini's Saffo starring *Primera donna mezzo soprano* Giuditta Galazzi. The owner invented a cocktail simply called the Giuditt-Cocktail.[4] Another bar, Café Nacional, owned by a man named George (or Jorge) Montell, became well-known for its "Robinson Cocktail" in 1873, though one writer accused Jorge of plagiarism: "The fame Jorge has gained in recent days is a usurped fame: it rightfully belongs to Orpheus, and no one else. He is the inventor of that delicious drink whose legitimate name is the 'Orpheus Cocktail.' To call it anything else from now on would be a punishable injustice."[5] It is not clear if the Orpheus in the cocktail name refers to Monteverdi's opera L'Orfeo, or the literal name of the inventor of the cocktail. Regardless, it is lamentable that the recipes for what might be two of Mexico's first original cocktails are lost.

The foreignness of cocktail consumption was stated outright in the satirical publication *El Padre Cobos*, which painted quite the scene in 1873: "Enter into the cafés and you will find wherever you like, in the corners that is, the Americans, English, French and German, drinking one punch after another punch or one cocktail after another cocktail but always face-down drunk."[6] In 1897, Ciudad de México's English-language newspaper, The Two Republics, compared, "If the 'gringo' takes to cocktails the Mexican prefers his aperitivo."[7]

During the peak years of the Porfiriato, European culture was held in esteem and foreign capitalists had fairly open access to the Mexican market. Cocktails would be served next to billiard tables in places like the Chicago Saloon, Águila del Oro, or Deaumont and Recamier. In this context, Americans and Spanish began to be an increasingly common presence behind Mexico's bars. By the time Díaz fell to the Revolution, it was a stereotype of the Spanish-born immigrants, pejoratively called *gachupínes*, that they operated bars, convenience stores, and loan shark dens.

In 1915, a Spanish writer commented on the extent of the situation: "It is calculated that here in this republic there are between forty and fifty thousand Spanish . . . the grocery and beverage stores, the bakeries, and the houses of credit being almost entirely in the hands of our compatriots."[8] Their control was such that, when Article 33 of the 1917 Constitution allowed for the expulsion of foreigners with little due process, many cantineros were deported. The typical American who was expelled from Mexico under Article 33 during the revolutionary years also tended to be a cantina owner.[9]

Finally, American Prohibition would go on to shape the border cities of Ciudad Juárez, Mexicali, and Tijuana. To serve the dry market just over the border, bars like The Kentucky Club and the Foreign Club appeared on the frontier in addition to new breweries (like Cerveceria de Mexicali in 1923), wineries (like Vinicola L.A. Cetto in 1926), and even distilleries (like Tecate's Donlevy Whiskey, which closed in 1932). Fleeing Prohibition south of the border, Americans would have been drinking cocktails alongside a freshly tossed Caesar salad.

The Birth of Mexican Mixology

Through the Mexican Revolution, the cocktail would have been a foreign import sold by foreign barmen to foreign consumers—but also to an increasingly wide audience of Mexican consumers. The nationalism and patriotic fervor of the Revolution helped to Mexicanize the cocktail as tequila became more popular and the foreign cantinero became the butt of the joke.

The Golden Age of Mexican Cinema, starting in 1936, corresponded with the most seminal years of Mexican mixology. As Mexico was coming out of its Revolution, Spain was embroiled in a Civil War. This allowed for Mexico to take center stage in the production of Spanish-language films. It also meant that many Spanish refugees sought a new home in Mexico away from the war. The Spanish cantinero became a well-known trope in Mexican cinema.

Simultaneously, on the coattails of the Revolution, tequila became a more patriotic drink of choice. A shot of tequila with salt and lime—a format known around the world today—was a Mexican folk medicine against influenza during the global outbreak of 1918 to 1920. In the 1930s and 1940s, many of Mexico's most iconic cocktails were born. The tequila-based drinks Margarita, Changuirongo, and Bertha all come from these decades, demonstrating a final and fruitful confluence of foreign cocktail culture and homegrown flavors and products.

By the 1950s, the famed Mexican author and gastronome, Josefina Velázquez de León, published a book on cocktails. Many of her recipes read as traditional, with gin and vermouth featuring prominently in drinks like Cocktail de Uva, Cocktail Bonifacio, and Bombero. Other recipes of hers included Coca-Cola and vino de jerez—two staples of twentieth-century Mexican mixology. Ginger ale, too, enjoyed mass adoption during these decades as the highball (sometimes written *jaibol*) became a staple drink made with rum, brandy, or tequila.

During these decades, Spain's influence would have continued to be felt in Mexican bars. Perico Chicote, owner of the world-famous cocktail bar Museo Chicote in Madrid, was serving tequila in Spain in the 1940s and imported Sauza in the 1950s. Chicote had visited Mexico and served margaritas at his bar. The Spanish barman's influence was such that a bar was opened with his very name in Mérida in 1969 by Arturo Ponce Alcalá, who was also involved in bringing baseball to the Yucatán.[10]

Finally, in the 1970s, mixology had sprouted into a formal career in Mexico. An Asociación Nacional de Barman's was created, presumably modeled after Chicote's 1964 founding of La Asociación de Barmans Españoles (A.B.E.). Yearly competitions sponsored by liquor brands like Bacardi, Brandy Presidente, and Sauza Tequila crowned national cocktail champions. The 1970 champion of one such competition was Barman J. Guadalupe Estrada with his cocktail called "Fuentes de Turismo."[11]

Mexican Cocktails in the World

The story of Mexican mixology is not only that of foreign influence in Mexico; it is also that of Mexican influence abroad. Tequila was introduced to Americans slowly following the end of Prohibition, when mixologists who had taken up shop south of the border migrated back north. Mexican cinema, too, developed iconic imagery associated with cantinas, tequila, and hard-nosed *charros*, or cowboys, that bled into Spaghetti Westerns. The margarita began to increase in popularity in the United States through the 1970s and 1980s, as tequila sales steadily climbed. Where pulque had long been considered the national drink of Mexico, tequila—hailing only from one region—began to usurp the title in the 1950s.

The development of Cancun and the Mayan Riviera starting in 1969 has also helped to position Mexico at the pinnacle of exotic, tropical, and tiki drinks. The hotel district in Cancun has become synonymous with drinking, and it is one of the only places where foreigners can legally purchase alcohol on Election Days.[12]

In the twenty-first century, though, something new has occurred. Mezcal's rise in popularity has complemented a renewed global interest in mixology and cocktails. The global recognition of Mexican cuisine and gastronomy has helped too. Mexican mixologists have thrown off the trappings of the Cuba Libre and left the cantina behind. Now, world-class cocktail bars and restaurants coax an international crowd of visitors to come to Mexico to drink. The 2011 opening of Licorería Limantour (whose name hearkens back to the early years of foreign cocktail bars) marked the beginning of Mexico's global renown in the world of refined cocktail experiences. Nowadays, the country is the cocktail capital of the Americas. With so many unique spirits and flavors, Mexico will continue to be a mecca for mixology in the decades to come.

* * *

Azulitos

Azulitos, or *pitufos* (referring to Smurfs), are twenty-first-century Mexican mixed drinks that are essentially flavored vodka Red Bulls. These cocktails call for vodka, curaçao, energy drinks, lime soda, and flavoring agents like blue raspberry and cherry. They are often garnished with a rainbow wreath of gummy candies tacked onto the cup by a thick smear of chamoy.

The infamous Ciudad de México neighborhood of Tepito may be the point of origin of the trend, which has now taken over bars across Mexico. The market of Tepito (where Chilangos say you can buy *anything*) is full of brick-and-mortar bars and market stalls that sell Azulitos in strange and humorous containers like Hello Kitty cups, blender bowls, and more phallic alternatives.

Bertha

The Bertha cocktail originates from a restaurant once owned by Bertha Estrada in the city of Taxco, Guerrero. The cocktail is mixed with honey, lime juice, silver tequila, and sparkling water. Bertha invented the drink in 1930. She is sometimes credited with inventing the not-so-different margarita too.

Bull

The Bull, referred to by its English name, is common along the west coast of Mexico in beach resort towns. It is a fortifying mix of white rum, simple syrup, and dark beer served on ice. One recipe calls specifically for the use of "Potosí," a kind of aguardiente from the Huasteca region.[13]

Coporitos

Coporitos are a new form of preparing a shot of mezcal inside a sour *xoconostle* cactus fruit that has been despined and hollowed out.[14] The process mingles the acidic juices of the fruit with mezcal and a bit of chili powder. The drink is local to San José del Torreón, Guanajuato, where the namesake El Cóporo archaeological site is located. Locals say that a man named José Bueno invented the form of consuming mezcal. He continues to sell coporitos at Lonchería el Volcán.

Cuba Libre

The Cuba Libre has been one of the most beloved mixed drinks of Mexico since the mid-1900s. Bacardi began producing rum in Mexico in 1931, around the same time that Coca-Cola was entering the Mexican market. Bacardi claims that their original factory at Calle de Cedro 380 was next door to a Coca-Cola bottler, earning the street the nickname "el paseo de la Cuba libre," or "Cuba Libre Way." FEMSA and Coca-Cola both still have facilities adjacent to the location in the Atlampa neighborhood. The high status of the Cuba Libre, and the proliferation of other cola-centric cocktails in Mexico, highlights the country's penchant for soda drinking.

The Cuba Libre would become a staple beverage in twentieth-century Mexican cantinas, keeping many solvent thanks to the excellent margins on the drink.[15] The association of drinking in cantinas with the Cuba Libre was such that the Mexican novelist José Agustín coined the term "Cubadicto" for a certain kind of alcoholic in his 1986 novel *Cerca del fuego*. There are also a variety of riffs on the Cuba Libre that have emerged in Mexico over the decades.

Campechana

Named after the Yucatán Peninsula state of Campeche, the Campechana, also known as the *Cuba Pintada* ("Painted Cuba"), is a normal cola-and-rum mixed drink which includes the addition of carbonated mineral water. Some drinkers believe that the Coca-Cola in the cocktail causes a hangover, so they must *despintar* ("strip the paint off") the dark soda with beer or *tehuacán* (slang for mineral water, named after the city in Puebla). This should not be confused with the edible Campechana cocktail, which is a shrimp cocktail with avocado and salsa.

Changuirongo

The changuirongo, sometimes called the *charro negro*, is a cocktail from Guadalajara that is essentially a Cuba Libre with tequila in place of rum. The drink contains cola, lime, and silver tequila. This drink is more commonly known as the Batanga, but all evidence points to the changuirongo being the original name and version. It should therefore be restored.

The typically Jalisciense concoction burst onto the scene in Guadalajara in the year 1940. Some say that it was the entry of Royal Crown Cola into the Guadalajara market that sparked the cocktail's invention.[16] That year, the Presidente Municipal of the city published announcements in the city's newspaper, *El Informador*, stating that "the owners of commercial stores, shops, restaurants, refreshment stands and places in general where the drink 'CHANGUIRONGO' is sold, are informed that the corresponding permit and contribution payments will be required as is of Cantinas."[17] This suggests that the sale of these cocktails was both widespread and occurring outside of traditional drinking spaces at this time (perhaps at new cola dispensaries).

The following day, the same newspaper wrote that the changuirongo contained tequila, cola, valerian, and "other drugs from a Yankee drink."[18] Other Cuba Libre riffs existed around 1940 Mexico, including the King Kong made with mezcal Potosino and the Ciudad de México Pantera Negra mixed with 96 percent pure alcohol. With salt, the changuirongo becomes a *Rusa* or "Russian."

Brandy, more popular than rum and tequila during the height of Cuba Libre consumption, was also used with Coca-Cola. Casa Madero, the largest producer of brandy, called the drink the Cubamadero. Josefina Velázquez de León's recipe for the cocktail "Miramar" includes vermouth, gin, sherry, sugar, and Coca-Cola.[19]

Heribertas

Heribertas are mixed drinks known in the university student community of Zacatecas that mix water, sugar, food coloring, tartaric acid, and 96 percent alcohol. Local lore suggests that Heriberto Campos Bernal, professor of chemistry at Unidad Académica de Ciencias Química in the 1960s and 1970s, helped some students prepare a mixed drink out of the supplies in his pharmacy, la Farmacia Lux.

Leche Caliente

Leche caliente literally means "hot milk," but the drink is a combination of freshly milked cow or goat's milk and strong liquor, whether it be tequila or aguardiente. The drink is a common breakfast beverage in the states of Colima and Jalisco where dairy farming and blue agave farming are common agricultural practices. The beverage is associated with life on the ranch but has also been adopted by popular culture as a way of capping off a night out (the following morning) or warding off a hangover.

Jalisco is the largest producer of both milk and tequila in Mexico. The combination of the two liquids is the result of their propinquity and complementary agriculture. The drink also borrows the name of several birds. Besides leche caliente, the raw milk and liquor combo is called *pajerete*, a sweet Spanish wine, *chereca*, or Sinaloan blue jay, *palomazo*, or big pigeon, *polla*, or baby chicken, and *galletera*, which literally means cookie-maker but likely derives from *gallo* for rooster. The last two, polla and galletera, are different drinks from the rest in that they include raw egg yolk in addition to raw milk and liquor.

Dairy farms have the obligation of milking their cows every morning of the year. As the drink has increased in popularity, some farms have converted a small area into a sort of bar, where morning drinkers arrive to prepare their own leche caliente along with tamales and other snacks during the morning chore of milking. Besides tequila or aguardiente, powdered chocolate, instant coffee, cinnamon sugar, or molasses can be added to the cup for flavoring. The mixture is then presented to the dairy farmer so that milk is introduced to the liquor directly from the udder. The drink is consumed immediately after milking.

Menyul

The menyul is a Mexican take on the Mint Julep popular in the state of Veracruz, which has existed since at least 1899.[20] The menyul is a refreshment on hot days on the beach in Córdoba, but it is not the same as the American Mint Julep. In place of the Mint Julep's usual bourbon, the menyul uses dark rum. A blend of sweet and dry sherry can be added, although some modern recipes call for Campari. Spearmint, angostura, and sugar or simple syrup finish off the cocktail.

Nalga Alegre

The Nalga Alegre, meaning "Happy Buttock," is a cocktail invented and sold by the famous Guadalajara cantina Los Famosos Equipales, founded in 1920 by Carmen Mancilla. The recipe was created in the 1940s and includes lime juice, gin, rum, red wine, and orange soda. It is served over ice. The legendary cantina, which closed temporarily in 2022 due to COVID-19, is also known for some of its other house cocktails, namely the *Charly* and the *Batido*.

* * *

Mixology-focused bars in cities like Ciudad de México and Guadalajara, and along the Riviera Maya have topped highly publicized lists that claim to rate the best bars in the world. Not only do Mexican bars innovate on cocktail classics, they also bring a range of native flavors to the greater world of bartending. Yet, these modern bars stand on the shoulders of a deep cantina culture, the best part of which is the famous botana—a snack that most traditional cantinas still provide drinking customers free of charge.

By the 1850s, Mexican cantinas had emerged in cities as places where working men could drink and socialize. Away from their family kitchens (women were not allowed in these spaces until President José López Portillo declared they be allowed entry in 1982), food would have been a key offering alongside intoxicating drink.

Botanas in cantinas range from simple chili peanuts or chips to more filling offerings like tacos, chicharrones, pozole, menudo, guacamole, caldo tlalpeño, or salsa borracha. Many dishes are hallmarks of the syncretization that occurred between Iberian and indigenous traditions, particularly in cantinas where Spanish owners were all too common over the last century. Such botanas might include snails in mole.

The botana often changes depending on the time of day and differs from day to day. It is a true *menu du jour* for the bar regular. In his 1999 book, *La Fiesta y La Muerte Enmascarada: El Distrito Federal de Noche*, the journalist Ignacio Trejo Fuentes wrote insightfully about the gendered allure of the botana in cantinas:

> The distinctive thing about cantinas is the splendid snacks that are served mainly during the day and even in the evenings, for a couple of beers one can eat as well or even better than in one's own house. (A couple of decades ago, when the cantina was an exclusive space for men, when entry to women was prohibited and those who entered were only of one class: prostitutes; at that time, they said, the cantina was the most dangerous rival to brides and housewives: they couldn't understand what the hell was behind those doors that their men ran towards them at the slightest provocation, they couldn't explain what the magic hook was. And they were unaware of the delights of privacy, the macho space and the wonderful goodness of snacks.)[21]

The cantinas of Guadalajara were once great purveyors of botanas. Nowadays, Mérida is an excellent city in which to eat a free lunch alongside the purchase of several beers, or perhaps the cantina classic, the Cuba Libre.

8

Atole

Atoles are a broad category of drinks, porridges, and gruels that derive from corn. Maize is the most consequential staple food of both ancient Mesoamerica and modern Mexico. It has been consumed there for millennia. Most theories point to Mexico's Tehuacán Valley as the point of origin of domesticated corn. The vestiges of ancient Mesoamerica are littered with references to the yearly agricultural cycle of corn facilitated by the maize gods who had to be appeased to ensure fertility and a good harvest. From the most distant Olmec times, Mesoamericans worshipped a rain god, who would go on to evolve into the Toltec (and later Aztec) rain god Tlaloc, who was closely associated with corn.[1]

The 1582 account of Juan Bautista Pomar describes a shrine to the god Tlaloc equipped with a stone basin full of a paste of a variety of common seeds, beans, and grains which he calls *olli*. The bowl atop the statue of the rain god's head "contained all the seeds that the natives use and sustain themselves with, such as white, black, red, and yellow corn, and beans of many kinds and colors, chia, *huauhtli*, and *michhuautli*, and chile peppers of all kinds that those in charge could afford, replenishing them every year at a certain time."[2] This "*olli*" paste was some kind of all-encompassing *atolli* replete with the many foodstuffs the rain god could provide. The Maya famously believed that the first humans were sculpted by the gods from corn dough.

In the ancient, foundational layers of Mexico's cuisine is the versatility of domesticated corn. Mexican cooks have transformed it into dozens of famous dishes: tortillas, sopes, gorditas, tacos, tlayudas, tamales, pozoles, esquites, elotes, and so many more. But in its liquid form, atole represents one of the most primitive maize-based foodstuffs. While technical diversity and complex chemical transformations exist in many atole preparations, some versions are more rudimentary than basic foods like tortillas and tamales. The thick drink of prehistory should not be discounted just because it lacks the glamour of Mexico's more global offerings. Atole is both profoundly simple and beautifully complicated.

The Timeless Tradition of Atole

Atole is not well-known outside of Mexico. While other cuisines in Latin America consume corn drinks such as Peru's *chicha morada*, Colombia's *chicha*, and Nicaragua's *pinol*, the hot and thick drink that Mexicans cherish is unique to the country. On the streets of Mexico today, it is commonplace for vendors to ladle an assortment of steaming atoles out of insulated containers into Styrofoam cups for their consumers. Most of these drinks are viscous, opaque, and sweet, tottering on the cusp between drink and porridge. The atoles are nourishing and filling—even serving as a meal replacement.

The pairing of an atole and a tamal is a timeless tradition. The names of both foods derive directly from Nahuatl. Atole, for the Aztecs, was *atolli*. Tamal was *tamal*. We need little imagination to picture the residents of the Valley of Anáhuac consuming the two preparations side by side for several centuries before the arrival of the Spanish. Millions continue to do so today.

In the 1777 work *Breve y compendiosa narración de la Ciudad de México*, Juan de Viera reported, "Also there is another street where are the tamaleras who sell their tamales . . . and those very people sell atole blanco . . . which is the regular breakfast of the poor and destitute people."[3]

The modern resident of Ciudad de México often eats the corny combination of atole and tamales for breakfast, and other cities find a hot and thick atole to be a nighttime comfort, especially during the winter. Other more cultural recipes are prepared for home consumption throughout the expanse of modern Mexico. Some versions are reserved for special occasions such as weddings and religious observations.

In 1780, Francisco Javier Clavijero described the basic atole-making process of the time:

> The atole are porridges, which are made with well-cooked corn dough, well ground, dissolved in water and strained. They put the filtered broth on the fire after, and there they cook it again until it acquires the desired consistency. To the palate of the Spanish, it is insipid, but they [the Spanish] use it for their sicknesses, sweetened with sugar, in place of the honey that the Indians use. For them it is such a delicacy, that they cannot live without it.[4]

The Spanish made it more to their liking with the addition of Old World products like milk and sugar.

The introduction of dairy to the Mesoamerican diet had far-reaching consequences. The Aztecs, who lived on an island, had to rely on floating *chinampa* farms and a probable threat of violence to extract sufficient food resources from the surrounding Central Valley (which was then more populated than any part of Spain). There were no pack animals in Mesoamerica, so bringing livestock into the valley would have disrupted the already strained use of land for production of cereals needed to feed millions of people.[5] Yet milk and refined sugar were pivotal in atole's transformation as another drink captured by Mexico's unrelenting mestizaje.

Describing atole as a "corn drink" does not properly explain the vast diversity that the category encompasses. While Francisco Javier Clavijero reported that there were seventeen distinct varieties of atole in the eighteenth century, it is safe to say that there are upward of 100 versions, deriving from a combination of added flavors and different preparation techniques.[6] Some atoles are regional specialties, while others are beloved at a national level.

For the most part, flavored atoles are straightforward mixtures of *masa* ("corn dough"), water or milk, and some kind of flavoring agent (usually fruit, flowers, other grains, or vegetables). A basic *atole blanco* could acquire the essence of nearly every flavor within the Mexican culinary universe, but some are more popular than others. The more notable differences in the diversity of the drink emerge when the base material corn is processed differently.

The Question of Nixtamalization

The most rudimentary atoles are likely older than other corn staples like tamales and tortillas (tamales are older than tortillas).[7] This is because tamales and tortillas rely on nixtamalized corn—corn that has been processed with *cal,* which is quicklime or calcium hydroxide, usually in the form of ashes from wood or seashells. Mixing corn in water with cal helps to remove the kernel's outer layers, called the pericarp and pedicel. The soaking process also helps to gelatinize starches. The calcium hydroxide even incorporates a calcium ion into the corn. All together, these transformations make maize a far more desirable food.

Thanks to nixtamalization, the dough is more resistant to potentially harmful microbes. It contains more calcium, vitamin B3, and amino acids. It contains fewer toxins like the chemicals known as fumocins.[8] On top of these nutritional factors, nixtamalization improves the texture of corn dough by increasing gelatinization, which makes for better tortillas. The process also makes the corn more yellow.

The nixtamalization process is at least 3,000 years old, and its discovery is one of the most consequential events in the history of Mesoamerica. Without nixtamalization, maize would not have played such a significant role in indigenous life in North and South America. We could count it among some of world history's greatest agricultural revolutions. In Mexico, the tamal emerged during the earliest years of knowledge of the quicklime process.[9] Atole blanco would have followed as well, but there exist atole recipes which call for non-nixtamalized tender, young corn.

The time before nixtamalization begs an intriguing question that remains largely unanswered: Why did so many societies cultivate corn without the culinary knowledge to optimize its usage as food? The answer, some have suggested, lies in the realm of beverages. Whether humans were using the corn stalks for sugar (and possibly to ferment a kind of prehistoric stalk juice wine), or were able to use the small seeds of wild teosinte in their cuisine is unclear, but corn was cultivated throughout the Americas prior to nixtamalization.

Culturally, Mesoamericans conceptualized non-nixtamalized corn as uncooked, raw, and alive. The atoles concocted from such corn dough, called *yotextli* in Nahuatl (meaning "living dough"), were called *yollatolli* ("living atoles").[10] When the corn was nixtamalized, the resulting atoles were known as *tenexatolli* ("atole of quicklime"), as well as *cuauhnexatolli* ("atole of ashes").[11] The distinction in corn processing has been pronounced for generations because the organoleptic, nutritional, and cultural attributes of an atole depend on it.

In total, there are four distinct genres of atoles, categorized based on the transformations that corn undergoes in becoming a drink.[12] There are atoles prepared with nixtamalization, atoles prepared with fermentation, atoles prepared with neither, and atoles prepared with both. In the modern context, a recipe will often reveal how the corn is processed simply by referencing a certain type of corn. The lexicon of Mexican corn vocabulary is vast and nuanced. While some corn terms are philologically Spanish, the meanings behind the terms invariably derive from indigenous culinary and agricultural knowledge. There are drinks made from fresh, unprocessed, non-nixtamalized corn which might call for *elote, esquites, izquiate, maiz nuevo* or *maiz tierno*. These are all terms for fresh, tender, and sometimes roasted kernels. Then there are drinks made from nixtamalized corn which use doughs like *nixtamal martajado, nixtamal picado* (both from coarsely ground corn), *puscua*, and, in Guerrero, *nixtamal nejo*, which derives from the Nahuatl for ash, *nextli*.[13]

Atoles and Their Flavors

Aside from the technique employed in producing a masa, atoles are made from different agricultural varieties of corn. There is dark corn like *maiz prieto, morado*, or *dorado*, white corn, or *maiz blanco*, blue corn, or *maiz azul*, and, in the case of the Maya, green corn to make their atole called *yax 'ul*. Not only do different varieties of corn influence starch content and natural sweetness, but the color of corn has also played a role in Mesoamerican cosmovision. One final variable in atole making is whether the corn kernels are toasted on a comal before being ground up. Toasted corn is used for *pinole*.

Certain atoles are also fermented, giving them a sour, lactic acid note. Such atoles can be distinct from traditional fermented beverages, but there is also overlap. Drinks like tesgüiño, sendechó, axokot, and chicha involve fermenting corn after it has been mixed into water. To complicate the issue, some fermented atoles involve fermentation of the corn dough before it is mixedwith water, like Chiapaneco pozol. This is considered a solid-state fermentation.

Once a corn base is prepared, regardless of the method, many atoles are flavored with fruits, vegetables, herbs, spices, and other creative alternatives like brand-name cookies! The compendium of flavors reported in a variety of modern Mexican recipe books is staggeringly vast. A non-exhaustive list of atole flavors includes the following, roughly separated into categories: raspberry, raisin, wild cherry, plum, hog plum, loquat, guava, strawberry, coconut, tamarind, mango, melon, apple, orange, plantain, banana, pineapple, sapote, custard apple (chirimoya), nance, prickly pear, peach, quince, fig, tejocote, coffee fruit pulp, sweet potato, radish, huitlacoche corn fungus, epazote leaf, squash, garbanzo bean, rice, amaranth, oat, barley, rye, cashew, walnut, almond, peanut, piñón nut, mesquite pod, pumpkin seed, barrel cactus, ash, *tequesquite*, aguamiel (agave sap), coyol palm sap, eggnog, dulce de leche, caramel, Galletas Marias, marshmallow, malanga root, peppercorn, the fruit of the *Schinus molle* tree, marigold, Mexican magnolia, cinnamon, and vanilla. Some recipes like banana mango call for a mix of these flavors. Also, virtually every flavored atole can be transformed by replacing a base of water with milk.

Certain atoles merit unique names. María Gorda is an atole made with corn, milk, sugar, and cinnamon. *Citum* refers to atole made with wild fruits, particularly plums. Real del Monte is made from extremely young and tender ears of corn. *Ollotolli* is produced with *olotes*, which are bare corn cobs (i.e., no kernels), roasted directly on a fire (a process called *tatemando* in Mexican cooking).[14] In Guanajuato and Michoacán, corn silks are burned and used to make *atole de chaqueta*.

There are more flavors cited in indigenous contexts that rely on the kind of native plants that are foraged rather than farmed. *Ojite*, the ramon nut of the *Brosimum alicastrum* tree, is used in traditional atoles in Huehuetlan, San Luis Potosí.[15] The ramon is also used in non-caffeinated coffee substitutes today. The *guamuchil* of the *Pithecellobium dulce* plant, as well as the *parota* or devil's ear seed of the *Enterolobium cyclocarpum* tree, are used in atoles in Acapetlahuaya, Guerrero.[16] The Mayo and Yaqui of northwest Mexico make a variety of flavored atoles from the berries of the *barchata*, or *Ziziphus obtusifolia* bush, the fruit of the garambullo cactus, and wild seasonal greens called quelites.[17] The Xi'ui of the Altiplano make atole from the seeds of a plant known as *patol*, among other things.[18]

Flavored atoles are not a new or isolated concept. Aztecs knew honeyed atole as *necuatolli* and chile atole as *chilinecuatolli*. The Aztecs also had a variety of atole that incorporated beans called *ayocomollatolli*. *Tequesquite*, a traditional foraged salt, has also long been used to flavor atole (and help with nixtamalization in lieu of cal). It is still used today to add a bit of flavor to atole blanco like soy sauce in a plain rice congee.

Additionally, there are certain beverages that fit into the category of atole which do not contain corn at all. Some modern uses of the word atole refer to wheat-based gruels. There are also seed flour drinks which have fit into the ancient atole category. The Aztec would have called such drinks *chianatolli* or *chiantzotzolatolli*. Pumpkin seeds, chia seeds, chan seeds, and patol seeds, among others, are dried, ground, and mixed with water or milk to make thick beverages. But beware the names. *Atole de maiz de teja*, contrary to the "maiz" name, is made not with maize, but with sunflower seeds!

Cultural Importance of Atole

If the culinary complexity and diversity of atole have not yet impressed, it is worth stressing how ingrained in Mexican culture atole is. Old Mexican cookbooks often use atole as a standard reference for the viscosity that the cook should look for in preparing the described dishes. Both its antiquity and ubiquity make it a suitable vehicle upon which cultural values can be grafted. Religion, language, and tradition have all taken to the cherished drink.

Several popular Mexican sayings feature atole as a prominent signifier. Single men are told "Con la que entiende de atole y metate, con ésa cásate," meaning that a good wife should have mastered the fundamentals of the traditional Mexican kitchen—that is, atole making and grinding with a metate. In Mexico, it is not uncommon for a woman serving you food to ask if she is ready to marry you. It is not a proposal, just a way of asking if the food is delicious. Additionally, a suitor could tell the object of his desire, "Contigo la milpa es rancho, y el atole champurrado," meaning "With you, the small farm is a ranch, and the atole a hot chocolate." "Dar atole con el dedo," meaning "to give atole with the finger," is a popular phrase in Mexican politics. When a politician gives the people atole with his finger, he satiates them, but only in the short term. The saying represents palliative measures.

In religious contexts, atole takes on many symbolic meanings. The most obvious example is the common use of atole as an offering on Día de los Muertos throughout Mexico, particularly in the famed celebration of San Andres Míxquic. These practices have roots in Mesoamerican religion where atole was offered to the dead and used in fertility sacrifices because the corn gods controlled fertility.

Many extant indigenous practices also prove that atole is a religious substance. The Purépecha use a drink called *atole de carrizo* made from cacao shells, roasted corn flour, and piloncillo in honor of the Immaculate Conception celebrated with adoration of a figure of the Virgin Mary they refer to as "la Virgen atolerita."[19] Some Maya people still prepare *santo uk'ul*, literally "sacred atole." They also prepare *saka'* and offer it to their nature deities. Beekeepers in Maní, Yucatán, present saka' to sacred Melipona bees at the time of hive division. In the north of Mexico, the Wixárika make a sacred corn atole fortified with amaranth and squash seeds used to wean children off breast milk.[20]

Two Notes on Atole

First, there is a group of foods around Mexico that exist on the edge of the atole world: pozole, chileatole, and nicuatole. The first two are kinds of soups, while the last is a dense Oaxacan confection. Nevertheless, they are historically, linguistically, and gastronomically related to atole.

Pozole is a common pork and corn-based soup in Mexico that utilizes large, tender corn kernels that have been crushed and boiled in broth.

Besides being an excellent hangover cure, the name of the soup hints at a history where it was not so distinct from atole. Pozol, with no "e," is a variety of atole in Chiapas. Both words derive from Nahuatl terms referencing foaminess in the corn boiling process. One historical recipe for pozole gives instructions to fully grind the corn: Corn was placed on the fire until it burst and then it was ground on a metate and left to ferment with water for 3 or 4 days.[21] This would render the corn into some kind of beverage or slurry. In certain communities of Oaxaca, pozole is still a nixtamalized masa beverage today.

Similarly, chileatole, a common delicacy from Puebla, exists on the edge of the beverage realm. The soup is a boiled combination of corn kernels and epazote herb that is seasoned with chiles. Eaten with a spoon, chileatole is more of a snack than a beverage, but its name demonstrates the underlying relationship. In Oaxaca, nicuatole is a thick corn-based dessert that can be flavored with a variety of fruits. The confection is pre-Columbian and its name derives from the combination of corn and honey. Still, it is decidedly solid. It is not an atole beverage.

Finally, there is an entire genus of corn-based beverages that incorporate the highly esteemed cacao. Even though these should be considered a subclass of atoles, the beverages will be discussed in the following chapter on chocolate because of the significance of cacao.

* * *

Atole Agrio

Atole agrio, also called *atole xoco* (literally "sour atole"), encompasses a diverse collection of atoles that are left to ferment at one or various stages of processing. For the Mexica, such atoles were designated as *xocoatolli*. Atole agrio exists in a variety of forms across Mexico, particularly in Chiapas, Oaxaca, Tabasco, and Veracruz.

Regionally, there are fermented atoles based on toasted corn pinol, nixtamalized corn, and raw corn. Axokot and xocoatol are known to be both nixtamalized and then fermented, while xocolat is fermented raw corn dough.[22] Within the world of fermented atoles, fermentation occurs at one of three stages in preparation (or a combination of those three). First, full kernels of corn can be left in water for several days at a time, as is the case in some Chiapaneco examples which soak corn for 4 to 5 days.[23] Second, the ground corn dough can be left to ferment as is the case with pozol or the atole agrio of the Tlapanec. Finally, the atole can be left to ferment after the corn dough is dissolved into water, as is the case with axokot. Yet another nuance is a hybrid process to make *jili Uat'ab* in Huehuetlán, San Luis Potosí, by which nixtamalized dough is left in water for 12 hours to ferment, only to be sieved out and boiled in a clay pot before serving.[24] After the fermented beverage is prepared, flavorings are sometimes added to atole agrio.

Atole de Elote

Atole de elote is an atole produced from elote or *maiz tierno*, a young, tender corn harvested before its prime maturity. Elote is the variety of corn that most Americans would call corn-on-the-cob. Most Mexican corn is allowed to mature and harden for storage and processing, while elote is picked early and has natural sweetness. Other names for similar products include *atole nuevo* and, toward Guatemala, *eloatol*.[25] This is an atole which involves neither nixtamalization nor fermentation.

To prepare atole from tender corn, the ears are shucked, and the kernels are stripped off. The corn is ground into a dough and then boiled. Floating particles are removed. Sugar, piloncillo, milk, salt, even more corn kernels, flour, or dough can be added during boiling to achieve the desired finished product. Another name for such an atole is Real del Monte. The Maya call this *aj sá*.

Atole de Frijol

Atole de frijol is a type of flavored atole that incorporates toasted and crushed beans. The coarse bean flour is introduced to *tejate* (in this context, meaning whipped corn dough) and left to boil as most atoles are. In place of bean flour, *frijol quebrada* ("broken beans") is also used. Most bean atole recipes call for the addition of tequesquite mineral salt.

The addition of beans to atole is common throughout Mexico. Bean atoles are pre-Columbian and were called *etlatolli* or *ayocomollatolli*. The inclusion of beans, as well as that of seeds or amaranth, adds to the nutritional value of the drink. In the case of amaranth, the drink is called *atole de alegría* and was known as *michihoauhatolli* in Aztec times. Pomar, in his 1582 memoir, wrote that "They have michihuauhtli which is a smaller white seed: of which they make loaves of bread like those made of huauhtli, and of which they usually drink after toasting it and grinding it and dissolving it in honey water."[26]

Atole de frijol is an ancestral tradition consumed at funerals in Triqui communities in Oaxaca, where they call the drink *nakinj runee* and produce it with *frijol ayocote*, a native species of large legumes.[27] Other recipes call for different varieties of beans. Communities in states including Guerrero, Morelos, and the Federal District prepare their own versions.

Atole de Granillo

Atole de grano or granillo is a nixtamalized corn atole produced from a mixture of coarsely and finely ground corn. It is one of the more basic forms of atole and is typical of southern Mexican states like Oaxaca and Chiapas. Corn is boiled with quicklime and then ground, separating out halves based on the fineness of the grind. The two halves are then boiled anew with cinnamon, sugar, water, or milk, and sometimes flavorings like clove. The same atole is also called *tezihuatole*.

Atole de Nalga

Atole de nalga is a ceremonial black or blue corn atole produced in certain communities in Veracruz for Día de Los Muertos. Its name literally means "butt cheek atole," and it is traditionally paired with *tamales de pedo*, or "fart tamales," which are made from the same black corn and filled with beans.

Atole de Puscua

Atole de puzua, also written *puscua*, is an atole produced from white corn. The same drink is called atole blanco or atole de masa. This is the most basic form of nixtamalized atole. Puscua is generally synonymous with nixtamalized corn dough. One nineteenth-century definition of puscua defines it as "corn cooked conveniently to make tortillas . . . also the name is given for a drink of cooked corn."[28] As it is used in tortillas, it is nixtamalized.

The drink is typical in Guanajuato, Hidalgo, Querétaro, and Michoacán. Traditionally, it is served as an accompaniment to sweet fritters called *buñuelos*. It is also a classic winter drink for warming the body. The Xi'ui use this kind of atole to cure hangovers.[29]

Atole de Tortilla

Atole de tortilla is a variety of atole produced from corn dough that is cooked into tortillas (and sometimes burned) and then ground into a dust and incorporated into water.

Tlaxcalatolli ("tortilla atole") was among the core pre-Columbian varieties of the drink. The preparation of tlaxcalatolli involved cooking thick tortillas on a comal, removing the crust, crushing the bread, mixing it with water, and then boiling.[30] Atole de tortilla is mentioned in Sahagún's Florentine Codex (lib. X, cap. 26). It is also called *atole quemado* ("burnt atole").

Axokot

In the northern hills of Puebla, indigenous Nahua people make a special kind of fermented atole known as axokot, axocot, or axocotl. The term roughly translates as "sour water," and is unique in that it requires several specific herbs. Chief among the additives is *axokotxihuit*, which is the plant *Fleischmannia pycnocephala*. Aside from adding flavor to the fermented atole, there is a belief that the herb is useful in childbirth, postpartum recovery, and as a sudorific agent.[31]

The Nahuas of Cuetzalan prepare axokot for momentous occasions like baptisms, marriages, deaths, festivals to saints, and the construction of new houses. The drink includes cal, two kinds of corn (red and white), and a paste prepared from the axokotxihuit. In the case of axokot, the base atole is both nixtamalized and fermented. The mixture is fermented in clay bowls that have been covered in the leaves of *Telanthophora grandifolia* for 1 to 3 days.[32]

Bate

Bate is an indigenous beverage that exists almost exclusively in a small region of Colima state in western Mexico. It is made from toasted and ground chan seeds which are then beaten with water and served out of a large balsa gourd with molasses or piloncillo syrup. While bate is not a corn atole, it is a descendant of the Aztec tradition of *chianatolli*, which were seed flour drinks. Writing in 1582, Juan Bautista Pomar discusses how chia was made into a drink by roasting, grinding, and boiling into water.[33] During the 1800s, Rémi Siméon, the Nahuatl-Spanish lexicographer, noted a mucilaginous drink made from chia seeds that he considered to be nutritious and refreshing.[34]

The chan seed that is the base of bate is a close relative of the chia. Chan, however, is a wider seed. The seeds come from the *Mesosphaerum suaveolens* plant. Bate makers harvest the seeds from spiky pods in October, usually asking permission from landowners who assume the wild plant growing on their land is just a weed. There are two varieties: short plants that bloom white and tall plants that bloom brown. Only the brown variety is used to prepare bate.

After harvesting, the seeds are cleaned, toasted on a comal, and ground by hand or in a milling machine. The mixture is then beaten or shaken (hence the name bate, from the verb *batir*, "to whip up"). The resulting liquid is extremely gelatinous due to the mucilage from the seeds. It has a cooling, toasted flavor, and mixes well with sweet molasses.

Bate supposedly has several medicinal benefits. Its gooey mucilage is a natural source of fiber and helps with digestion and gastritis. Local claims also suggest that the drink helps with kidney health, blood circulation, and even cancer. Today, local women from the small town Suchitlán are the main individuals upholding the tradition. Chan grows in the hills of Suchitlán, and several women from the town sell prepared bate in downtown Colima. Bate El Merced, the famous stand run by the late Doña María Cipriana who is immortalized in a bronze statue next to Jardín Nuñez, is still operated by her daughters and granddaughters every day of the year.

Pinol/Pinole

Pinol or pinole is a common beverage made from ground, toasted corn kernels. Pinol is a generic term for the flour that is made from toasted corn that derives from the Nahuatl word *pinolli*. Roasting and grinding corn into dry flour is a useful way to preserve and store the grain for several months. Basic pinol would be an example of an atole that is neither nixtamalized nor fermented.

While atole de pinol can feature just pinol mixed into water or milk, it is common to add flavorings to the drink such as cacao, anise, and cinnamon. There are also examples of pinol prepared with corn flour mixed with the flour of a variety of proteinaceous foods like beans or amaranth. Generally, pinol has a darker, roasted, more bitter flavor compared to unroasted corn atoles. It also has a noticeable grainy texture in comparison to the oatmeal-like, dissolved atoles.

In Chiapas, pinol is known as *poote*. Some communities in the Altos de Chiapas call a similar drink *chilim*.[35] For the Tarahumara people of the Chihuahuan Desert, toasted corn dissolved in water has been called *esquiate* or *izquiate*, like *atole de izquitl* (toasted, tender young corn), although the term may have once referred to tesgüiño.[36] *Elisquiate* is apparently a derivative of this northern pinol, sweetened and flavored with chile. The Aztecs also made *izquiatolli* from toasted corn and chiles. The Maya know this drink as *k'aj*.

Piznate

Piznate is a refreshment made from ground, roasted corn, piloncillo, and cinnamon. It is typical in Nayarit and Sinaloa. Roasted corn is ground and strained until a homogeneous beverage is achieved. The liquid is then boiled with the piloncillo and cinnamon. In some cases, it is chilled and served as a sort of corn agua fresca. The existence of this drink is noted in the Nayarit towns of Ruiz and Acaponeta.[37]

Pozol

Pozol is a native atole produced from fermented corn dough and water. It is still a daily drink in both Tabasco and Chiapas and can also be found in Veracruz and the Yucatán Peninsula. Pozol vendors usually produce both corn pozol, called *pozol blanco*, and chocolate pozol, called *pozol de cacao*. In Tabasco, pozol with cacao is sometimes known as *chorote*.

The pozoleras (traditionally women) who sell the drink boil corn with cal and then grind the cooked corn into a fine dough. If they are preparing pozol with cacao, they mix roasted and ground cacao into the dough. In both cases, they leave the resulting dough to ferment for around 2 days. Markets in Chiapas have vendors offering large piles of white and black doughs ready to be mixed into water at home to prepare the finished beverage. Pozoleras also sell prepared drinks from large vats filled with chunks of ice. The drinker's prerogative is to add coconut, sweet potato, and peanut to the mix as well.

Pozol is a hardy atole that lacks the sweetness of more popular drinks in the north. The beverage is thought to be energizing and fortifying in addition to refreshing. In both Tabasco and Chiapas, pozol takes on an outsized role in social and religious celebrations as a traditional beverage. It is a key source of nutrients for many in the region. The Maya know pozol as *k'eyem* and consume it in the fields as an energizer.[38]

To consume pozol, the drinker must constantly swish the liquid around in the jícara cup to keep the grainy dregs, sometimes called *xix*, *poso*, or *coladura*, from settling.[39]

Saká

Saká, also *sakab*, is a ceremonial corn atole prepared by the Maya as an offering to the *dueños* of the environment around them, particularly the gods of the mountain and Chá Chaak, the god of rain.[40] Before a hunt or the sowing of a new milpa farm, saká is prepared and presented in traditional jícaras. In April, beekeepers in Maní, Yucatán, open the harvest with offerings of saká sweetened with the first drops of honey of the harvest. It is commonly accompanied by the other sacred Maya beverage, balché.

Saká is produced from nixtamalized corn and is lightly cooked in virgin water from subterranean cenotes. The combination of corn and water is physical proof of its religious significance; saká offerings show gratitude for both corn and rain. Often, fresh honey is added to the atole. It remains a religious substance. The majority of contemporary Maya beekeepers in Campeche offer saká to the mountain gods to ask permission to harvest honey.[41]

Tejuino

Tejuino is a refreshing beverage made from the masa of nixtamal of white corn and piloncillo. In the states of Jalisco and Colima, and to a lesser extent Nayarit and Oaxaca, tejuino is popular during peak hours of heat in the early afternoon. Push carts and bicycle stands open around public plazas and parks to sell cups of the brown drink with plenty of ice. Upon serving, it is common to add sugar, lime juice, and even salt. The drink is invariably served cold, with some versions being served as sorts of slush. In cities like Guadalajara, some restaurants mix lime slush with tejuino. There are also vendors who sell *tejuichelas*, or beer mixed with tejuino.[42]

Tsinari

Tsinari or *chinari* is a unique atole produced with *huitlacoche* ("corn smut"), a fungus of the species *Ustilago maydis* that grows on maize. Huitlacoche has been used in both Mesoamerican cuisine and traditional medicine for centuries. The Wixárika make an atole from nixtamalized corn and add metate-ground huitlacoche (called *kiau* locally) to color the drink black, which is then left to rest in a dark, cool place and may be sweetened with piloncillo before drinking.[43]

* * *

Even as traditional Mexican cooking enjoys global acclaim for even its most rudimentary dishes like corny tamales and tortillas, humble atole has been largely unexplored by modern gastronomes. La Atolería by Tierra del Sol in Oaxaca brings a modern, chic approach to the ancient corn gruel, but it is mostly still relegated to street corners, push carts, and home kitchens.

A walk through San Luis Potosí's Museo Leonora Carrington, though, reminds us of the spiritual importance of atole to the soul of Mexican nutrition. Carrington, a British expatriate who came to Mexico to continue her career as a surrealist painter exploring female power, the occult, and witchcraft, sculpted a large statue toward the end of her life in 2011. The statue depicts a strange, goddess-like figure that had appeared throughout her work since 1951. The figure is hunched and robed and holds a bowl in its hands resting on its lap. It is titled *La inventora del atole*—The Inventress of Atole.

Whosoever invented atole deserves the deification that Carrington gave her in this sculpture. Just as Mesoamericans mythologized the originators of pulque and corn in Mayahuel and Tlaloc, respectively, the primordial corn stew that is atole was a groundbreaking moment for sustenance in this part of the world. It has persisted in providing succor to generations of different people in this land for thousands of years.

While atole has not garnered the respect that it properly deserves, a cup of hot atole on a brisk night can be an ambrosia that teleports you back to the warm, fuzzy, and fulfilled time when a motherly figure attended to all your needs.

9

Cacao

The Spanish chronicler Bernal Díaz del Castillo wrote that Moctezuma served golden cups brimming with a chocolate beverage to Hernán Cortés and his soldiers in 1519. The drink was strange to the European palate, but the Spanish could not understand the status, power, and luxury that they held in their cups. Cacao was not grown in the Central Valley of Mexico. Moctezuma's supply of the drink's raw material represented the geographical extent of the Aztec empire, as well as its coercive tax and tributary systems. Since the 1480s, the Aztec alliance had secured passage across the Mixteca, through the Valley of Oaxaca, onto the Isthmus of Tehuantepec, and into the distant, southern, cacao-producing region of *Xoconochco*.[1]

Cortés would find the drink compelling enough to exchange it (in addition to salt, shrimp, and fish) with the lords of Tlaxcala at Quiahuitztlan who had given him and his soldiers their daughters as offerings of their alliance.[2] The Conquistador brought nibs of cacao back to Spain as early as 1528.

These first intercontinental exchanges of chocolate would herald the global expansion of the cacao tree and a select few beverages derived from it. As chocolate traveled around the world, it transformed in the hands of different cultures. The hot chocolate that Americans drink after the hard labor of building a snowman is not the same drink that Cortés consumed in Tenochtitlán. Ours is sweeter, less bitter, foamless, and devoid of cocoa butter. Solid milk chocolate bars, too, are a nineteenth-century European innovation.

The reality is that the world has forgotten where chocolate came from and is ignorant of the fact that chocolate is still consumed in a variety of delicious beverages in its original geography. This history of chocolate is a history of Mesoamerican beverages like no other.

While the Aztecs introduced Europeans to chocolate, they were by no means the keepers of the drink. In fact, they would have traded for cacao or forced conquered peoples in southern Mexico to pay tribute in kind. The cacao tree did not (and does not) grow around Ciudad de México, where the Aztecs had built Tenochtitlán. Cacao is much more deeply ingrained in the Maya culture to the south.

Ancient Roots of Cacao

By the time the Aztecs rose to power, cacao had nearly 3,000 years of use and consumption within the Mesoamerican world. The new empire simply inherited the drink and the cultural importance that came along with it. Evidence suggests that ritualistic cacao consumption facilitated by trade had, in fact, traveled as far north as modern-day Utah prior to the arrival of the Spanish. Cacao was a sought-after commodity—even in the remotest corners of the Mesoamerican sphere of influence.

Over the course of the last two decades, archaeologists with increasing access to chromatography, a technology that allows them to test pot shard residues for specific compounds, have pushed the antiquity of the use and consumption of cacao further back. It is firmly established that the domesticated plant originates from the Amazonian highlands that are shared between Brazil, Ecuador, Peru, and Colombia. South Americans have been using cacao for around 5,300 years .[3] But Mesoamericans had the most developed culture of cacao beverage consumption in the New World.

In southern Mexico, particularly in Chiapas and Tabasco, as well as in Honduras and Guatemala, evidence of cacao consumption dates to the advent of pottery in the region. The Early and Middle Formative periods currently yield the most antiquated evidence of cacao residues in pottery.[4] That would put the infancy of cacao use in Central America at around 1500 BCE, a precursor to the Olmec civilization, which is considered Mesoamerica's first "great" civilization and was foundational in establishing the region's basic cosmovision. To corroborate this fact, the word cacao likely emerged from the Olmec region as well, where Mije-Sokean language lent its word *kakaw* to neighboring and subsequent Mesoamerican languages.[5]

For the Maya who lived within the tree's natural range of cultivation, cacao acquired overt religious significance. Many samples of ancient pottery that test positive for cacao residues were used in Maya funerary rites. The naturalist Francisco Hernández de Toledo wrote about a drink made from a mix of cacao and *pataxte* in the 1500s, which may have been a ritual aid for those who died to reach the afterlife. Chocolate drinks would have been presented as offerings to the gods of the Olmec, Maya, and Chontal worlds.

One god, labeled God L by scholars of Mesoamerica, ruled over commerce and transportation, and was closely related to cacao because the drinkable commodity was closely associated with exchange and currency.[6] A similar Maya god, Ek Chuah, was also patron of both merchants and cacao. In the old Xinka language of Guatemala and El Salvador, the word *tuwa* meant both cacao and money.[7] As late as the 1910s, ethnographers noted that the modern Maya were willing to exchange money for only a select few commodities—one of which was cacao.[8] Cacao was in such demand that it became a common form of exchange. It stored value as a luxury commodity that indicated status and could be trusted to be useful in future exchanges. Such a ubiquitous and coveted substance can easily be imbued with cultural significance.

For much of Mesoamerica, cacao was reserved for the elite. Only the wealthy could afford to drink a substance that could be used as currency.

Nezahualcóyotl, who ruled Texcoco from 1402 to 1431, had a cacao orchard planted 400 units long and 200 units wide, and his court allegedly consumed 32,000 cacao beans a day.[9] Sahagún picked up on the common Nahuatl phrase *Yollotli, eztli*, meaning "the price of blood and of heart": "This saying was said of cacao, because it was precious; nowhere did it appear in times past. The common folk, the needy did not drink it."[10] Cacao tribute in Mesoamerica was measured in *zontles*, which contained 400 beans, and *xiquipiles*, which contained 8,000 beans and weighed an estimated 20 pounds.[11] Juan de Torquemada reported that Moctezuma had a supply of 40,000 loads of cacao in one storehouse. Only in the late sixteenth century did the value of cacao begin to fall and its use as a currency slowly phase out.[12]

Today, cacao still has religious significance in indigenous communities in Chiapas and the Yucatán Peninsula. Traditional cacao drinks are often prepared for holy days or social occasions. Cacao has even been co-opted by certain strains of modern Western culture in the form of the cacao ceremony. While these ceremonies continue the spiritual legacy of cacao consumption, they do not derive from indigenous practice. Instead, they are more closely related to European astrology, Pagan, and Wiccan ritual—though tourists in Tulum can easily find a Western cacao ceremony in chocolate's ancestral home.

Cacao Cultivation

The culture of cacao in southern Mexico was born of the auspices of geography and botany. The cacao plant generally grows below an altitude of 600 meters, thrives under shade, and requires temperatures between 24 degree Celsius and 28 degree Celsius. Accordingly, the tree has been cultivated in the low altitude regions of the tropical southern states, mainly Tabasco, Chiapas, Oaxaca, Guerrero, and Veracruz. In this range, strong traditions of drinking complex cacao beverages have flourished.

Chocolate drinks derive predominantly from one of two species of cultivated (and sometimes wild) cacao. Overwhelmingly, chocolate is produced from the fruit of the species *Theobroma cacao*. This is the plant that has found an endearing place in the sweet tooth of the world. But another larger species of tree in the genus has remained in use in South and Central America without any interest from the West. Mesoamericans—and today Mexicans and Guatemalans—have long enjoyed the taste of *Theobroma bicolor*.

In southern Mexico, *Theobroma bicolor* is commonly known as *pataxte* (from the Nahuatl *pataxtli*), as well as *huapataxtle*, *macambo*, *bacao*, and *balam te'* ("jaguar tree"). In Mesoamerican thought, both cacao and the jaguar are associated with concepts like nighttime and the Underworld. While pataxte is less bitter than normal cacao, it does not contain caffeine, which may make it less attractive as a base for daily beverages. It also ferments for longer. Ethnobotanical research points to the occasional use of the species *Theobroma angustifolium* in cacao production. Low-quality cacao pods that desiccated on the tree before reaching maturity are still consumed as well. In Tabasco, this shriveled version of the pod is called *cocolbox*.[13] On the other hand, Sahagún wrote that a drink made from young cacao pods was called *xoxouhqui cacahuacintli*. Modern commercial varieties of the *Theobroma cacao* species include the bitter but fruitful *Forastero*, the mellow *Criollo* (native to Central America and Southern Mexico), and the *Trinitario*.

The Original Cacao Beverages

The juice of the cacao pulp, known in Tabasco today as *cacahuada* and in Guatemala as *refresco de pocha*, would have been one of the earliest culinary uses of the cacao pod. Producing chocolate from the nibs requires solid-state fermentation. Using the pulp surrounding the nibs is the most basic method to prepare a cacao drink: Harvest the inner pulp of the cacao pod, press out its juice, and enjoy the sweet and tangy flavor. That same juice will spontaneously ferment into a sort of cacao wine if left alone. Cacao residues discovered at the archaeological site of Puerto Escondido in Honduras point to the extreme antiquity of cacao pulp wine.[14] Later, when Mesoamericans developed more complex fermentation and drying processes of the solid fruit, a bitter cacao nib drink would have been born.

Even in ancient times, significant diversity existed between and within communities in how cacao was prepared for consumption, from enriching mole sauces to bittering foaming beverages. Corn, *achiote* ("annatto"), vanilla bean, and honey, among many other ingredients, were mixed with cacao and frothed with special cacao mixing tools. Early Spanish chroniclers provide a window into the gamut of diverse New World cacao beverages.

Sometime between 1541 and 1555, the Milanese merchant Girolamo Benzoni observed one method of producing a local cacao beverage in Central America:

> when they wish for the beverage, they roast them [the nibs of cacao] in an earthen pan over the fire, and grind them with the stones which they use for preparing bread [tortillas]. Finally, they put the paste into cups, made out of the calabashes produced by a certain tree that grows all over India [the Americas]; and mixing it gradually with water, sometimes adding a little of their spice, they drink it, though seeming more suited for pigs than for men.[15]

Traditional chocolate was bitter, and the oenophilic southern Europeans were not always impressed.

The Italian Benzoni does not specify which spices were used, but other sources enumerate an eclectic menu of cacao mixtures. Sahagún mentions cacao mixed with ingredients like flowers, honey, pulque, chili, vanilla, and magnolia, among other things. Similarly, during his trip to the New World, Spanish naturalist and royal physician Francisco Hernández de Toledo described the use of *pochotl* ("ceiba tree"), as well as several different combinations of corn in cacao beverages. The king's doctor specified how different species of cacao were used and sometimes combined in the same drink. Francisco Javier Clavijero similarly mentions cacao prepared with *tlilxochitl*, or vanilla, *xochinacaztli*, or ear flower of the *Cymbopetalum penduliflorum* species, and the fruit of *mecaxochitl*, which could be *hoja santa* or perhaps *higuillo de limon*.[16] Other flowers, especially those of *Plumeria rubra*, *Piper auritum*, and *Quararibea funebris*, have long been used in chocolate drinks.

Tepexonacate was a historical cacao beverage produced by communities in Oaxaca from cacao and wild onions.[17] One inscription on a Maya vessel suggests that wild cherries may have been used in cacao drinks.[18] It is also likely that peanuts were mixed into cacao drinks. Peanuts are a New World product and the Mexican name for peanut, *cacahuate*, roughly translates as "ground [earth] cacao." Sapote and mamey seeds were toasted and ground into a powder and then added to chocolate drinks.

Some herbal mixtures imbued cacao drinks with medicinal properties beyond the well-known power of the aphrodisiac. Sahagún recorded that cacao mixed with the rubber tree (*Castilla elastica*) was good for infections, cacao mixed with an herb called *tlayapoloni xiuitl* was good for infantile diarrhea, and cacao mixed with corn and *tlacoxochitl* (*Bouvardia termifolia*) helped with fevers.[19]

Cacao Across the Atlantic

During the colonial period, cacao beverages continued to be popular in indigenous communities, but Europeans and enslaved Africans living in New Spain also adopted them. Chocolate even made appearances on the transpacific Manila Galleon, where a 1678 crossing involved a theatrical trial of the captain of the ship which concluded with a sentencing in which he had to give the crew hardtack, sweets, and chocolate.[20]

The term "chocolate" itself first appeared in Spanish in 1590 in *Historia Natural y Moral de las Indias*. Etymologies of the word often suggest that it derived from a pre-Columbian term. The most common theory is that the word derives from *xocolatl*, composed of the Nahuatl terms for sour (*xoco*) and water (*atl*). There is scholarly disagreement over the etymology, though.

The term "chocolate" is not mentioned during the first decades of colonization, casting doubt on its pre-Columbian origins.[21] On the other hand, it may originate from the cacao-growing Izalcos Nahua speakers from present-day El Salvador.[22] It is worth highlighting that some fermented atoles have remarkably similar names such as *xocoatol* and *xocolat* that are pre-Columbian in origin. While these drinks do not necessarily contain cacao, the close relationship between corn and cacao beverages could provide a potential etymology for chocolate.

When Europeans began drinking cacao, they made some major changes. They introduced key ingredients from the Old World like milk, sugar, and cinnamon, and other commodities like rice, anise, black pepper, and sesame seeds found their way into cross-cultural chocolate recipes. The drink also moved to Europe via Spain. After samples were shipped in 1528, the first commercial cargo of cacao did not arrive from Mexico until 1585.[23] The Spanish Crown jealously guarded cacao as a secret, but by the mid-1600s, other Europeans had caught on. New Spain conducted a booming trade in cacao with Venezuela (even though the Crown prohibited such intercolonial exchange) from the 1620s to the 1720s, buying cacao from Guayaquil via Maracaibo for silver from the northern mountains of Mexico.[24]

In 1728, King Phillip V put a stop to the intra-American trade and sold the royal cacao monopoly to a private society, the Caracas Company. By 1776, the first French chocolate factory had opened.[25] In 1828, Dutch chocolatier Coenraad Johannes van Houten invented a press to separate the fat (or cocoa butter) from the rest of ground cacao. When dry, over 50 percent of cacao is fat, so the removal of cocoa butter means that our modern hot chocolate powder is entirely different from locally made Mexican drinks which use buttery cacao pastes.

The drink, already religious in its indigenous context, would undergo religious scrutiny by the Catholic church. Carmelite nuns took a vow to abstain from drinking chocolate starting in 1616. The vow against chocolate was of equal weight as their other vows of chastity, poverty, obedience, and cloister and likely had something to do with the aphrodisiac properties that cacao was said to have. The Sisters must have felt that temptations would be harder to resist when drinking chocolate. In 1636, Antonio de León Pinelo wrote *Cuestión moral: si el chocolate quebranta el ayuno eclesiástico* (Whether chocolate breaks ecclesiastical fast: a moral question), to explore the problem of the New World drink in Old World religion. There was real European concern regarding chocolate's power over the soul. Pope Gregory XIII eventually declared that chocolate was permissible and did not break fast.

This was a strange new drink with impressive powers. Cacao is a biologically active drink. It contains a triad of chemicals called methylxanthines, namely theobromine, caffeine, and theophylline, which are all stimulants. Chocolate was known to most Europeans earlier than other caffeinated staples like coffee and tea. It would have been their first time being perked up by a drink.

As cacao consumption spread to Europe, its production also moved away from southern Mexico. Cacao nibs first arrived in the Netherlands in 1606 and had hit London by 1657. European demand drove expanded supply. In the 1600s and 1700s, cacao plantations were established in the Caribbean and Brazil. Much later, in 1879, cacao was brought to West Africa. Within 50 years, the newly cultivated continent would become the world's leading producer, a title it still enjoys today, even as African plantations are fighting widespread disease and unpredictable fluctuations in climate.

The Cultural Heritage of Cacao Processing

Regardless of where cacao is grown in the modern world, the basic process of transforming it from a raw agricultural good to a foodstuff still reflects the traditional agricultural knowledge of Mesoamericans. After harvesting, cacao pods are broken open, the beans inside are fermented, dried, roasted, and then ground. The fermentation of the cacao pulp develops alcohol and acids that penetrate the bean and break down cell walls. Enzymatic interactions then develop the compounds that give cacao its famous flavor. Certain fermentations, like that of pataxte for *chocolate atole* in Oaxaca, occur underground for many months with water regularly being added. While the peoples of southern Mesoamerica would not have known all the chemical details, they transmitted these complex processes generation by generation across thousands of years. Thanks to this culture, the world enjoys modern versions of chocolate.

Today, Mexicans drink both modern and traditional cacao beverages. There are some chocolate drinks that are nearly universal in distribution, such as *champurrado*, but most traditional drinks are found only in the southern part of the country where cacao is still cultivated. In many of these cases, beverage producers roast and grind their own cacao, preserving the ancestral tradition.

Cacao is an accepted part of Mexican life and has a role in popular culture. In Chiapas, the phrase "*pedir cacao*" (literally "to ask for cacao") means to beg pardon. Also, if someone is "*como agua para chocolate*" (literally, "like water for chocolate"), it means they are fuming or boiling mad.

Chocolate and the cacao from which it derives are one of Mexico's greatest culinary gifts to the world, yet the world knows so little of the beverages that Mexicans have traditionally made with the bitter nibs.

Maize and Cacao

In the world of cacao beverages, there is an impressive array of recipes that include some form of corn. In fact, most traditional Mesoamerican cacao drinks were based on corn. Yes, cacao was sometimes consumed on its own, but so many other preparations add nixtamalized masa or pinol. It may be that the earliest form of using cacao nibs in beverages was as a seasoning or flavoring in boiled atoles.

In 1577, Francisco Hernández de Toledo described *atextli*, a beverage made from cacao and corn, as well as an unnamed beverage made from cacao, pataxtle, and corn. Today, the combination of the two ingredients is still the backbone of daily cacao drinks like pozol. The two ingredients were so closely related that they had religious associations. There are overt depictions of cacao and corn together in ancient Maya iconography. Both ingredients were key offerings to the gods, representing a "binomial of sacredness."[26] For the Maya, the cacao tree was one of the nourishing gifts that emerged from the body of the sacrificed corn god.

Some Maya glyphs depict the corn god with cacao pods growing out of his body. The god of corn is sometimes embodied as a cacao tree, or *iximte'el kakaw*, which might translate as "Maize Tree-like Cacao."[27] It is not that the corn god is a cacao god; rather, the corn god is the source of all the world's fruits, and cacao is the most coveted of all of them. Maya vessels were traditionally inscribed with glyphs that indicated the vessel's use, its contents, and its owner.[28] Corn and cacao often appear together in these descriptions.

Modern Maya groups in southern Mexico and Guatemala still use cacao as an offering to ask for a bountiful corn harvest.[29] In certain regions of Oaxaca, atole de pataxte is prepared for Día de los Muertos. There were at least twenty-two distinct pre-Columbian corn and cacao beverages and seven post-contact novel corn and cacao drinks.[30] These numbers are even conservative.

Within Mexico, the nuances in producing corn and cacao beverages are sundry. It becomes complicated to differentiate hyperlocal practices and define beverages as distinct. Some beverages are made using identical ingredients but have different names according to dialect. Other terms may be used for more than one recipe. This chapter attempts to present broad classifications of cacao beverages, knowing that local terminologies are far more diverse. For example, there are various names and recipes for drinks made of corn, cacao, and achiote, but the combination is discussed generally as tascalate.

Today, corn and cacao are still a common pairing, even outside of Mexico. Nicaraguans enjoy a toasted corn flour and cacao drink called *pinolillo*. Guatemalans, too, produce corn and cacao drinks with other flavorings such as *tiste*, a combination of cacao, corn, sugar, cinnamon, and achiote.

* * *

Bu'pu

Bu'pu is a foaming cacao beverage made by layering an unsweetened, hot atole blanco with a cool foam made from sweetened cacao and either the *Plumeria rubra* or *Bourreria huanita* flower (in Zapotec, *guie' chaachi* and *guie' xhuuba'*, respectively). The drink is produced in the Isthmus of Tehuantepec by Zapotec communities for festivities. It is also sold door to door by some vendors, and some bu'pu vendors are for hire at family parties and events. In Juchitán de Zaragoza, Oaxaca, Zapotec women sell bu'pu and champurrado in the afternoons and evenings on the side of the city's Parque Central. It is consumed when it is cooler out, which is a relative term in the sweltering heat of Juchitán.

The Zapotec name for Juchitán is *Guidxi Guie'*, meaning Flower City. The flowers that flavor the foam paste are most bountiful in May. For the Zapotec, the flowers have importance beyond their perfumed aroma in the bu'pu foam. Women harvest the flowers to make necklaces, headdresses, and floral arrangements for religious ceremonies and offerings.[31]

Bu'pu is a drink of contradictions. The atole is hot, thick, and heavy. The cacao foam is cool, fine, and light. The fusion of heat and cold supposedly helps with lack of appetite and coughing. To serve a fresh cup of bu'pu, a vendor ladles hot atole into a jícara and then begins beating the cacao-and-flower mixture into a fresh foam with a molinillo. She will ladle off only the finest part of this foam onto the atole base.

Cacahuada

Cacahuada, also spelled *cacagauda*, is a beverage known in English as cacao water or cacao juice. It is the liquid that is pressed from the unfermented white pulp of the cacao pod. That same liquid can then be fermented, but is generally consumed as a sweet refreshment, though the juice must be refrigerated to prevent fermentation. It has an entirely different flavor from chocolate and tastes slightly tart, sweet, and unctuous, like syrupy lemonade. The pinkish pulp of the *Theobroma bicolor* species is also made into a similar beverage.[32]

Due to its brief shelf life, cacahuada is only consumed in cacao-producing regions, particularly Tabasco around Comalcalco. The same drink is produced and known by different names throughout the cacao-producing regions in the Americas, including in Guatemala and Peru.

Champurrado

Champurrado is a corn atole flavored with chocolate and cinnamon and sweetened with sugar. It usually contains milk. It is like a thick and filling hot chocolate and is often consumed during colder months alongside tamales or bread. It is also a hearty breakfast.

Of all the corn and cacao drinks, champurrado is perhaps the most widely consumed. Its name is also a perfect metaphor for the corn-cacao relationship. *Champurrar* has been used in Spanish since the seventeenth century to describe the process of mixing liquors, usually of two different qualities. While neither atole nor chocolate is truly a liquor, the mix of corn and cacao is indeed a champurrado. Champurrado was used to describe a corn and chocolate drink in a text by Francisco Santamaría from 1782.[33] Milk and sugar were both Old World additions to the Mexican diet.

In Chiapas, *cacapote* is another name for hot chocolate atole with cinnamon. It is a common breakfast as well. Other names for nearly identical beverages might include *atole de carrizo*. Street vendors around Mexico sell champurrado out of insulated coolers alongside steaming pots of tamales. Usually, the drink is served in a large Styrofoam cup.

Chilate

Chilate, or *chilatl*, is a foaming beverage typical of Guerrero made from two varieties of cacao, corn, rice, piloncillo, sugar or honey, cinnamon, chiles, and rain water. In this case, both *Theobroma bicolor* (called *huapataxtle* in Guerrero) and *Theobroma cacao* are roasted and ground together into a paste with the other ingredients, which is then diluted and mixed with water.

Chilate is famous for its style of service. Vendors place a cup or jícara on the ground and pour the prepared chilate from a height to mix it, cool it, and form a froth. Women in Guerrero are experts at the pouring process and spill no liquid. Chilate is consumed as a refreshment and is often served with ice. When dried, the paste becomes a powder, called *tlahuasol*, and keeps for 2 weeks without refrigeration to be rehydrated on long journeys or during work away from home.[34] Modern Mexicans also freeze chilate paste and use a blender to prepare the drink anywhere in the country.

Mixtec and Tlapanec communities in Guerrero reportedly observe a ritual during which they parade the image of the Virgen de Guadalupe from house to house, at which point the homeowners must greet their neighbors with jícaras of chilate.[35]

Chocolate de Mesa

Chocolate de mesa is the simple mix of toasted cacao paste and hot water. The toasted and ground cacao forms a suspension in the water. This form of cacao consumption is pre-Columbian, but modern versions also include milk and sugar. When sugar is added, the drink is usually called *chocolate dulce*. It was this version of cacao that gained popularity in Europe and is now available globally. Still, powdered chocolate mixes are devoid of cocoa butter. True *chocolate amargo* would have more fat than modern versions.

Mexican chocolate is traditionally sold in solid blocks, called *chocolate de tablilla*, to be ground and mixed into water to produce bitter chocolate. Cinnamon can also be added. Vendors of pure chocolate sell the drink in large gourds or clay pots and continually whip the suspension with a wooden mixer called a *molinillo*. The device resembles a large honey dipper with vertical grooves. The lacquered wood devices are commonly sold to tourists across much of Mexico. Some local versions of chocolate beaters are not round but are cut out of flat sticks with teeth.

Chorote

Chorote is the regional term for pozol de cacao in Tabasco. The drink is made by mixing boiled and ground corn with toasted and ground cacao in water. Pataxte may be used in place of cacao without any change in name.[36] The cacao can also be left in water to ferment for several days before the drink is prepared. Usually, the corn dough is left to ferment overnight in its solid state. It is served cold and has a grainy texture with a bitter and earthly flavor.

Historically, chorote represented several corn and cacao combinations in Tabasco. In 1868, the newspaper El Siglo Diez y Nueve discussed the Tabasco drink, "chorote and tlascalote [*sic*] is an horchata of well-cooked corn, broken with a little cacao from the country, accompanied by a small quantity of powder of the roasted red sapote seed, and of cinnamon."[37]

The drink is considered nutritious and hardy. An 1895 report stated, "A mixture called pozol or chorote made of ground pop corn, piloncillo (brown sugar) and cacao, is used in water by the wearied traveler or by the fatigued peon in the field as a nutritious and refreshing drink."[38] On long journeys from home, Tabasqueños will bring chorote dough to mix with water for sustenance.

The term "chorote" likely derives from the Maya term "*sholote*" related to the word for "pieces."[39] The term "chorote" exists in Colombia and Venezuela for chocolate beverages and in Cuba for any number of thick beverages. Like pozol blanco, chorote is sold in markets as a dough ready for mixing with water. It is generally drunk from jícaras or coconuts around noontime. The same drink is called pozol de cacao in Chiapas.

Chorreado

Chorreado, which means "dirty" or "grimy" in Mexico, refers to several different drinks, but one unifying factor is that they have been thickened with additional ingredients. The name, however, does not derive from the term "dirty"; rather, it references a *chorro* or a "jet of liquid," indicating that it is poured. In Tabasco, chorreado is a chocolate drink thickened with tree sap and consumed during festivities.[40] In Guerrero, it is chocolate or coffee made with water or milk and thickened with egg, often with a shot of mezcal or grape brandy added.

An exception is the usage in the Bajío region, where it is a kind of horchata made from almond.[41]

Polvillo

Polvillo is a typical corn and cacao drink from Tabasco. The difference between polvillo and champurrado lies in the sort of atole each one is based on. Unlike champurrado, which is essentially an atole blanco, polvillo is made from pinol, or toasted and ground corn kernels. Instead of being thick, sweet, and smooth like champurrado, polvillo has the graininess of pinol and has more of a toasted and bitter chocolate flavor. The most basic polvillo is just pinol and cacao, but some variations include cinnamon, pulverized cookies, and sugar. A drink known only as *bebida* (literally "drink") may be a hot version of polvillo consumed at dinner.[42]

Popo

Popo is a ceremonial and refreshing drink made from cacao and an herbal foaming agent known as *cocolmeco*, *cocolmécatl*, or *bejuco de popo* of the *Smilax cordifolia* species which contains bubble-forming saponin compounds. Other ingredients include pataxte, piloncillo, cinnamon, honey, rice, sugar, cassava peel, and the root of *chupipe* of the *Asclepiadaceae*family.[43] The same drink is sometimes called atole de popo.

An alternate recipe from Tlacotalpan, Veracruz, is produced from a base of boiled rice, but still has cacao, cassava, chupipe, and sugar.[44] In fact, many variations of popo exist across the cacao growing region of Mexico. The prototypical popo would have been based on cacao, corn, honey, a floral flavoring agent, and a foaming agent like chupipe. Popo is consumed during times of celebration including Christmas, All Saints' Day, the New Year, patron saint celebrations, and weddings, but primarily in November and December. Versions of the drink exist in Veracruz and Oaxaca. *Pozonque* or *pozontle* is a similar Zapotec beverage made with corn, cacao, and a native vine.

Tanchuca

Tanchuca is a beverage produced by mixing anise seed into corn and cacao. While most sources suggest that tanchuca is a pre-Columbian beverage, actual anise is an Old World product. Mesoamericans cultivated and harvested herbs that were analogous to anise and fennel in flavor, often using them in medicinal drinks. The native species *flor de San Juan* (*Telosiphonia hypoleuca*) and *acueyo* (*Piper sanctum*) would all have imparted a similar "*anisado*" flavor when mixed into pre-Columbian drinks.[45] Tanchuca is typical in Yucatán and Tabasco.

Tascalate

Tascalate, also written *texcalate*, is a beverage typical of Chiapas made from cacao or pataxte, corn, and toasted achiote. Achiote, commonly referred to as annatto in English, is a seasoning and colorant derived from the seeds of *Bixa orellana*. It is the ground achiote seed that gives the drink a muddy red color. Usually, the corn component is ground corn pinol, but dried or toasted tortillas can be ground up and used as a base for the drink as well.[46] The drink can be prepared with a base of cold water or milk. Sugar is sometimes added, as well as other flavorings like papaya or cinnamon.

Tascalate is sold in markets at juice stalls and customers can also buy the orange-red powder to mix it at home. The achiote does not impart a particularly strong flavor, and the drink, with milk, tastes like grainy breakfast cereal. A similar drink in Tabasco, consisting of achiote, cacao, and sugar or honey, is known as *xochistle* or *xochisle*.[47]

Tejate

Tejate is a variety of corn and cacao drink made in the Central Valley region of Oaxaca. It is traditionally made from corn, ash, white cacao, *flor de cacao* (which is not actually the flower of the cacao tree, rather the flower of *Quararibea funebris*), and *pixtle* (the seed of the mamey). Modern versions include cane sugar and can be flavored with coconut and *corozo* ("palm nuts").

The corn and ash are soaked overnight and then ground into a mixture called *nicuanextle*. The remaining ingredients are toasted, ground, and mixed with the corn dough. Tejate is mixed from the dough by manually massaging iced water into the dough for an hour or more. The slow mixing process leads to the development of chunks of white foam. According to Oaxacan vendors, the foam is the result of acids in the cacao binding with other ingredients to form a solid.

The foam is called the "flower of tejate," which is a literal translation of the Zapotec name for it "*ghilo cu'uhb*."[48] Equating beverage foam with flowers was common in Mesoamerican thought; Nahuatl songs recorded in the sixteenth century discuss foam as a bloom.[49] The term "tejate," according to Oaxacan native Ricardo Salvador, derives from the Nahuatl combination of *textli*, meaning flour or dough, and *atl*, meaning water.[50] In certain contexts, the term "tejate" does not refer to the finished beverage; rather, it refers to whipped corn dough and appears in certain atole recipes as an ingredient or an intermediary product. The drink tejate has a mellow chocolate flavor, and the foam is a custardy mix between chocolatey and floral.

Tejate has long been commercialized and is available in the main markets and streets of Oaxaca City. Women predominantly from two communities on the northeastern outskirts of Oaxaca City (San Andrés Huayapam and San Agustín Yatareni) sell the drink. Huayapam also hosts a yearly event Fiesta de Tejate to attract tourists. However, families throughout the Central Valley prepare tejate for domestic consumption.

In Tabasco, *chorote*, a mix of corn and cacao, can also include the seed of mamey which they call *pixte*. When adding this ingredient to pozol or chorote, they say they are "*pixteando*."[51] Drinks found in indigenous communities with extremely limited range are likely localized versions of tejate. Many such versions of whipped cacao and corn drinks exist in Oaxaca including *bitxiin* of Zaachila, *Kuxtasy* from San Juan Juquila Mixe, and *Chaw Popox* from San Mateo Del Mar.[52] There is also a ritual beverage like tejate called *qátouj* produced by the Tz'utujil Maya that is made from pataxte, cacao, corn, and sapote seeds.[53]

* * *

The whole world knows chocolate, yet we are largely ignorant of its drinkable origins in Mesoamerica. It is beautiful as a coating on a sweet strawberry, a delight when whipped up into a fudgy ganache, a staple of summertime nostalgia on a s'more, but where does chocolate belong?

In a jícara, of course! The fruit of the higuero tree of the genus *Crescentia* is emblematic of many of Mexico's drinks, but is especially associated with the traditional chocolate preparations of the cacao-growing south.

Sahagún wrote of the close relationship between chocolate drinks and the gourd *xicalli* (Nahuatl for jícara) cups in the 1500s:

> And they would serve it in some xícaras that they used for drinking [cacao], which are of many types. One of these is called tecontlacuilolli, "xícara painted with various designs," and its lid, called atzaccayotl, is very beautiful, as well as its turtle spoon, used to stir the cacao; other types of xícaras are called ayotectli tlacuilolli, "black xícara painted black," along with its circular base made of tiger skin or deerskin, used as a rest or seat for this gourd, called ayahualli, ocelohuatl, or cuetlaxayahualli.[54]

Today, chocolate, balché, pozol, and pulque are all still served in jícaras. Regionally, the cups made from the tree are called by many names including *bux*, *bule*, *guaje*, and *tecomate*. But don't spill the chocolate! As Sahagún mentioned, round-bottomed cups call for a cup rest (lest they wobble and spill). Where he describes rings made from leather and pelts, fibers are woven into rings today like the *yagual* coiled from lengths of *mimbre* (of genus *Salix*) or other vines.

Not the chocolate bar, not the globular truffle, not the aluminum-wrapped "kiss"; instead, the ancient history of chocolate consumption takes shape in the simple hemisphere of the jícara.

10

Coffee

There are the hallowed halls of Ciudad de México's legendary coffee shops like Café De Tacuba and Café El Popular and there are the ancestral brown clay *jarros* filled to the brim with aromatic *café de olla* at market stalls around the country. There are the cobblestoned streets at the heart of Coatepec's cloud forest *cafetales* and there is the cacao-and-coffee coexistence of the western slopes of Soconusco.

Coffee in Mexico presents a lucrative case of surplus—the production of the beverage is more consequential than its consumption. While around 60 percent of Mexican households consume coffee, the country's annual output, which ranks tenth in the world, outpaces its caffeine habit. Mexico produced an estimated 3.89 million 60-kilogram bags of coffee from 2024 to 2025.[1] Mexican coffee drinkers only consumed around 1.3 million of those 60-kilogram bags.

Coffee came to Mexico relatively recently and has long been associated with foreign investment. Since the mid-1800s, Mexico's eastern and southern states have built out large *cafetales*, or coffee farms, to send coffee out into the global commodity market. Today, the average Mexican coffee farm is a small, indigenous-owned operation. Still, many Mexicans enjoy a cup of *aromático* as they start their day each morning.

The Arrival and Spread of Coffee in Mexico

Coffee, originally from the Horn of Africa, slowly spread to the New World via the Caribbean islands. Between 1723 and 1730, the first coffee plants arrived in Martinique, transplanted by the French. By 1730, Jamaica was growing coffee. A year later, it was planted on Hispaniola at Santo Domingo. While some sources claim that coffee cultivation arrived in Mexico as early as the 1740s, it is more commonly believed that coffee did not land in Mexico until around 1790, when the first plantations were sown around Acayucan, Veracruz. By 1792, the Spanish had issued a Royal Order which levied taxes on coffee mills in New Spain.[2] Compared to other colonial cash crops like sugarcane, coffee was a latecomer.

The first exports of Mexican coffee occurred as early as 1802, but production would have been limited to the east coast.[3] As the nineteenth century wore on, the cultivation of coffee slowly expanded from its outpost in Veracruz. From the coastal plain around Acayucan, cafetales crept northward into the hilly regions of Córdoba and Orizaba. From there, coffee directly migrated into the mountainous Huasteca across Puebla, Hidalgo, and San Luis Potosí. Independently, in either 1828 or 1831, General José Mariano Michelena brought Moka coffee seeds directly from the Arabian Peninsula and planted them in Hacienda de la Parota in Taretan, Michoacán. Chiapas was introduced to coffee largely from its southern neighbor, Guatemala, where an industry had developed along the Costa Cuca just across the Mexican border.

Coffee was spreading, but large-scale commercial production did not develop until after the 1870s. It was the period of liberalization that came with the regime of Porfirio Díaz at the turn of the twentieth century that gave the final push to industrialize the sector. Matías Romero, a Mexican statesman under both the Juárez and Díaz governments, was the foremost advocate for the expansion of coffee production in Mexico. Romero and Díaz implemented tax breaks, infrastructural development plans, and labor policies that helped to develop coffee production on what were predominantly foreign-owned coffee estates.[4]

The industry's development came in three waves over the last three decades of the nineteenth century. First, a wave of immigrants from the northern Mexican states moved south to start plantations in the 1870s. Then, in the 1880s, independent US investors arrived without financial backing. Finally, fully funded ventures emerged at the end of the century pushing Mexican coffee production to a critical level of maturity to supply a robust export market.[5]

Veracruz, the first coffee-growing region in Mexico, benefited disproportionately during the Díaz era thanks to its strategic position between Ciudad de México and the east coast. In 1873, a railway opened connecting the capital with the port of Veracruz, giving producers easy access to domestic and foreign markets. Towns like Coatepec, Veracruz, developed by growing coffee and sending it along the rail to the port of Veracruz. Coffee regions like Orizaba had rail access directly to the populated Central Valley as well. Almost all coffee consumed in Mexico in the nineteenth century would have come from Veracruz.

Starting in the 1870s, the states of Oaxaca and Chiapas both saw their fledgling coffee sectors expand, blossoming into full-blown industries by the 1890s. Matías Romero himself was a landowner in Chiapas and had planted coffee on his estate, but he had a falling out with the local cacique, Sebastián Escobar, who had Romero's workers confiscated and his coffee plants destroyed.[6]

Escobar's qualm with the statesman had to do with the then poorly defined border with Guatemala. Mexico's southern neighbor was making claims in the Soconusco region where Chiapas's coffee industry was beginning to put down roots. Romero worked with the United States in delineating the national border. A treaty was signed in 1882 and came into effect in 1893, the same year that the cacique Escobar was assassinated.[7] The agricultural potential of the region (which had attracted Aztec conquest to *Xoconochco* in the late fifteenth century with the aim of securing a supply of cacao) attracted coffee farmers on both sides of the border.

Simultaneously, in 1883, the Mexican government passed the Ley de Colonización y Compañías Deslindadoras, which granted vast land concessions to investors and coincided with political turmoil in Brazil (an event which drove up global coffee prices).[8] Coffee looked like a lucrative investment, and suitable land was available for cultivation in Mexico. Foreigners arrived in Chiapas and immediately planted coffee. They also sowed sugarcane so they could produce piloncillo and aguardiente while waiting for their coffee bushes to mature.

Ultimately, coffee production helped to colonize Chiapas, which had always been a highly indigenous region. Investors like Compañía Mexicana de Colonización de San Francisco and Chiapas Land & Colonization Company declared the mission of colonization in their very names! A coastal railroad was built between 1901 and 1908, and the port at San Benito was redeveloped. Soconusco became a German-Guatemalan enclave where prefabricated Sears-Roebuck summer houses overlooked vast cafetales well into the twentieth century.[9] Some of these imported American houses still stand, evidence of the foreign element that brought coffee production to Mexico's most productive coffee-growing region today.

In Oaxaca, Romero credited the 1880s collapse of the price of *cochinilla* (cochineal, a valuable red pigment made from insects of the *Dactylopius coccus* species which live on prickly pear cacti) as a regional impetus toward coffee production.[10] Around the same time, demand for coffee was taking off in the United States, the perennial consumer of the majority of Mexico's exported coffee. Oaxaca's governor, José Esperón, issued Decreto Número 15 in 1875, which exempted coffee investors from paying taxes.[11]

Similarly, coffee expanded from Uruapan, Michoacán, starting in 1860 into the neighboring regions of Colima and Jalisco. While Veracruz dominated volume, the coffees from Michoacán and Colima were almost immediately considered to be of superior quality. Coffee from the Platanarillo of Colima was domestically considered the best during these years and Uruapan coffee won international renown at Philadelphia's Centennial International Exhibition of 1876.[12]

Coffee Becomes Part of Mexican Life

By the end of the century, Mexico and Central America represented the world's third largest coffee-producing region. Coffee, next to henequen fiber, was the most profitable commodity in Mexico during this time, which saw exports grow by a factor of nine between 1877 and 1911.[13]

The boom in production also meant that domestic consumption of coffee had become increasingly common. The coffee-loving statesman Romero commented, "a few years ago coffee was barely drunk in the Republic, while now it is beginning to compete with cocoa and even corn . . . coffee production is not even enough to satisfy local consumption."[14] Mexicans had stimulating (even caffeinated) hot beverages in the form of atole and chocolate before coffee arrived, so when it became available, it was immediately substituted in their place. Indigenous Chinantec communities in Oaxaca, for example, adopted coffee where atole was once used, even blurring the line between the two by mixing ancestral corn into coffee sweetened with piloncillo.[15]

When the first cafés did open in Mexico (the first was on Calle de Tacuba in Ciudad de México), they invariably served coffee with milk. These cafés, including early examples like Café Águila de Oro, El Cazador, and Café del Sur, occupied stalls around central plazas in the capital. If you visit Ciudad de México's grand Zócalo today, the storefronts to the west of the plaza near the Gran Hotel would have once been home to the country's pioneering coffee shops. Mexico's first cohort of independent politicians were known to congregate in these cafés, even meeting at Café de Águila de Oro to discuss the controversial arrival of Santa Anna and Gómez Pedraza to Ciudad de México in 1833.

Coffee with milk was the norm, as it was considered French and thus in vogue. A subsequent wave of coffee shops was opened by Chinese immigrants who had come to Mexico between 1880 and 1943 en masse to build Mexico's expanding rail system. These became famous for their affordable coffee with milk.[16] By the early 1900s, coffee consumption was firmly established as a daily habit in Mexico.

Once the haunts of Mexico's post-independence political milieu, the *capitalino* cafés transformed into centers for the literati, artists, and political thinkers of the post-revolutionary, mid-twentieth century. Diego Rivera, the famous muralist, celebrated his first marriage at Café de Tacuba. The brother of muralist Jose Clemente Orozco owned Café de los Monotes where some of the painter's larger-than-life characters decorated the walls. Café Europa, which later became known as Café de Nadie after Arqueles Vela wrote a novel about it, was a notorious meeting place for Stridentist thinkers. The poet and chronicler of Ciudad de México, Salvador Novo (who also wrote the excellent culinary history *Cocina mexicana: o, Historia gastronómica de la ciudad de México*), noted that Café Paris was a bohemian buzz of writers and artists in the 1940s, ultimately representing a European mode of leisure.[17]

In the wake of the Spanish Revolution, the dictatorship of Francisco Franco displaced coffee-drinking peninsular refugees who continued their beloved habit in Mexico. Tupinamba, a café originally from Barcelona, opened a shop in Mexico and attracted the expatriates looking for coffee with milk and *molletes*.

The Fickle Coffee Market

The twentieth century would see Mexican coffee production boom and bust. Brazil, the largest global producer of coffee, pulled back on exports to push up global prices in the 1920s, giving Mexico an opportunity to reap a profit. As coffee became increasingly lucrative, the Mexican government became more involved. They established the Consejo Nacional del Café in 1946, injecting capital and technology into the industry. Following the Second World War, the global demand for coffee exceeded the supply for the first time in history (and would exceed supply until 1957). A bonanza occurred as international quotas were canceled. The boom was punctuated by the establishment of Instituto Mexicano del Café (INMECAFE) in 1958.

At first, INMECAFE dealt only with large producers who in turn would purchase and process coffee from small producers, but President Luis Echeverría moved toward allocating more assistance to small producers in 1972.[18] Capital from BANRURAL and fertilizers from FERTIMEX were distributed to small growers.[19] By 1982, INMECAFE was purchasing 47 percent of all of Mexico's annual production, but, as neoliberal policies swept across Mexico, INMECAFE was dissolved in 1989. Unfortunately, the disappearance of INMECAFE price-setting coincided with the global collapse of coffee prices due to the suspension of the International Coffee Agreement the same year. Small producers, no longer profitable due to plummeting prices, left the industry and Mexico was plunged into a "coffee crisis" for much of the 1990s.

Today, Chiapas represents around 38 percent of Mexican coffee production, Veracruz is still in second with 26 percent, and Puebla produces around 18 percent.[20] Coffee cultivation exists in other states including Oaxaca, Colima, Michoacán, Guerrero, Hidalgo, Nayarit, San Luis Potosí, Tabasco, and Tamaulipas. Two of these states, Veracruz and Chiapas, have denominations of origin for their beans from the government. A third, Oaxaca, requested a denomination in 2003 for Café Pluma Hidalgo, but no declaration has been made, although the pluma coffee is distinguished internationally for its quality. Around 85 percent of Mexico's output is of the Arabica variety, with the remaining 15 percent being robusta.[21] More than anything else, though, coffee production is largely an indigenous activity in Mexico. Over 90 percent of producers are smallholders and around 61 percent of Mexican coffee producers are indigenous.[22]

Modern Mexico consumes coffee in a variety of formats, but *café soluble* ("instant coffee") still dominates. An estimated 60 percent of domestic consumption is instant coffee, with the remaining 40 percent roasted grain coffee.[23] Nestle's Nescafé product is ubiquitous in Mexican households, and the Swiss company controls a massive share of the Mexican coffee market. As far as hot beverages go, coffee is by far the most consumed by volume and value when compared to teas and tisanes. Mexico's signature coffee preparation is sweet and infused with cinnamon—*café de olla.*

* * *

Café Chiapas

Café Chiapas is a denomination of origin protected coffee produced in twelve regions in the state of Chiapas. The denomination of origin was approved in 2003, protecting Arabica beans grown in plots at least 800 meters above sea level regardless of subsequent processing. In 2007, the standards for café Chiapas were codified in NOM-169-SCFI-2007.

Within the café Chiapas category, there are four sub-classifications of quality: Prima Lavado and Extra Prima Lavado (800 meters), Altura (900 meters), and Estrictamente Altura (1000 meters.) Today, Chiapas produces the most coffee of any state in Mexico. Production was historically centered in the Soconusco area, but is now dispersed throughout the state.

Café de Olla

Café de olla is a common way to prepare coffee in Mexico with sugar, cinnamon, and piloncillo. It is usually served in clay jarros reminiscent of the native traditions of *alfarería*, or pottery. Some recipes include anise seed or cloves. Most food vendors in Mexican markets prepare café de olla in large pots that simmer throughout morning breakfast service. The coffee is dark, aromatic, and sweet.

One theory suggests that café de olla has indigenous roots in a cacao, corn, and honey beverage, perhaps saká. While it is true that coffee fits into the cacao and corn niche of pre-Columbian hot beverages, all the key ingredients in café de olla came from the Old World: coffee, sugarcane, and cinnamon.

Café Pluma

Pluma coffee is from the town of Pluma Hidalgo in Oaxaca. A group of investors first brought coffee to the region and attempted to plant it at a high-elevation town called San Isidro del Camino. When locals pushed back, the coffee farmers went on to plant at Cerro de la Pluma. Thanks to its altitude and long-standing cafetales, the region produces some of the finest coffees in Mexico, which are often noted to be sweet.

Café Veracruz

Café Veracruz is a denomination of origin protected coffee produced at least 750 meters above sea level in the state of Veracruz. The denomination of origin was granted in 2000 and standards were established in 2001 with NOM-149-SCFI-2001. Veracruz has the longest history of coffee cultivation and was the first region to receive a denomination of origin for coffee.

* * *

The Mexican coffee industry is still waking up from the dark decade of the 1990s. Many other countries have outpaced Mexico in recent years, and a realignment of value in coffee, moving toward Robusta varieties, has enabled new stars, like Vietnam, to shine. Worse, Mexico struggled with the scourge of coffee leaf rust (the fungus *Hemileia vastatrix*) during the 2010s, infecting over two-thirds of the country's crop, but the industry's outlook is beginning to look more positive.

Most of the coffee farmers in Mexico operate small, rural farms with their families. A majority of farms belong to indigenous groups or families farming on communally held ejido land. For these growers to continue making their livelihood, selling to both international and domestic markets will be necessary.

To help these farmers, the Mexican government launched its own brand of instant coffee, Café Bienestar, in 2024. In effect, the federal government is reentering the coffee market, following in the footsteps of INMECAFE with more modern branding. The goal is to purchase coffee directly from smallholders to avoid the middlemen who often take money out of their pockets. The concept also highlights another positive trend for coffee in the country, which consumes less coffee per capita than other producers like Brazil and Colombia: Mexicans are increasingly drinking more coffee.

11

Soft Drinks

Soft drinks represent one of the most consequential categories of beverages in regards to consumption in Mexico today. Between juices, sodas, and aguas frescas, Mexicans of all ages drink a dazzling array of colorful, sweet beverages daily. Soft drinks are also the most modern of the country's many drinking habits.

Starting in the late 1970s, Mexico ranked second place globally in terms of annual soda consumption after the United States. Then, in 2012, Mexico became the number one consumer of soda in the world. By 2019, it was reported that the average Mexican was consuming 163 liters of soda annually, 40 percent higher than the second-highest country, the United States.[1] The southern state of Chiapas has experienced incredibly high consumption rates, thirty times the global annual average. In 2019, the average consumption of Coca-Cola in Chiapas was a superfluous 683.8 liters per person per year.[2]

The relentless consumption of sodas and sweet drinks in Mexico has had dire health consequences ranging from cavities to obesity, heart disease to diabetes. It has also infiltrated home economics, with reports suggesting that the average Mexican family expends 10 percent of all household income on soda.[3]

Yet, of the many kinds of drinks in the country, soda has only been in Mexico for a short period of time. Most studies consider the 1980s to be a watershed moment in domestic soft drink consumption after the Mexican government adopted neoliberal economic policies that allowed commodity prices, including that of sugar, to float freely, making sweet drinks cheaper—at times even cheaper than bottled water.[4] Then, during the 2000 to 2006 presidency of Vicente Fox (who cut his teeth as a young man working for Coca-Cola), consumption of soda tripled among Mexican adults.[5] The road to this high consumption has been heavily influenced by the United States and its two giant soda companies, Pepsi and Coca-Cola. But soft drinks have a broader story too.

The Early History of Mexican Soft Drinks

In the late 1700s, during the viceroyalty of Matías de Gálvez y Gallardo, fruit juices, lemonades, and drinks similar to aguas frescas were widely popular—but these were flat (i.e., without carbonation). As early as 1875, European companies were advertising state-of-the-art equipment for the production of "*bebidas gaseosas*" in Mexico. At this time, "*aguas de Seltz*," limonadas, soda water, and sparkling alcoholic beverages like wine and cider were the main market for these carbonation contraptions. By the end of the century, the global trend of patent medicines, tonics, phosphate sodas, and extracts had hit Mexico's urban centers.

As the US soda market matured, entrepreneurs (both Mexican and foreign) launched Mexican-based soft drinks, selling sodas and bottled waters in the cities of their founding. Mexico's Secretaría de Economía notes that La Montañesa's founding in 1886 marked the beginning of the *industria refresquera* (soda industry) in the country. The bottler Sidra Pino of Mérida claimed to have been in existence since 1880, while other sources suggest its founding occurred in 1888. In 1920, Mundet, who had begun to produce crown corks and glass bottles in 1902, launched Sidral Mundet, a nonalcoholic apple-flavored soda he developed in the 1910s. In 1912, Don Leo Fleishman founded La Pureza in Tampico, the predecessor to Grupo Tampico. During these early years, sodas would have been sold at *droguerías* and *boticas*, akin to American soda fountains in drug stores.

The 1930s saw the introduction of automatic bottling machines which fomented a wild boom in bottlers, spiking to an estimated 2,300 independent facilities.[6] Following this boom, the Mexican bottling market has experienced a period of near constant consolidation for almost a century. The general trend has been that regional bottlers with prominent brands grow, establish new plants, form groups with others, and (sometimes) sign bottling contracts with international brands. In the 1950s, the number of bottling facilities had shrunk to 1,073 and by 1970 had further reduced to 478.[7] By 2002, that number was around 220.[8] Don't let this shrinking trend confuse you—modern bottling facilities are massive and well-equipped factories and Mexican soda consumption by volume has increased decade over decade for nearly a century.

Ironically, growth in soda production was underpinned by a widespread marketing campaign that equated soda with health. With the advent of soda, sanitation of potable water was becoming a public concern. Most soda companies were also bottlers of purified water, and many publicized that all their drinks were cleaner than tap water. Two different early bottlers (in Tampico and Guadalajara), for example, were both called "La Pureza," or "The Purity." Advertisements boasted state-of-the-art pasteurization and purification of water. One vintage advertisement for Chaparritas El Naranjo depicted a child peeing in a pond behind some reeds while another child drank from the same water—a lineup of colorful Chaparritas bottles in the background presented a more sanitary source of refreshment.[9] Soda, full of sugar, was also touted as energy-giving.

As the market expanded, assisted by the infrastructural development of the beer market which manufactured crown corks, carbonation, and glass bottles domestically, President Manuel Avila Camacho moved to protect the soda market from foreign control. In 1941, the president decreed that only a company funded with majority Mexican capital could produce sodas.[10] Well-intentioned, the law was futile against Coca-Cola's franchise strategy of expansion that took off following the Second World War. The Atlanta-based soda giant would sell the rights to bottle and distribute Coke to local Mexican bottlers. Many of Mexico's earliest regional successes in the soda space resorted to bottling Coke (and to a lesser extent Pepsi). Thus, the line between Mexican soda and American soda has long become blurred, with a wide array of different legal entities serving regional markets in the country with the American brands.

The Arrival of Coca-Cola

Some writers suggest that Coca-Cola would have been imported into Mexico in the final years of the nineteenth century, but advertisements for Dr. Pemberton's products did not appear until an English-language newspaper in Ciudad de México began notifying their readership that a shop called La Imperial was selling Coca-Cola in 1908.[11] In all likelihood, the first bottles were smuggled in from Texas.

In 1920, Botica del Leon was selling ice cream sodas, root beer, and Coca-Cola in Monterrey, and the American brand formally launched in Guadalajara in 1928.[12] In 1926, Tampico's La Pureza and Monterrey's Bebidas Mundiales received the first two concessions to bottle and sell Coca-Cola in Mexico.[13] The following year, the Arizpe family's bottler, Arma, established a Coca-Cola concession in Coahuila. Arturo Mundet began bottling Coca-Cola in 1929 in Ciudad de México. These early bottlers have all since been consolidated and absorbed into Coke's two main bottlers in Mexico, FEMSA and Arca Continental.

Today, consolidation of bottlers, particularly those contracted with Coca-Cola, has led to an oligopolistic market. Coca-Cola products account for over two-thirds of soft drink sales in Mexico, followed by Pepsi, and then Danone. Over the years, the distribution of Coke products has been consolidated into the hands of only a few entities: FEMSA, Arca Continental, and Bepensa. Both FEMSA and Arca Continental are based out of Monterrey, each descended (in part) from one of the two first bottlers granted contracts in 1926.

Generally, FEMSA distributes in the southern states and Arca Continental has the contract for the north. Bepensa controls the three states in the Yucatán Peninsula. In addition to divvying up distribution territory, the large bottlers have absorbed some of Mexico's homegrown soda flavors and brands.

FEMSA, which evolved out of Cervecería Cuauhtémoc, is now the single largest independent bottler of Coca-Cola in the world (it operates in much of Latin America, not just Mexico). Yet the business did not get its first concession to bottle Coca-Cola until 1979. The growth of FEMSA is the best example of how quickly soda consumption has taken hold in Mexico since the 1980s. Acquisition has been the weapon of choice that has brought the Monterrey juggernaut to its current level of control.

In 2001, Promotora de Marcas Nacionales, better known as Grupo Mundet, was bought by FEMSA. Sidral Mundet, one of Mexico's first iconic brands, joined the de facto Coke family. Grupo Fomento Queretano (FOQUE) combined with FEMSA in 2008. Along with it, Victoria sodas, another local line of regional renown, was brought under the Coca-Cola umbrella. La Pureza, better known as Grupo Tampico, merged its soft drinks division with FEMSA in 2011. Along with the bottling operation went Escuis de Hierro, a vanilla cola only available around Tampico. In 2013, Grupo Yoli of Guerrero was acquired by FEMSA along with its line of sodas, Yoli Lime being the most emblematic.

What do all these twenty-first century mergers have in common? Each of the regional brands had been a bottler for Coca-Cola for some time: Mundet since 1929, FOQUE since 1945, La Pureza since 1926, and Grupo Yoli since

1938. While FEMSA is a Mexican company, its success has been driven by consumption of American soda brands.

For the other half of the country, Arca Continental presents a slightly different model. Unsurprisingly, it is the second largest independent bottler in Latin America. In 2011, Arca merged with Grupo Continental. A decade earlier, in 2001, three smaller bottlers, Proyección Corporativa, Empresas del Carmen, and Argos, had merged to form Arca. These key entities had mostly been dedicated to the sale of Coke products and did not have the iconic brands that FEMSA's portfolio did (except for Topo Chico, which Coke bought outright in 2017 from Arca Continental, having been owned by Proyección Corporativa and the Barragán family, who had also signed one of the first two Coca-Cola contracts in 1926).

Outside of the Coca-Cola and Pepsi ecosystems, some Mexican bottlers have survived independently, bolstered by sales of some of the country's regional and iconic brands. Sinaloa has ToniCol, a vanilla cream soda. Chihuahua's Refrescos Unión has Elite, a line with a variety of flavors. One company now produces two legendary Veracruz brands: Jarochitos and Zaraza, a peachy chocolate soda. Ciudad de México is home to the business known for Boing!, Pascual, and Lulú. Oaxaca has Gugar. Finally, two of the larger Mexican soda makers have developed through mergers. Embotelladora Aga produces Jarritos, Caballitos, and Titán, while Del Fruto owns Chaparritas, Sangría Señorial, and Treból. In 2014, the company making Yucatán's beloved sodas Soldados de Chocolate and Sidra Pino went bankrupt and disappeared for good.

The Politics of Sugar

Through all of this, politics have been involved in the background. The soda business requires two key commodities above all else: sugar and water. Both have been politicized to the benefit of business for the better part of a century.

Sugar production in Mexico was once the pain point of New Spain's chinguirito rum problem, but has become deeply interwoven with the country's soda addiction. During much of the 1900s, the government became the price fixer in the sugar market. After the sugar mills came together in 1941 to form Unión Nacional de Productores de Azúcar S.A. (UNPASA), the Secretaría de Agricultura began to regulate which plantations sold to which mills in 1943, an affair that lasted through the 1950s.[14]

Not only did UNPASA publicly promote the healthfulness of sugary beverages, but the soda industry became the single largest consumer of Mexican sugar by the 1970s.[15] Due to the PRI party's post-revolutionary monopoly on power, the sugar union decided to work within the partisan system, pledging loyalty to the ruling party in a mutually beneficial relationship.[16] With plantations beholden to the financing that came from selling to mills, the PRI could also exert influence over large swaths of land and a sizable class of sugar laborers. All the way through the early 1980s, Mexico's government controlled the sugar trade and did business with soda producers. Between 1970 and 1982, the assets of sugar mills that were indebted to the state bank, Financiera Nacional Azucarera, S.A. (FINASA), went directly into the hands of the state. At the time, this was more than 75 percent of the factories in the country, and the indebtedness had resulted from state policy that favored soda, alcohol, and confectionery end uses of sugar.[17]

PRI control of the sugar industry would cease as Mexico liberalized its economy starting in 1988. But the process of privatization drove sugar production directly into the hands of soda producers. Soft drink companies had achieved a consequential degree of ownership over these sugar refining facilities by 1992.[18] Some factories were sold to political allies. Enrique Molina came to own Mexico's largest sugar consortium.[19] He also bottled Pepsi.

Up until today, the soda industry has been adept at lobbying against adversarial legislation (like soda taxes in 2008 and 2012) while ensuring they get government concessions on water. Those water concessions, generally, do not benefit the communities from which water is extracted. The soda companies do business with the federal government, not the local authorities. Even today, bottles of soda might be distributed to voters by campaigning politicians.

Mexican Soda Culture

It is this history that has led to the development of a Mexican Coca-Cola and an American one. They taste different. Even after the Mexican government privatized sugar mills, they aimed to protect the domestic sugar industry from imported high fructose corn syrup. Mexican Coca-Cola has long had a stable, reliable, and politically savvy supply of cane sugar to sweeten their sodas, while the American recipe relies on corn syrup.

Outside of the high levels of consumption and the backroom dealings of production, soda has achieved cultural importance in Mexico. In its early years, soda consumption would have had a certain prestige of consumption, associated with wealth—something that has tarnished over the years as health concerns and disputed water rights rein in the impunity once enjoyed by the industry.

Regional soda brands, some of which are now owned by Coca-Cola, are points of pride and nostalgia. Tampico's Escuis de Hierro (owned by Coke), for example, might be purchased at specialty Huasteca shops in cities like San Luis Potosí, but only because the merchants have brought the soda from its region of distribution as a representative gastronomical delight.

Famously, in Chiapas, where the rate of soda consumption is highest, Coca-Cola has achieved religious significance. At the church of St. John the Baptist in Chamula, Coca-Cola, alcoholic pox, and other sodas are consumed as a rite of religious confession.

* * *

Agua Fresca

Agua fresca is one of the most consumed beverages throughout Mexico. As a category, aguas frescas are fruit juices, starches, flours, or seeds mixed with sugar water and served cold. They have been associated with the *vitrolero* barrel-shaped, glass container for over 100 years, although some vendors use large plastic pails.

Aguas frescas are incredibly diverse and can be made from just about any fruit or flavor. Common and seasonal fruits make popular flavors like coconut, strawberry, soursop, kiwi, passion fruit, tamarind, and pineapple, among many others. During the celebration of Mexico's Independence on the 16th of September, three of the most common aguas frescas are popularly presented in a patriotic flag: green *chia con limón*, white *horchata*, and red *jamaica*.

Some regional flavors of agua fresca include coyol palm fruit in southern Mexico, *garambullo* cactus berries in the Tehuacán Valley, Biznaga de Tuna (*Ferocactus hamatacanthus*) in Nuevo León, jícama root (or *saya* in the Cahíta language) in Sonora, and *jobo* or jocote in the Huasteca region. In Jalisco, the berries of *Rhus trilobata* ripen in the early spring and are consumed as *agua de agrillo*.

Agua de Betabel

Agua de betabel is an agua fresca made with beetroot that is common in the state of Guanajuato. The drink's significance derives from its deep red color. It has become associated with Semana Santa, the week leading up to Easter. It is commonly called *agua de obispo* ("bishop's water"), *agua de cuaresma* ("Lenten water"), and *lágrimas de la virgen* ("the Virgin's tears"). In Guanajuato, people drink agua de betabel on the Friday of Sorrows. It is believed that betabel is a diuretic and helps to eliminate kidney stones and disinfect the urinary tract.

Agua de Matalí

Agua de matalí is prepared from the leaves of the native *Tradescantia zebrina* plant, commonly called the silver inch. The refreshment is common in Tabasco and Chiapas and has an attractive pink color. To prepare matalí, the leaves of the plant are boiled in water, and lime juice and sugar are added to taste. The drink is supposedly a strong diuretic and cleanses the kidneys.

Chaya

Chaya is the leafy green of the plant *Cnidoscolus chayamansa* and is consumed as an agua fresca predominantly in the Yucatán Peninsula. The plant has been part of ethnic Maya diets since before the Conquest and continues to be used in many regional dishes. The raw chaya leaves are blended with sugar, lemons, or pineapples to make agua fresca. The drink can be found in any of Yucatán's cities and is comparable to a spinach smoothie.

Chilacayote

The chilacayote is a gourd of the species *Cucurbita ficifolia*. Agua fresca is prepared from the gourd by washing it thoroughly until the natural foam of the fruit disappears. The fruit is chopped and boiled with cinnamon. Simultaneously, piloncillo is boiled into a molasses-like syrup. Once the gourd is cooked and the piloncillo is dissolved, the two are combined. Lime rinds and pineapple can be added for flavor.

The gourd is known throughout Mexico, but the drink is almost exclusively consumed in Oaxaca. Often, vendors serve the sweet drink on ice with squash seeds and stringy pulp in the cup. It is found in most markets in Oaxaca, where the *tejateras* often also sell agua de chilacayote alongside their foamy cacao tejate.

Horchata

Horchata is an agua fresca prepared from ground rice or almonds and sugar. Cinnamon is often added. It has a milky color and texture. Rice and cinnamon are left to soak in water overnight and are then blended. Sugar and vanilla are added to taste.

The drink arrived with the Spanish from the Mediterranean world, where other ingredients were used. Today, different countries in Central America have different recipes. Mexican horchata is generally made with rice.

Arguably, one of Mexico's most famous *horchateras* was the late Casilda Flores Morales. Her family began selling pineapple beer, nicuatole, and agua de chilacayote in the city of Oaxaca in 1890. They later developed a famous recipe for *horchata de almendra con tuna*, or almond horchata with prickly pear fruit. The drink, along with other agua frescas, is still served by the family of Casilda in Oaxaca's Benito Juarez Market.

In Sonora, a horchata-like drink is made by the indigenous Mayo from wheat pinol, cloves, cinnamon, salt, sugar, and piloncillo. It is called *bajicopo* or *jipoko*.[20]

Jamaica

Jamaica is the infusion of the hibiscus calyx, known as *rosa de jamaica*, with sugar and water. The calyx of the *Hibiscus sabdariffa* swells after the actual flower falls off. Where other hibiscus-producing countries tend to harvest them by trimming the plant calyces, Mexican cultivation technique involves cutting down the entire plant to harvest the useful parts.[21] The Spanish brought hibiscus flowers to the west coast of Mexico in the fifteenth century from the Philippines. Unsurprisingly, that region still dominates domestic production, with the state of Guerrero accounting for over three-quarters of domestic supply.[22] The municipalities of Tecoanapa, Ayutla, Juan R. Escudero, Acapulco, and San Marcos are home to the heartland of hibiscus farming. Growers plant the seeds in July and harvest in December. While there are over 100 cultivars of hibiscus, Mexico specializes in the la Criolla, Alma Blanca, Rosalíz, Cotzaltzin, and Tecoanapa varieties.[23] Agua de jamaica is available everywhere in Mexico and has a refreshing, sweet, and tart flavor.

Uvate

Uvate is a sort of agua fresca made from grape marmalade and soda water that is typical in Aguascalientes. The name, uvate, is the name of a candy or marmalade that is made from grapes, *uva ate*. Traditionally, these colonial sweets, called *ates*, were made from both red and white grapes, as well as figs, prickly pears, peaches, pears, and apples. To prepare uvate, marmalade is mixed with sugar over ice and carbonated water is added with a splash of lime.

* * *

Mexico's soda industry grew up in the shadow of beer, but it has now come into the light—for better or worse. The high rates of consumption of these sweet beverages have become the focus of legislation, health campaigns, and mobilization around water rights. But the well-funded soda industry continues to be equipped to lobby the government against antagonistic legislation.

A 2014 sugar tax seems to have led to a small decrease in soda consumption, but legacy brands continue to be staples on Mexican tables. Still, the country is not immune to the global health trends that are eating away at the market share of sugary drinks. Better-for-you craft sodas are poised to reach urban Mexican consumers looking for low-calorie alternatives. Even FEMSA is moving to get ahead of the trend by marketing Coke Zero, locally called Coca-Cola Sin Azúcar, more aggressively in Mexico.

Where many of Mexico's homegrown sodas have been sold off or consolidated, a new craft soda moment is primed to allow new, local flavors to come to the market in a healthier, more sustainable way.

12

Herbal Infusions and Decoctions

In the course of Mexican history, medicine and hydration have collided as leaves, flowers, roots, barks, and fruit of both native and introduced plant species have been infused and decocted into a wide range of tisanes, endearingly termed *tecitos* today. These drinks are almost all medicinal (and can be toxic and dangerous if dosed incorrectly), but they can also be consumed for flavor, ritual, or quotidian hydration. Over half of all families in Mexico continue to purchase herbal infusions to consume at home.[1] While modern herbal teas might use similar plants as their indigenous counterparts, a lot has changed over the centuries as well.

What we know about herbs in Mexican medicine derives from around 500 years of observation. Some of the earliest and most informative medicinal texts, though, were nearly lost to history. It was shortly after the Conquest that an indigenous author, Martín de la Cruz, wrote a book in 1552 recording herbal knowledge (including the uses of 270 different plant species) which has become known as the Cruz-Badiano Codex. The text had been translated into Latin at Colegio de Santa Cruz de Tlatelolco, only to be lost for nearly four centuries. In 1929, the same Latin text, titled *Libellus de Medicinalibus Indorum Herbis* (Little Book of Indian Medicinal Herbs), was rediscovered by a researcher in the archives of the Vatican Library. Also in the late 1500s,

King Philip II sent his personal physician, Francisco Hernández de Toledo, to New Spain to study medicinal plants. Based on his 7 years of research, he wrote *Historia de las Plantas de la Nueva España* comprising seventeen vast volumes, most of which was ultimately destroyed in the 1671 fire at El Escorial library.[2] In 1777, Francisco de la Mota, a priest at San Martin Tilcajete, noted that native communities had more success in healing with herbs "than with medicines from the pharmacy which kill them."[3]

In more recent history, Mexico has invested in documenting its medicinal herbs. Porfirio Díaz founded the Instituto Médico Nacional in 1888 under the direction of Fernando Altamirano, which had the express charter of researching medicinal plants. This marked the beginning of the modern cataloging of medicinal plants in Mexico and introduced a focus on chemical explanations for medicinal properties. Later, in 1975, the Instituto Mexicano para el Estudio de las Plantas Medicinales was founded. Indigenous Mesoamerican knowledge of native plants has impacted global medicinal knowledge. Just one example is that of the modern birth control pill invented by Gregory Pincus. It was based on progestin extracted from the wild tuber known as *cabeza de negro*, which was traditionally used by indigenous women as an herbal contraceptive.[4]

Traditional Mexican Medicine

Traditional medicine in Mexico does not limit its herbal uses to drinks like tisanes and decoctions. In fact, some of the herbs used in beverages could also be smoked, snuffed, rubbed on the body, used as suppositories, dissolved in water for soaking the body, or used in temazcal herbal steam baths. Some medicinal herbs are also consumed as condiments, like *pericón*, or as vegetables, like *epazote*. Moreover, traditional Mexican medicine does not just stop at herbs—stones, soils, waters, and parts of animals are also employed. The Cruz-Badiano Codex lists one formula meant to cool the body when hot.

The prescribed elixir is a juice made from a mixture of root powders, red soil, whitish soil, cactus spines, and the little rocks that are in the crop (part of a bird's esophagus) of both roosters and sparrows.[5]

The ingestion of herbs as beverages is by far the most common method of taking herbal medicine. Aqueous solutions have the benefit of evenly distributing the active herbal compounds of plant matter into a consistent dose. In both modern usage and usages listed in the Cruz-Badiano Codex, the decoction is the most common form of consuming herbs.[6] While drinking reigns supreme, we are not beholden to water. Many other medicinal draughts result from ground herbs soaked and macerated in other drinks like atole, pulque, and even blood.

Preparing Herbal Beverages

There is not just one way of preparing or consuming herbal drinks in the Mexican tradition. Technical differences exist as to when herbs are added to water, if those herbs are boiled, and how long they are left to steep or soak. These distinctions give rise to separate categories, but recipes for utilizing a particular herb are not always specific.

English describes aqueous herbal preparations using different terms. Herbs can be prepared in water by infusion, decoction, or maceration. Infusion involves boiling water and then pouring it over the herb, allowing the herbs to soak for a brief period, perhaps 5 minutes. These drinks could also be termed tisanes, and common usage will call them teas. A decoction involves boiling water, adding herbs, and continuing to boil or simmer for some time. A maceration does not necessarily require hot water but involves soaking an herb for an extended period, for days or even weeks.

The form of preparation often influences an herb's end use. Many prescriptions recommend that a decoction be consumed while fasting. Some medicines should only be served hot, while others like *té de monte* and *pericón* are often drunk cold. Mexicans also use the term "*agua de tiempo*" to refer to the practice of replacing pure water in the daily diet with herbal drinks. Agua de tiempo is usually a maceration of cold-soaked herbs. At times, when preparing herbs for children, they can be boiled into milk instead. Examples of this include the expectorant *gordolobo* of the species *Gnaphalium* and the digestive *té de menta* of the species *Hedeoma piperita*.[7] Atole could also be used as a base for herbs such as *nurite*. Strong alcohol is used to produce tinctures of many plants in Mexico's pharmacopoeia by long-term maceration. Old-school pharmacies around the country still make and sell their own tinctures. Cacao drinks have historically been used as a base for herbs. And, for a long time, pulque has been used as a vehicle for medicine.

Pulque as a base for herbal medicine was noticed by the very first chroniclers of the New World. Writing in the sixteenth century, the missionary Motolinía noted that "All the medicines that are to be drunk are given to the sick with this wine; once it is placed in their cup or goblet, they pour over it the medicine they apply for the cure and health of the sick person."[8] Records of the measles outbreak in 1595 mention that an herbal mix with pulque called *eloquiltic tletlematzin* was a common cure for the epidemic disease.[9]

The root mixed into fermenting pulque prior to the arrival of the Spanish was known as *octpatli*—translated literally, this means "pulque medicine." Similarly, an herb called *popotle* and the stick known as *cuapatle* have been used to ferment pulque. Finally, the Manuscrito de Sotuta, which describes practices in the Yucatán between 1823 and 1846, details how the Maya soaked rooster testicles in wine (though not necessarily pulque) to drink in the morning to ward off faintness.[10]

Pulque, even without herbs, has appreciable medicinal qualities. In 1897, Francisco Martínez Baca, a Poblano physician, found that the fermented sap cured scurvy in prisoners. It was not until 1933 that vitamin C was discovered. Generally, though, Mexico has moved away from pulque and favors water for its herbal consumption today.

Centuries of Herbs

Much has changed in the world of herbal medicine in Mexico. When comparing the 1552 Cruz-Badiano Codex with modern practice, between 35 percent and 50 percent of the herbs mentioned in the codex are not reported as in use today.[11] Plus, some of modern Mexico's favorite herbs come from the Old World, like chamomile, basil, rue, and certain varieties of mint.

Herbal infrastructure has also transformed. In Aztec times, the herbs came from individuals known as *teixpatil* or *texpitiamil.* Today, they are bought in markets like Ciudad de México's Mercado Sonora, from *hierberías*, and even at supermarkets in commercialized tea bags. The emperors of Tenochtitlán maintained large greenhouses and botanical gardens to supply doctors with a diversity of herbs.[12] Today, only the most demanded herbs, like chamomile or basil, are farmed at scale in states like Baja California Sur, Baja California, Mexico, Nayarit, Morelos, Puebla, Oaxaca, and Tlaxcala. Most modern herbal production still derives from foraging wild plants in the countryside.

Today, experts count between 3,000 and 5,000 unique medicinal plant species in Mexico.[13] While diverse, the most popular herbal tisanes derive from a group of plants that fit into two main botanical families: *Asteraceae*, the daisy family including herbs consumed in Mexico like *manzanilla*, *cempasúchil*, and *gordolobo*, and *Lamiaceae*, the mint family including herbs consumed in Mexico like *toronjil*, *poleo*, and *nurite.*[14] The citrus family *Rutaceae* is also of notable importance, including tisanes made from *flor de azahar*, *hojas de naranja agria*, and *ruda*. In total, over half of all the species in the Mexican herbarium belong to only eight botanical families.[15]

Finally, a note should be made about the difficulty in relying on common names to identify many medicinal herbs. Some herbs have names that vary by region, while other common names often refer to more than one species. For the most popular herbal teas consumed, we have attempted to separate out discrepancies that exist surrounding common names and species.

* * *

Albahaca

Albahaca is basil or *Ocimum basilicum*. It is the most commercially cultivated herb in Mexico and is exported to other countries, although more cilantro is produced and consumed domestically. Used as a condiment but also as an herbal tea, the leaves and stems of basil are infused and drunk to calm nervousness. Common usage in northern Mexico attributes gastrointestinal properties to basil tea, while southern Mexico generally consumes the tea for psychological disturbances like *susto*, or fright.[16]

Aguacate

Avocado pits and leaves are used in medicinal teas in many parts of Mexico. For people in the Yucatán Peninsula, avocado leaf tea is suitable for colds and fevers.[17] The stones of avocados can also be macerated in strong liquor for a week with rosemary to address a wide range of illnesses. It is generally accepted that avocado tea is a good antidiarrheal.

Ahuilote

Ahuilote is the tree *Vitex mollis*. In Jalisco, it is common to use the leaves in a tea for a variety of medicinal purposes including diarrhea, menstrual cramps, and acne. One etymology of the term "ahuilote" suggests that it is a combination of *ahuitl* ("aunt") and *octli* ("wine").[18] Perhaps, in the past, the tree's berries were fermented into a kind of alcohol.

Cuachalalate

Cuachalalate is the astringent bark of the *Amphipterygium adstringens* tree. It is commonly used to prepare infusions and decoctions that help with stomach ulcers and gastritis. In Nahuatl, the plant is known as *quauhchalálatl*. The bark can be mixed with sarsaparilla as a hydrating drink, and the seeds can be made into a tincture with white wine, pepper, copal seeds, and eucalyptus. The plant grows in Morelos, Puebla, Nayarit, and Oaxaca, but overexploitation of its bark has put pressure on the species, which is now vulnerable. The bark is also used to treat wounds when applied topically to the skin.

Damiana

Damiana is the desert plant *Turnera diffusa* that is consumed as a tea mainly for aphrodisiac, anti-inflammatory, and tonic properties. The harvest and production of damiana are heavily concentrated in Baja California Sur, where the flower has traditionally been harvested from the wild. The flower is also used as a flavoring for regional liqueurs in the Baja Peninsula. The leaves are used as tea and can be called *pastorcita, hierba del pastor, hierba del venado,* and *damiana de california.*

Around the turn of the eighteenth century, Father Juan Maria de Salvatierra wrote about how native populations used the flower to help with libido and arousal, but its use as an aphrodisiac may have been his invention.[19] Its use is indigenous and is traditionally believed to help bring on childbirth.

Epazote

Epazote, also *ipazote, epazótl,* or *pazote,* is a prominent food herb and has been used as a drink so frequently that it has earned the English nicknames Jerusalem Tea, Jesuit's Tea, Mexican tea, and Spanish Tea. Epazote is considered a *quelite,* or edible green, and is still commonly used to season beans. There are two distinct kinds of epazote. The first is *epazote de comer, Chenopodium ambrosioides,* and the second is *epazote de zorillo, Chenopodium graveolens.*

Normal epazote tea has widespread uses for women who want to stimulate lactation when nursing or encourage menstruation.[20] It is also used for deworming. Epazote de zorillo tea is consumed for nervousness and depression.

Estafiate and Ajenjo

Ajenjo, sometimes called *yerba maestra,* is the generic term for grand wormwood, or *Artemisia absinthium,* of European origin which arrived in Mexico during the Conquest. Mesoamericans were already familiar with *estafiate,* or *Artemisia ludoviciana,* which has a similar flavor and chemical composition. The two wormwoods can be mixed and consumed as a decoction or infusion to treat liver issues, bile, diabetes, and stomach pains. Alternatively, ajenjo can be mixed with *chaparro amargo, gobernadora, estafiate, marrubio,* and *simonilla* to make a tea consumed while fasting.[21] Estafiate, known as *iztauhyatl* to the Aztecs, was a symbolic herb of the Tlaloc rain god cult.[22]

Flor de Azahar

Flor de azahar, a generic term for the flowers of any of the species of citrus in Mexico (orange, grapefruit, lemon, etc.), is drunk as a calming tea and for amelioration of blood pressure.

Flor de Manita

Flor de manita is the native hand-shaped flower of *Chiranthodendron pentadactylon.* In Nahuatl, it is called *macpalxóchitl.* The plant has both medicinal and ritual uses, including its flower being used in an infusion for the treatment of dysentery, nervousness, and heart disease.[23] It is also commonly infused alongside magnolia and tila.

Flor de Tila

Tila is one of the most prominent staple herbal teas of Mexico. Tila is widely available at herbal markets around the country and is even sold in industrial pre-made tea sachets. However, usages diverge on what exactly tila is. This confusion arises from the fact that two families of plants are commonly called tila:

Pentaphylacaceae and *Lauraceae*. Both families have native Mexican species that are used in herbal medicine and both generally have yellowish-white flowers.

First, tila refers to *Ternstroemia*, mainly of the species *T. lineata*, also called *T. pringlei*. According to La Comisión Nacional para el Conocimiento y Uso de la Biodiversidad (CONABIO), common usage of the name tila also extends to the flowering cousins in the same family as *Ternstroemia*, specifically within the genus *Cleyera* (these may not have medicinal use). A decoction of *T. lineata*'s fruits and flowers is a calming tea. It can also be macerated for 2 to 3 days in water or alcohol.

Alternatively, tila is the linden flower, often of the species *Litsea glaucescens*, or Mexican bay leaf, although all introduced species of linden are called tila. Tila, literally translated into English, is linden but, in Nahuatl, would have been *ecapatli*. This version of tila is similarly used to form a decoction for calming anxiety, fright, and nervousness. Linden leaves are also used as an herb in cooking like bay leaf normally would be. Sometimes, a mixed tea is prepared combining linden leaves with mint, cinnamon, lemon balm, and lemon verbena.[24]

In either case, both plants lay a legitimate claim to the name tila in modern Mexico and both have widely accepted uses as medicinal teas.

Guásima

Guásima is the beverage produced from the bark, leaves, or ripe fruit of the *Guazuma ulmifolia* tree, or bay cedar, made in the state of Tabasco. The fruit is also called by the names *guásimo*, *cuaulote*, *pixoi*, and *aquiché*, among others.[25] While the "piña chiquita" fruits (like lychees in size) are fermented into a drink, infusions of the leaf and bark are far more common throughout southern Mexico.

The ancient Maya of the Late Classic period (600–900 C.E.) fermented the fruit of *Guazuma* trees to produce a ritual beverage.[26] Francisco Hernández de

Toledo depicted a plant labeled "*Quaucholotl, vel Guacimo*" in his sixteenth-century work for King Philip II. At the time, the botanist noted the plant was medicinal. The Maya utilized the infusion of the bark against diarrhea, and the Books of Chilam Balam indicated that the tree was the legendary "*pixoy*," which was planted by the gods following a mythical deluge that had destroyed the world.[27]

Cacao and guásima are relatively closely related and are part of the same botanical family, *Malvaceae*. Today, it is common to make an unfermented infusion out of the dried fruits, sometimes called *cualote* or *tapa*. It has intended uses including sugar regulation for diabetics. Drinkers also attribute liver and kidney cleaning properties to the decoction. Traditional Maya medicine utilized the tender tips of the tree to cure dire digestive issues.[28]

Hojas de Naranja Agria

The leaves of sour oranges, *Citrus aurantium*, are commonly used to produce tea in the Yucatán Peninsula. The tea is believed to calm nerves and help with loss of appetite. Most stomach pains are cured with an infusion of these leaves. Fever, cold, the flu, and even hangovers are treated with naranja agria tea.[29] In Yucatán communities, these leaves are one of the most common folk medicines. The plant is a valuable source of vitamins C and E as well as other phenolic compounds. Outside of the Yucatán, other varieties of orange are also used to produce tea. Orange leaf tea is a common accompaniment to breakfast.

Hojas de Guayaba

Guava leaves are a native Mexican medicine used for gastrointestinal problems like dysentery, nausea, and diarrhea throughout all of Mexico. The Cruz-Badiano Codex echoes this use of the guava leaf tea, which they would have called *xaxócotl* or *xalxócotl*.

Manzanilla

Manzanilla is the European herb chamomile, or *Matricaria chamomilla.* Chamomile was introduced to Mexico during the Conquest and was quickly accepted as a key part of the domestic herbal tradition. It is one of the most consumed herbs in the world. Chamomile is prized for its digestive properties, soothing gastritis, colic, and other stomach pains.

Chamomile is now farmed at scale in Mexico. For example, 80 percent of agricultural output in the small community of San Matías Cuijingo in the municipality of Juchitepec, Mexico, derives from chamomile.[30] This industry has grown considerably in the last five decades as Mexico industrialized its herbal production.

It is common to find elderly *marchantas*, or roaming street vendors, selling small quantities of chamomile on the streets of most Mexican cities alongside other humble offerings like garlic and cilantro.

Mints

Hierbabuena

Hierbabuena is the generic name given to spearmint and peppermint teas sold in nearly every herbal market across Mexico. It is perhaps the most recognized herbal tea in Mexico. Despite its popularity, *Mentha piperita* is not one of Mexico's native mint varieties. Consumed with vinegar, it is traditionally used to kill worms, and the tea helps with stomach pain.[31]

Menta

Té de menta refers to a variety of spearmint teas made from several mint species, mainly the imported *Mentha spicata* and the native *Hedeoma piperita*. The tea is good for digestion and may also be prepared with vinegar.

Poleo

Poleo is one of the most common herbal teas throughout Mexico. While the actual scientific species that the common name poleo refers to differs, it is generally infused from the leaves, stems, and flowers of the *Lamiaceae*, or mint, family. Some species which might use the common name poleo include *Satureja macrostema*, *Mentha pulegium*, *Cunila lythrifolia*, and *Hedeoma drummondii*. The herbs are widely used in both cuisine as a spice and in teas as a flavorful infusion. The tea soothes sore throats. Use of poleo is indigenous, and the Nahuatl name for the herb is *atóchietl*.

Pelos de Elote

The silks, *pelos*, *cabellos*, or *estigmas*, of corn cobs, which are the female inflorescence of the plant, have long been used in infusions to treat urinary issues and to induce urination or clear kidney stones. Corn silk tea is one of the most widely distributed herbal medicines in all of Mexico.[32] The Maya consider the infusion helpful in stopping incontinence or bed-wetting.[33] The Rarámuri mix male corn inflorescences, the pollen-bearing tassels of the stalk, with milk.[34] Corn silk tea is still used today and likely works as a diuretic due to secondary metabolites present in the corn silks.

Pericón

Pericón, also known as *yerbanís* of the native species *Tagetes lucida*, is both a condiment and an herbal medicine. It is taken as a decoction for stomach pain, diarrhea, and dysentery. For the Aztecs, pericón was called *cuahuyaúhtli*, meaning either "herb of the clouds" or "dark brown," and was used for more mystical purposes like helping those traversing waters and as a cure against lightning strikes.[35] When smoked with tobacco, the herb was believed to induce hallucinations. The herb was closely related to the cult of the rain god Tlaloc and was used in rain-bringing and fertility rituals well into the post-contact era. On September 28 and 29, the Feast Day of St. Michael the Archangel, farmers in some regions of Mexico still make crosses out of pericón to mark the four corners of their milpas against the wind.[36] It is also laid on tombs. It must be harvested in advance of the festival, as one informant in Naolinco, Veracruz, explained, because the devil would bespoil the flowers with his urine.

Pingüica

Pointleaf manzanita, of the species *Arctostaphylos pungens*, is a native Mexican herb used to make a diuretic tisane that can also help with inflammation. The Mexica knew it as *tomozquítl*. The Codex Badiano lists the herb as a diuretic and as a treatment for fatigue. Pingüica can be substituted for water and consumed throughout the day as agua de tiempo.

Prodigiosa

Prodigiosa is either the species *Brickellia squarrosa* or *Brickellia cavanillesii*, commonly called Brickell bush in English. The flowers of the plant are infused in either water or alcohol to produce a bitter tonic that helps with bile, salivation, and stomach pain. The alcoholic tincture of prodigiosa has become a common liqueur in Querétaro. An infusion of the aerial portion of the plant is one of the most common supplementary treatments for Type 2 diabetes in all of Mexico.[37]

Nurite

Nurite, also *nurhitini*, is one of the most culturally significant herbs used as a tea and medicine. Many indigenous communities attribute religious and social significance to nurite and consume it as daily water, medicinal tea, coffee substitute, culinary spice, and ceremonial offering. Accordingly, nurite has many names (some of which overlap with other herbal teas) including *poleo, tabaquillo, té de monte, tabaquillo grande, tiochil, hierba del borracho, menta, té nurite, tunche, garañona,* and *hediondilla*. Nurite is the minty scented plant *Clinopodium macrostemum* (sometimes written *Satureja macrostema*).

The tea of nurite alleviates colic, intestinal infections, and assists with digestion. Reports also suggest that the leaf is consumed by women in hopes of becoming pregnant.[38] Indeed, ethnographic evidence shows that nurite is generally considered a symbol of fertility and is distributed to guests at weddings alongside the cacao beverage tejate. Zapotec communities also adorn Catholic altars with the branches of the nurite plant during festivals.

The herb has strong associations with Purépecha communities in Michoacán. In Uruapan, nurite is sold on the streets and in markets and is also infused into local charanda rum to add flavor and medicinal potency. It is also used as a flavoring in atoles.

Ruda

Ruda is rue, of the species *Ruta graveolens*, and is an introduced species in Mexico that has achieved widespread consumption. It is mainly used by women as a tisane to promote menstruation and may also be employed as an abortifacient. The seeds are reportedly made into a tea to calm nervousness.[39]

Tlachichinole

Tlachichinole is a flowering, medicinal shrub used in Veracruz of the species *Mousonia deppeana*. It is used topically for scars and wounds, but the tea treats ulcers, kidney health, and chronic diarrhea. It is also prepared in an alcoholic tincture.

Yoloxóchitl

Yoloxóchitl, or *Flor del Corazón*, is the name of the Mexican Magnolia of the species *Talauma mexicana*. In both Nahuatl and Spanish, the Heart Flower's name points to its medicinal use. Tea made from yoloxóchitl flowers is prescribed to those who have had heart attacks. A tea of its bark is believed to be a heart stimulant as well. The flower could be mixed into chocolate for flavor. In the sixteenth century, Sahagún wrote that *eloxochitl*, another name for magnolia, was given to boys, while *eloxuch* was given to women.

* * *

In the kaleidoscope of herbal drinks we find throughout Mexico, we find Old World and New World species intermingling in an entirely novel pharmacopeia. While modern medicine is at the forefront of Mexican healthcare, herbal infusions still feature prominently in daily life.

Whether a drinker takes an agua de tiempo to fight off a sickness or sips a mint tea to help with digestion, the popular knowledge surrounding the use of these herbs is still alive and well. But much of the herbal industry is still informal. For many of these ingredients, foraging outpaces farming. As Mexico continues to develop a sophisticated agricultural industry, profitable herbs will likely be moved into greenhouses. Others, though, may fall into obscurity, though it is impressive how long many of these herbs have been used in tisanes over the centuries.

13

Hallucinogenic, Narcotic, and Alkaloid Drinks

All evidence points to Mesoamericans having profound mastery over their natural environment. Their knowledge of the invisible endowments of native flora and fauna is uncanny. They harnessed microbes in spontaneous fermentations of pulque and colonche and balché. They foraged thousands of unique herbs for medicinal end uses. They employed ash and seashells to nixtamalize corn into a civilization-building foodstuff. Yet their exploitation of naturally occurring alkaloid compounds in native plants still resounds as remarkable.

When ingested, many organic alkaloidal compounds can be toxic—even lethal—but in the right dosage they cause hallucinations, euphoria, disorientation, and other strange and inebriating sensations. Accordingly, psychotropic and other alkaloid plants have long been entheogens, that is a key part of religion and spiritual life in Mesoamerica.

It turns out that, while not always the primary mode of consumption, the beverage is a common method of ingesting some of Mesoamerica's most common psychotropic plants and fungi. Four or five substances emerge as culturally salient including tobacco, peyote cactus, psilocybin mushrooms, morning glory seeds, and certain nightshade species. Other roots, barks, seeds, and flowers have been rumored to have strong and poorly understood effects on humans when consumed in various preparations.

While this category of beverages may be surprising, it is not unprecedented. In most parts of the world, alkaloid-containing plants are transformed into drinks. For starters, many of the world's most popular beverages contain biologically active compounds of the alkaloidal chemical class, which can have stimulating, psychedelic, narcotic, and even deadly effects. Coffee's principal alkaloid is caffeine. Tea produces theine, which has a unique name but is chemically identical to caffeine. Kola nut, which gives its name and bitter flavor to Coca-Cola, also contains caffeine. Chocolate has theobromine.

On the psychedelic and narcotic spectrums, ancient Indians drank the mysterious beverage called *soma*, the specific ingredients of which are still hotly debated. Indians have also long consumed *bhang*, or cannabis, in beverage form, particularly as a dairy drink (perhaps because cannabidiol (CBD), which is not an alkaloid, is fat soluble). A drink called *post* has been produced in western India from the poppy plant which contains the alkaloids morphine and codeine. Coca, which is consumed as a hot infusion in Bolivia and Peru, holds the infamous cocaine. In ancient Greece, *kykeon* was a barley-based brew that occasionally contained ergot, *Claviceps purpurea*, the fungus that contains the alkaloid lysergic acid, better known as the basis for LSD. LSD itself, in its early years of modern consumption, was famously consumed by Ken Kesey and the Merry Pranksters in the form of Kool-Aid. The general conclusion? Humans like to drink their stimulants, narcotics, and hallucinogens.

Still, it is striking how many different hallucinogenic and inebriating substances Mesoamericans consumed from their environment. Richard Evans Schultes, a pioneer of ethnobotany, counted over 150 native plants and fungi species used for hallucinogenic effect.[1] Mesoamerica had established what was perhaps the most complex system of botanical knowledge of psychotropics in the world.

The Mystery of Mesoamerican Hallucinogens

Tobacco contains nicotine; peyote, mezcaline; mushrooms, psilocybin; morning glory, lysergic acid alkaloids; and jimson weed, scopolamine. While morning glory seeds are mostly used in drinks, the other entheogens are primarily smoked, eaten, chewed, or rubbed on the skin. Their use in beverages is medicinal or acts to potentiate an already inebriating drink such as pulque, corn beer, or aguardiente. In one form or another, all appear in traditional beverages.

We know that all these substances have been consumed in indigenous contexts for centuries before the Conquest. Almost all the early chroniclers mention the consumption of one of these substances, starting as early as the 1528 Magliabechiano Codex, which depicts mushrooms being eaten in the presence of Mictlantecuhtli, god of the underworld.

However, actual research into the world of hallucinogens in Mexico has only taken off since 1950. The Biblioteca Digital de la Medicina Tradicional Mexicana, for example, bemoans the fact that the field of Mexican mycology was not firmly established until the 1960s, all but ensuring that a significant amount of indigenous knowledge surrounding fungi has been lost to the long historical campaign of destruction against indigenous culture.

Modern scholars still have difficulty conclusively identifying the plants that historical sources discuss as potential hallucinogens. The substances called *poyomate* and *pipiltzintzintli* (consumed as a beverage in water) still have no agreed-upon botanical identity, although some have suggested that *Salvia divinorum* could be *pipiltzintzintli*. Similarly, the substance called *tlitlitzin* has been theorized to be *Ipomoea violacea* (which Oaxacan Zapotecs called *badoh negro* and consume like morning glory seeds).[2] Spain's ecclesiastical and legal opposition to the consumption of these plants and fungi drove them underground and into obscurity.

The Surprising Effects of Alkaloid Drinks

Not all of Mesoamerica's alkaloid drinks are "hallucinogenic." Each plant or fungal compound produces a unique effect on humans when ingested. Morning glory seeds induce trances, peyote and mushrooms induce visions, and others, like sinicuichi, create mostly auditory effects.[3] Tobacco, when drunk, may create some kind of disorienting effect, but is generally not considered a hallucinogen at all. In the Florentine Codex, Sahagún even mentions that the stimulant cacao is conceived of in the same category as other hallucinogens: "And also it was said of it [cacao] that it was like jimsonweed; it was considered to be like the mushroom, for it made one drunk; it intoxicated one."[4] Sahagún's statement is a clear attestation to the intimate knowledge that Mesoamericans had of their surroundings. They were able to conceptually group dissimilar substances that all contain alkaloids, without knowing what alkaloids were in the first place.

In addition to alkaloid drinks, there is another forgotten category of chemical beverages. The geographer Henry J Bruman delves into the topic of some of the strange additives that are used in pulque and other fermentations. He terms these substances "auxiliary herbs" and separates them into three categories: those added to drinks occasionally but mostly consumed alone like peyote, tobacco, and jimsonweed; those added to drinks only for flavor; and those added to drinks to induce an inebriating effect. The last category, he argues, is composed of plants containing cardiac poisons. It is worth quoting his theory at length.

> The final group is the most interesting of all. It includes plants that may contain in their bark or root certain saponins that act as cardiac poisons. Such heart poisons have for the most part a cyclopentanophenanthrene nucleus in their molecules, and hence are closely related to the digitalis complex [found in common foxglove it can improve heart function and

> also lead to cardiac disturbances]. . . . The various barks and roots, to which ocpatli, quauhpatli, limacatlín, tepesimatl, mecate colorado, and balché belong, and perhaps gotóko and mesquite likewise, not to mention the many unrecorded plants utilized in this area elsewhere, often contain tannin as part of their chemical composition. . . . However, we may be quite certain that the roots and barks just listed are not added to beverages because of their tannin content. The tannin may result in a slightly better flavor and a clearer liquid, but such considerations are set aside. Intoxicating power is the prime consideration.[5]

His theory, which has not been examined more thoroughly since, is that the ingestion of small quantities of plant saponins with cyclopentanophenanthrene nuclei will increase the pulse rate in a human, perhaps giving a sense of stimulation or euphoria followed by marked fatigue. Of course, these are poisons and an overdose is possible—a bout of deaths in late seventeenth-century Puebla was attributed to the pulque medicine root, *ocpatli*.[6] Substantiating Bruman's cardiac poison theory becomes particularly difficult given that the botanical identity of ocpatli, the most well-documented pulque additive, is not known for certain today.

Religion and Hallucinogens

What we can say is that the many peoples of Mesoamerica were aware of the properties of the plants around them. Some of these intense properties seemed mystical or god-given. The discovery of the pulque root ocpatli was attributed to the god Pátecatl. Psilocybin mushrooms were known as *teonanácatl*, meaning "flesh of the gods." Morning glory seeds were in the realm of the god of ripe corn, Cinteotl-Itztlacoliuhqui.[7] The unknown plant *pipiltzintzintli* was in the purview of Piltzintecuhtli, a young god associated with pleasure, food, and unripe corn.[8] Piltzintecuhtli was also an avatar of Xochipilli, the goddess of sacred plants. Tlaloc, the god of rain and fertility, reigned over all hallucinogenic plants.

Due to the religious associations with these plants and mushrooms, the Spanish Inquisition saw their consumption as idolatrous—even a form of devil worship. In 1529, the Spanish outlawed ocpatli in pulque. Friar Motolinía wrote about the consumption of psilocybin mushrooms in his 1558 chronicle and considered it the devil's doing, while Sahagún described them as bad mushrooms that made people lose their reason. One 1582 Inquisitorial Edicto General de Fe outlawed beverages made from herbs and roots.[9] Peyote was formally banned in 1620 because the authorities cast it as a substance that made drinkers vulnerable to possessions by the devil. Later, a 1769 edict reiterated the ban on hallucinogens again because they facilitated pacts with the devil. Between 1620 and 1820, the church conducted at least forty investigations into diabolical peyote use.[10]

In the natural range of peyote cactus in the northern deserts, where the Spanish Conquest arrived much later, the Rarámuri consumed the cactus ritualistically as part of the Jíkuri cult. When the Spanish set up mission towns in the region and implemented *reducción*, or forced relocation, indigenous groups pushed back in a series of uprisings through the 1690s. But this outward resistance was eventually quashed, resulting in the withdrawal of the Tarahumara Jíkuri cult and other native cultural practices from the public sphere, though they persisted within community spaces.[11]

By the time Mexico gained independence, use of these substances was esoteric and hidden. It remained so for most of the intervening 200 years. The new government would not regulate the consumption of peyote, ololiuqui, or hallucinogenic mushrooms until 1971, when global interest in hallucinogens drew many keen eyes to Mexico's offerings.[12] It has slowly begun to resurface.

While many of the more obscure plants have been lost to the erasures of Conquest, the main hallucinogens of Mesoamerica still exist in Mexico, even if their beverages are not as common. Peyote and morning glory seeds are the two most consumed as drinks today.

* * *

Ololiuqui/Morning Glory Seeds

Ololiuqui, the seeds of the morning glory *Ipomoea corymbosa*, are ground up and mixed into water, pulque, and even strong spirits such as aguardiente. The psychoactive components of the seeds are lysergic acid alkaloids, specifically ergine. Where peyote consumption is largely isolated in northern Mexico, morning glory is distributed throughout the south.

Among the many names for ololiuqui are some that reference Christianity such as *flor de la Virgen*, *semilla de la Virgen*, *yerba de la Virgen*, *la señorita*, and *pascua*. Other names are more indigenous or derive from the Nahuatl name for the plant, including *coatlxihuitl* or *coatlxoxouhqui*, meaning "snake plant." Other names include *manto*, *yerba de las serpientes*, *cuexpalli*, and *piule* (administered by medicine men called *piuleros*). In the Yucatán, morning glory seeds are called *xtabentún*, which is also a Maya beverage made from liquor and the honey produced by bees feeding on morning glory nectar.

Most early chroniclers of New Spain noted the use of ololiuqui, including Sahagún and Hernández. One priest in particular, Hernando Ruiz de Alarcón, led an Inquisitorial campaign against the seed and its consumption. In 1629, he wrote, "The ololuhqui is a kind of seed like lentils, produced by a kind of ivy of this land, and this seed once drunk deprives one of judgment, because it is very vehement; and by this means they communicate with the devil."[13] For the Aztecs, the god of ripe corn, Cinteotl Itzlacoliuhqui, was closely associated with the seeds.

Colonial era consumers drank a *bebedizo*, or potion, of the seeds to divine the location of gold mines near Querétaro.[14] In Acapulco, Afro-Mexican women consumed or "worshipped" ololiuhqui in order to divine the date of the arrival of the Manila Galleon to the city's port.[15] Due to Spanish prosecution under the Inquisition, consumption of the seeds was clandestine, thus Westerners did not positively identify what plant ololiuqui referred to until the 1800s (but really the mid-1900s), when research into psychedelics was taken more seriously.

Peyote

Peyote is the small cactus of the species *Lophophora williamsii.* The buttons of the cactus contain the compound mezcaline, which is a strong psychotropic. While peyote is often consumed as a solid, by soaking it in the mouth and swallowing it whole, it is also macerated in water and consumed as a drink.

Reports from the late eighteenth century indicate that peyote was fermented in water with a few tobacco leaves and subsequently drunk during the most solemn rituals.[16] The prominent Mexican anthropologist Gonzalo Aguirre Beltrán wrote of the plant, "Peyote was ground on a metate until converted into a dust or dough and thus it is ingested. Most of the time, however, dilution of the dust or dough is resorted to in water . . . or in wine, a generic name that commonly indicates the distilled liquor of agave that the mezcal produces."[17] The Otomi reportedly mixed it into pulque.

The cactus is still consumed today and evidence suggests that it has been ingested for millennia, perhaps as early as 5,000 BCE. The Spanish Inquisition formally banned the consumption of peyote in New Spain in 1620 due to its perceived diabolic nature, yet the cactus had a variety of religious nicknames during the colonial period including *Niño Jesús, Santísima Trinidad, Nuestra Señora, Yerba Santa María, Rosa San Nicolás, Cristo Crucificado, San Antonio, Señor San Pedro,* and *Santa Rosa María.*[18] In more indigenous contexts, the cactus is also called *piote, jículi,* and *hikuri.* For the Raramurí, the healers known as Sipáame oversee the Jíkuri ritual during which peyote is consumed; the cactus has been identified with the brother of the supreme Raramurí deity Onorúame.[19]

Peyote consumption is common across northern Mexico as the cactus grows in Zacatecas, San Luis Potosí, and Coahuila. It was associated with the Chichimecas during the colonial period and is still common in Wixárika communities, particularly around the sacred desert of Wirikuta near Real de Catorce, where international tourists visit to consume the hallucinogen. Due to tourism, overexploitation of the cactus has become a pressing issue.

Peyotl, the Nahuatl word, derives from the phrase meaning "a thing that glimmers." By coincidence, many reports of peyote consumption during the colonial period point to its use in precious metal divination. Special seers called *Zahorí*, often non-European, non-Indigenous peoples from Asia or Africa, would drink peyote to find lost valuables, seek veins of ore in the soil, or predict future events. Afro-Mexicans participated in the peyote cult as early as the sixteenth century. The cactus has also been employed by some indigenous peoples to cure alcoholism. There is also the cactus *Ariocarpus fissuratus*, sometimes called false peyote, which is prepared in a similar intoxicating beverage.[20]

Piçietl/Tobacco

Tobacco is a New World product belonging to two main species, the common *Nicotiana tabacum* and the wild *Nicotiana rustica*, although dozens of varieties exist. The plant is in the nightshade (*Solanaceae*) family. *Piçietl* or *piciete*, meaning "small tobacco," specifically refers to the snuff produced by grinding fine tobacco of *Nicotiana tabacum* with calcium hydroxide, or lime.[21] The Aztec referred to the inferior *Nicotiana rustica* as *yetl*.

When consumed as a beverage, nicotine can have extremely harmful effects. Nevertheless, tobacco beverages were consumed throughout the leaf's traditional range of consumption, from Brazil to Mexico. Tobacco in

Mesoamerica was smoked, chewed, snuffed, smeared on the skin, and drunk in medicinal drinks. Several sources discuss how a powder of tobacco could be mixed into beverages to be consumed against swelling of the stomach and other intestinal pain.[22] The Kaqchikel of southern Mexico used tobacco as an ingredient in mead and the Sumu of Honduras employed it in corn chicha.[23] Tzotzil Maya communities in Chiapas prepared a medicine in the form of a tisane or spirituous maceration of tobacco.[24]

Conversely, beverage substances like cacao, flowers, molasses, and alcohol were all added to piçietl for snuff and smoking, sort of like flavored cigarettes.[25] A drink of peyote fermented in water with a few tobacco leaves is reported toward the end of the eighteenth century. New archaeological evidence of pot shard residues containing nicotine points to tobacco beverage production during the Late Classic Pantaleón Phase (AD 650–950) in Cotzumalhuapa, Guatemala.[26]

Sinicuichi

Sinicuichi is the plant *Heimia salicifolia*, the leaves of which are consumed in a fermented beverage that creates euphoria and giddiness. The leaves are wilted, then crushed in water, and left in the sun to ferment. When consumed, the hallucinations are mostly auditory.[27] The plant contains the alkaloid cryogenine or vertine.

Teonanácatl/Psilocybin Mushrooms

Teonanácatl, meaning "flesh of the gods" in Nahuatl, is one of the many names given to a variety of mushrooms that were consumed in Mesoamerica for their hallucinogenic effects. As early as the 1528 Magliabechiano Codex, Europeans observed the culture of mushroom consumption. While the mushrooms are normally eaten, many instances of consumption involve incorporating the mushrooms into pulque or cacao beverages, as well as eating the bitter mushrooms in conjunction with a beverage as a sort of chaser.

Black mushrooms called *nanacatl*, for example, were sometimes eaten in tandem with a cacao and honey beverage.[28] Alternatively, the mushrooms could be mixed into cacao drinks. In 1661, Jacinto de la Serna wrote that natives drank pulque mixed with the mushrooms.

Psilocybin mushrooms are also called *nanáctl*, *niños santos*, *hongos divinos*, *apipil*, and *xochinanactl*. UNAM's database of medicinal fungi includes over 100 species of mushrooms and lichens used in traditional Mexican medicine. Today, the consumption of these mushrooms is common in Mazatec indigenous communities in Oaxaca.

Toloache/Datura

Toloache is jimsonweed of the genus *Datura*. Mesoamericans consumed the seeds, roots, and stems in water and alcohol for medicinal and hallucinogenic effects. The plant contains the alkaloids atropine, hyoscine, and hyoscyamine. Other names for the plant include *tlapatl*, *higuerilla del infierno*, *toloatzin*, *toloa*, *quiebraplatos*, *nexehuac* (usually referring to aquatic species), and *hermana del ololiuqui*.

Sahagún wrote about the use of *toloa* as a light infusion drunk to abate a fever, in addition to a mixture of the leaf with egg whites to be used as a poultice.[29] He notes that *toloatzin* or *tlapatl*, sometimes equated with toloa, is not potable. A variety of *Datura* called *iztac toloatzin* has a kind of milky liquid in the stems that was drunk as a cure for cholera.[30] When consumed in wine, the jimsonweed is highly somniferous. Like other hallucinogens in Mexico, toloache has been consumed to find things that were lost.

In modern contexts, *Datura* is still consumed as a drink by the Rarámuri in northern Mexico. Typically, they mix the plant into corn tesgüiño for ceremonial consumption.

It is likely that the closely related, but highly toxic, *floripondio* of the *Brugmansia* genus was mixed into pulque as well. There are many examples of fermented beverages mixed with the dangerous angel's trumpets flowers in indigenous South America.[31]

* * *

Where the pre-Columbian mystic rites of ingesting hallucinogens were forced underground for much of the colonial era, recent interest in these plants and the active compounds they contain among recreational and pharmaceutical users has begun to put pressure on tradition. In the Wirikuta, the sacred desert of the Wixárika people, the increasing presence of industrialized, greenhouse agriculture is eating up land that peyote once grew on. The cactus buttons themselves are also being overexploited by a burgeoning psychedelic tourist industry that supplies itself via an unsustainable and even furtive foraging practice. The buttons are even illegally trafficked internationally by organized groups.

Reports of shortages of peyote in the United States, where members of the Native American Church consume the cactus as a sacrament, have pointed to modern pressures on the species. Where it was once a religious rite, peyote has become a business. The commodification of the medicinal plant is threatening its original cultural role.

As the world reawakens to the idea of consuming these alkaloid-rich plants that Mesoamericans once respected, it is important to avoid the pitfalls of commodification.

14

Conclusion

In his 1970 essay, *The Other Mexico: Critique of the Pyramid*, Mexican Nobel Prize laureate Octavio Paz argued for the heredity of power between eras of the country's history.

> The fact that the whole country was given the name of the city of its oppressors is one of the keys to the history of Mexico, her unwritten, unspoken history. . . . Although the Conquest destroyed the indigenous world and built another and different one on its remains, there is an invisible thread of continuity between the ancient society and the new Spanish order: the thread of domination. That thread has not been broken: the Spanish viceroys and the Mexican presidents are the successors of the Aztec rulers.[1]

The national name of Mexico, Paz noted, derived from the ethnic name of the Aztecs: "Mexica." He saw how Ciudad de México was built atop the ruins of Tenochtitlán, how the Basilica of Our Lady of Guadalupe emerged from the former shrine to the goddess Tonantzin on the Cerro del Tepeyac. While one theory suggests that the name of the Mexica, and thus Mexico, translates as "el ombligo de la luna" or "belly button of the moon," Fray Juan de Torquemada offers up another translation in his seventeenth-century history *Monarquía Indiana*. "But the natives themselves affirm that they took this name from the principal god they brought with them, who had two names, one Huitzilopuchtli and the other Mexitly [*sic*], and this second name means navel of the agave plant."[2]

Mexico, the name of a city founded on the location of a prickly pear cactus, became the name of a country governed from what was once the watery center of the Valley of Anáhuac. Mexico, the belly button of the agave, sits at the fulcrum of vast epochs of North American history, radiating well-defended fronds of influence out into the distant periphery.

And what do we find in the agave's navel? Pulque, of course. Even if the moon etymology is correct, the Aztec moon was conceptualized as a rain vessel imprinted with the shape of a rabbit, a hallmark of the cult of pulque which saw Mexica priests drink from rabbit-shaped bowls called *ometochtecomatl*. The pulque gods wore *yacameztli*, half-moon nose rings, and brandished *ometochchimalli*, shields emblazoned with the crescent moon. Mesoamericanist Eduard Seler proposed that the cult of the pulque gods originated in what is now Hidalgo state. For the Aztec, this area was known as Metztitlán, or "the land of the moon."

What we find is an umbilical connection. A taproot runs deep through the centuries of Mexican history and draws its power from the now-hidden waters of Lake Texcoco. The sweet sap of the bleeding navel of the agave was the amniotic fluid of an empire, a colony, and a nation. Whether subliminal or intentional, the continuity that we find across the pre-Columbian, colonial, and independence eras reverts to one primordial fermentation, one perennial source of nourishment, one emblematic symbol of Mexican civilization.

Just as we find Christianity donning the garb of pre-Columbian worship and colonial power co-opting Aztec modes of influence, drinks have subsumed each other's roles. There is the original economic supremacy of cacao, replaced by the robust pulque tax mechanism of the viceroyalty, replaced again by the cash cow of beer during the independence era. There is the rite of offering atole to the gods that some Maya replaced with distilled pox and eventually even Coca-Cola in Chiapas. There is corn stalk beer that became sugarcane beer that became aguardiente in Veracruz. There is an evergreen cultural utility in the beverage, and while the species of beverage may change, the underlying practice remains intact.

In the pages of history, we find dates and names and places, but there are slower undercurrents that move imperceptibly over vast periods of time. In our relationship with the plants and animals and fungi that provide us with our lifeblood and nourishment, we find such an epochal tale. Mexico is the product of its foodways. Mexico is synonymous with its ancestral drinking culture. It is corn-and-agave-and-prickly-pear incarnate.

Is this guide, as the title suggests, complete? I could never answer in the affirmative. In reviewing thousands of written sources, I have come across countless permutations in spellings, recipes, and theories relating to hundreds of different Mexican drinks. In traveling around the states of Mexico and interviewing dozens of producers, I have come to understand that no two recipes are the same. There is more work to be done in documenting the nuances of drinks in different parts of Mexico today, as well as drilling more deeply into the antecedents of Mexican drinking culture. I welcome additions and amendments and corrections to this work. There is also further work to be done in revalorizing ancestral traditions and preserving ancient drinkways from gradual degradation. But the broad scope of this book should serve as proof that the beverage deserves careful attention—in Mexico, yes, but also in culture more generally.

I hope the reader will come away from this book with a deeper appreciation for Mexico's diversity. Despite the continuing centrality of Tenochtitlán-turned-Ciudad-de-México, Mexico is a vast country of over 130 million people. Mesoamerica was not just the Aztecs. Colonial New Spain was more than Spaniards. Modern Mexico is a mosaic of strains of distinct cultures that have become amalgamated and morphed into a nation. When mixed, what a cocktail it all makes!

More than food, drinks demonstrate a kind of dynamism that can only be the property of a liquid. Drinks meld and mix and take new forms depending on the circumstances and vessels into which they are placed. They permeate the fabric of culture and flow through the passage of time. In presenting this book, it is my intention to use the exemplar of Mexico as a proof of concept that the beverage surpasses its mere material. Drinks are serious business that can teach us about our own lives, cultures, and civilizations.

So, grab a cup and select your tipple from the great Mexican tradition. Whether it be a refreshing tepache, a frothy tejate, or an ice cold Tecate, there is drink enough for all!

¡Salud!

BIBLIOGRAPHY

Adams, Leon D. *The Wines of America*. Boston: Houghton Mifflin, 1973.

Aguado, Albino. "El Pulquero." In *Los Mexicanos Pintados por Sí Mismos: Tipos y Costumbres Nacionales*, 13–20. México: Imprenta de M. Murguía y Compañía, 1854. https://archive.org/details/losmexicanospint00mexi.

Águila Mexicana. "Avisos," August 22, 1824, NO. 130. Hemeroteca Digital Nacional de México.

Aguirre Beltrán, Gonzalo. *Medicina y magia: el proceso de aculturación en la estructura colonial*. 3a reimpresión. México: Instituto Nacional Indigenista, 1987.

Albornoz, Rodrigo de. "Carta del contador Rodrigo de Albornoz, al emperador." In *Colección de documentos para la historia de México*, tomo primero, edited by Joaquín García Icazbalceta. Mexico: García Icazbalceta, 1858. https://archive.org/details/bub_gb_WJk6nlChEKYC.

Alemán Saavedra, Tania. "Chaparritas, el refresco de nuestra infancia." *México Desconocido*, February 27, 2020. https://www.mexicodesconocido.com.mx/chaparritas-el-refresco-de-nuestra-infancia.html.

Alfaro Bates, Rita Guadalupe, Jorge Ángel González Acereto, Juan Javier Ortiz Díaz, Flor Alicia Viera Castro, Ana Isabel Burgos Pérez, Enrique Martínez Hernández, and Elia Ramírez Arriaga. *Caracterización palinológica de las mieles de la península de Yucatán*. Mérida, Yucatán: Universidad Autónoma de Yucatán and Comisión Nacional para el Conocimiento y Uso de la Biodiversidad, 2010.

Alva Ixtlilxóchitl, Don Fernando de, Amber Brian, Bradley Benton, Peter B. Villella, and Pablo García Loaeza. *History of the Chichimeca Nation: Don Fernando de Alva Ixtlilxóchitl's Seventeenth-Century Chronicle of Ancient Mexico*. Norman: University of Oklahoma Press, 2019.

The American Star (Mexico City). "Theater Coffee House," December 30, 1847, 30 ed. Hemeroteca Nacional Digital de México. https://hndm.iib.unam.mx/consulta/publicacion/visualizar/558075bd7d1e63c9fea1a108?pagina=558a34187d1ed64f16a05f53.

Anales del Museo Michoacano. "Imp. y Lit. del Gobierno en la Escuela de Artes, a cargo de José Rosario Bravo," January 1, 1888. https://hndm.iib.unam.mx/consulta/publicacion/visualizar/558a32d97d1ed64f168be6b8?intPagina=103&tipo=pagina&anio=1888&mes=01&dia=01&butIr=Ir.

Anonymous Conqueror. *Narrative of Some Things of New Spain and of the Great City of Temestitan, Mexico*. Translated by Marshall A. Saville. New York: The Cortes Society, 1917. https://archive.org/details/narrativeofsomet00savi/mode/2up.

Aparicio Prudente, Francisca. *Sazón de la cocina afromestiza de Guerrero*. 1. México, D.F: Consejo Nacional para la Cultura y las Artes, 2007.

Arango, Oscar Montaño, José Ramón Corona Armenta, Héctor Rivera Gómez, Enrique Martínez Muñoz, and Gustavo Erick Anaya Fuentes. "Evaluación del nivel competitivo de un desinfectante de alimentos desarrollado a partir de cálices de flor de Jamaica." *Revista CEA* 9, no. 19 (2023).

Ariza-Flores, Rafael, Víctor Serrano-Altamirano, Salvador Navarro-Galindo, Manuel E. Ovando-Cruz, Enrique Vázquez-García, Aristeo Barrios-Ayala, Alejandro C. Michel-Aceves, Salvador H. Guzmán-Maldonado, and M. Antonio Otero-Sánchez. "Variedades mexicanas de jamaica (Hibiscus sabdariffa L.) Alma Blanca y Rosalíz de color claro, y Cotzaltzin y Tecoanapa de color rojo." *Revista fitotecnia mexicana* 37, no. 2 (2014): 181–5.

Arvigo, Rosita, Nadine Epstein, and Marilyn Yaquinto. *Sastun: My Apprenticeship with a Maya Healer.* 1st ed. San Francisco: HarperSanFrancisco, 1995.

Asencio, Domingo. *Tes Curativos Mexicanos: Recetario de Herbolaria para la Salud.* Mexico City: Selector, S.A. de C.V., 1995.

Ávila, Ricardo, Martín Tena, and Peter Hubbard. "Lime as the Key Element: A 'Non-Food' in Food for Subsistence." In *Consuming the Inedible: Neglected Dimensions of Food Choice*, edited by Jeremy MacClancy, Jeya Henry, and Helen Macbeth, 6:113–26. New York: Berghahn Books, 2009.

Bahena, Lola. "Tés e infusiones: bebidas que se han adaptado al gusto de México," February 23, 2024. https://thefoodtech.com/tendencias-de-consumo/el-te-una-bebida-que-se-ha-adaptado-al-gusto-de-mexico/.

Barros, Cristina, and Marco Buenrostro. "Pozol, popo, champurrado." *Revista Digital Universitaria* 12, no. 4 (2011): 1–9. https://revista.unam.mx/vol.12/num4/art41/art41.pdf.

Basurto Peña, Francisco Alberto, Itzel García Rivas, Lizeth Carrión Santos, and María Socorro Orozco Almanza. "Uso actual de las plantas del Libellus de Medicinalibus Indorum Herbis o Códice de la Cruz-Badiano en México." *Anales del Jardín Botánico de Madrid* 80, no. 1 (2023): 135–135.

Beliaev, Dmitri, Albert Davletshin, and Alexandre Tokovinine. "Sweet Cacao and Sour Atole: Mixed Drinks on Classic Maya Ceramic Vases." In *Pre-Columbian Foodways: Interdisciplinary Approaches to Food, Culture, and Markets in Ancient Mesoamerica*, 257–72. New York: Springer, 2009.

Beltrán-Rodríguez, Leonardo, Ignacio García-Madrid, and Alfredo Saynes-Vásquez. "Apropiación cultural de una planta europea en la herbolaria tradicional mexicana: el caso del Ajenjo (Artemisia absinthium L. Asteraceae)." *Etnobiología* 15, no. 2 (2017): 46–67.

Benavente Motolinía, Toribio de. *Historia de los indios de la Nueva España: Escrita a mediados del siglo XVI.* Barcelona: Herederos de J. Gili, 1914. https://archive.org/details/historiadelosind00moto/page/n3/mode/2up.

Benzoni, Girolamo. *History of the New World.* Translated by Rear-Admiral W. H. Smyth. London: Printed for the Hakluyt Society, 1857. https://archive.org/details/historynewworld00smytgoog/page/n12/mode/2up.

Bergmann, John F. "The Distribution of Cacao Cultivation in Pre-Columbian America." *Annals of the Association of American Geographers* 59, no. 1 (1969): 85–96.

Bernard Menna, Alicia Inés, and Maribel Lozano Cortés. "Las bebidas sagradas mayas: el balché y el saká." *Sincronía* 28 (2003): 5.

Bristol, Joan. "Health Food and Diabolic Vice: Pulque Discourse in New Spain." In *Substance and Seduction: Ingested Commodities in Early Modern Mesoamerica*, 128–46. Austin: University of Texas Press, 2017.

Bruman, Henry. "The Culture History of Mexican Vanilla." *The Hispanic American Historical Review* 28, no. 3 (1948): 360–76.

Bruman, Henry J. *Alcohol in Ancient Mexico*. Salt Lake City: University of Utah Press, 2000.

Bruman, Henry J. "Early Coconut Culture in Western Mexico." *The Hispanic American Historical Review* 25, no. 2 (1945): 212–23.

Buenrostro, Marco. "¿Cuáles bebidas se pueden preparar con maíz?" In *Respuestas acerca del maíz: La voz de 72 autores*, edited by C. Morales-Valderrama, C. Mapes-Sánchez, C. Rodríguez-Lazcano, and J. A. Serratos-Hernández, III:91–2. Mexico City: INAH, 2021.

Cabañas, G. "El comercio entre México y España." *El Trimestre Económico* 4, no. 13 (1937): 55–73.

Cabrera, Ehécatl. "El alto consumo de refrescos en México es resultado del entramado de procesos económicos, políticos y culturales," October 24, 2019. https://www.iis.unam.mx/blog/el-alto-consumo-de-refrescos-en-mexico-es-resultado-del-entramado-de-procesos-economicos-politicos-y-culturales/.

Calva González, Juan José. "El movimiento de Independencia de México y su repercusión en las necesidades de información de los agricultores que cultivan Vitis vinífera." In *Procesos revolucionarios, bibliotecas y movimientos culturales*, edited by Jaime Ríos Ortega and César Augusto Ramírez Velázquez, 85–106. Universidad Nacional Autónoma de México, 2011.

Carrera Stampa, Manuel. "La Ciudad de México a Principios del Siglo XIX: Aspectos Económicos." *Memorias de la Academia Mexicana de la Historia: Correspondiente de la Real de Madrid* 2, no. Tomo XXVI (June 1967): 184–231.

Castillo Girón, Víctor M., Alfredo M. Coelho, and Suhey Ayala Ramírez. "Las marcas, la denominación de origen y la región de origen:¿ Qué estrategias de marketing en la globalización de la industria tequilera?" *Mercados y Negocios* 12 (2005): 15–34.

Centurión-Hidalgo, Dora, Judith Espinosa-Moreno, Lourdes Baeza-Mendoza, and José Alberto García-Centurión. "Comidas y bebidas en celebraciones y ritos como rasgo de identidad cultural tabasqueña." *Estudios sociales. Revista de alimentación contemporánea y desarrollo regional* 31, no. 57 (2021). https://dx.doi.org/10.24836/es.v31i57.1055 ID e211055

Cervecería Cosaco, los pioneros de la cerveza artesanal en CDMX. Vol. 5. El Universal, 2021. https://youtu.be/VtkI8XKjpAU?si=y2m7xNjCimhqQvHK.

Chemín Bässler, Heidi. *Recetario pame de San Luis Potosí y Querétaro*. 1. México, D.F: CONACULTA, Dirección General de Culturas Populares e Indígenas, 2000.

A Citizen of the United States. *Notes on Mexico, Made in the Autumn of 1822, Accompanied by an Historical Sketch of the Revolution, and Translations of Official Reports of the Present State of That Country*. Philadelphia: H.C. Carey and I. Lea, 1824.

Clavijero, Francisco Javier. *Historia antigua de México: Sacada de los mejores historiadores españoles, y de los manuscritos y de las pinturas antiguas de los indios: Dividida en diez libros . . . e ilustrada con disertaciones sobre la tierra, los animales y los habitantes*.

Translated by Joaquin de Mora. Mexico: Departamento Editorial de la Dirección General de Bellas Artes, 1917. https://archive.org/details/historiaantiguadem01clav/page/n7/mode/2up.

Corcuera de Mancera, Sonia. *El Fraile, El Indio Y El Pulque: Evangelización Y Embriaguez En La Nueva España; (1523–1548)*. Fondo de cultura económica, 1993.

Córdoba, Fernández de. "Actualidad de La Vitivinicultura Mexicana." *El Informador* (Guadalajara), May 27, 1991. Hemeroteca Nacional Digital de México. https://hndm.iib.unam.mx/consulta/publicacion/visualizar/558075be7d1e63c9fea1a303?pagina=558a3bf27d1ed64f1708f52e.

Corona Núñez, José. "Religiones indígenas y cristianismo." *Historia mexicana* 10, no. 4 (1961): 557–70.

Coutiño, Beatriz, A. C. Flores, G. Vela-Gutiérrez, L. Sepúlveda, Cristóbal N. Aguilar, M. Chavez-Gonzalez, and Raúl Rodríguez. "Tavern or Coyol Wine: A Beverage From Palm Sap With Biotechnological Potential." In *Biotechnological Progress and Beverage Consumption*, edited by Alexandru Mihai Grumezescu and Alina Maria Holban, 233–52. Academic Press, 2020. https://doi.org/10.1016/B978-0-12-816678-9.00007-2.

Crocker-Sagástume, René, J. L. Vázquez-Castellanos, and V. G. García-Serrano. "La identidad etnocultural en la formación de multiplicadores en salud y nutrición maternoinfantil con el pueblo wixárika." *Revista Española de Nutrición Comunitaria* 16, no. 2 (2010): 105–10.

Crosswhite, Frank S. "The Annual Saguaro Harvest and Crop Cycle of the Papago, with Reference to Ecology and Symbolism." *Desert Plants*, 1980. http://hdl.handle.net/10150/550735.

Cuatro Bebidas Típicas Nicaragüenses. Managua: Banco Central de Nicaragua, 1997.

De Los Angeles De Las Vilas, María. "La Puebla de los Ángeles y su Arte Culinario." *Artes de México*, no. 81/82 (1966): 13–19. http://www.jstor.org/stable/24314048.

Dehouve, Danièle. "Simbolismo de las técnicas de preparación del maíz. Análisis de unos platillos tlapanecos (me'phaa) del estado de Guerrero (México)." *Itinerarios* 29 (2019): 97–118.

Dentral de Noticias Diario Judío. "Familia Fleishman, Cuatro Generaciones Engrandeciendo Nuestro País," June 21, 2012. https://diariojudio.com/comunidad-judia-mexico/familia-fleishman-cuatro-generaciones-engrandeciendo-nuestro-pais/8837/.

Departamento de Salubridad Pública. "Relación de los productos comestibles, bebidas, y similares, aprobados durante los meses de diciembre de 1937 y enero y febrero del presente año." *Periódico Oficial del Estado de Baja California Norte*, October 30, 1938, LI, 30 ed. Hemeroteca Nacional Digital de México.

Díaz y de Ovando, Clementina. *Los cafés en México en el siglo XIX*. México: Universidad Nacional Autónoma de México, 2000.

Domingo Schievenini, José. "A Small Distinction with a Big Difference: Prohibiting 'Drugs' but Not Alcohol, from the Conquest to Constitutional Law." *The Social History of Alcohol and Drugs* 34, no. 1 (2020): 15–47.

Dreiss, Meredith L., and Sharon Greenhill. *Chocolate: Pathway to the Gods*. 1st ed. Tucson. Ariz: University of Arizona Press, 2008.

El Chisme. "El Arte de Matar En Un Cuarto de Hora: Boticarios, Curanderos, y Medicos de Oficio," March 18, 1899. Hemeroteca Nacional Digital de México. https://hndm.iib.unam.mx/consulta/publicacion/visualizar/558075bd7d1e63c9fea1a199?pagina=558a333c7d1ed64f16926262.

El Continente Americano. "Literatura: Reeleccionista," November 29, 1899, 232 ed. https://hndm.iib.unam.mx/consulta/publicacion/visualizar/558075be7d1e63c9fea1a1c1?pagina=558a35e87d1ed64f16bf7171.

El Informador (Guadalajara). "Al Día," July 5, 1940. Hemeroteca Nacional Digital de México. https://hndm.iib.unam.mx/consulta/publicacion/visualizar/558075be7d1e63c9fea1a303?pagina=558a34b97d1ed64f16aaa909.

El Informador (Guadalajara). "Aviso Importante," July 4, 1940. Hemeroteca Nacional Digital de México. https://hndm.iib.unam.mx/consulta/publicacion/visualizar/558075be7d1e63c9fea1a303?pagina=558a34b97d1ed64f16aaa724.

El Informador (Guadalajara). "El Brandy 'Presidente' Hace la Felicidad de un Barman Mexicano, al Ganar Valioso Premio," October 12, 1970. https://hndm.iib.unam.mx/consulta/publicacion/visualizar/558075be7d1e63c9fea1a303?pagina=558a38db7d1ed64f16eae54e.

El Informador (Guadalajara). "Madero," August 29, 1964. Hemeroteca Nacional Digital de México. https://hndm.iib.unam.mx/consulta/publicacion/visualizar/558075be7d1e63c9fea1a303?pagina=558a381a7d1ed64f16e19cc8.

El Informador (Guadalajara). "Ventas," September 23, 1928, sec. SECOND. https://hndm.iib.unam.mx/consulta/publicacion/visualizar/558075be7d1e63c9fea1a303?pagina=558a33b97d1ed64f169a32eb.

El Mundo: Diario Vespertino de Política e Información. "Regreso de Nueva York El Sr. V. Fernandez de la Reguera," September 6, 1922. Hemeroteca Nacional Digital de México.

El Museo Mexicano, Tomo IV (Mexico City). "Trages y Costumbres Nacionales: El Jarocho (Departamento de Veracruz)," January 1, 1844. Hemeroteca Nacional Digital de México. https://hndm.iib.unam.mx/consulta/publicacion/visualizar/558075be7d1e63c9fea1a376?pagina=558a32d77d1ed64f168bcaf1.

El Padre Cobos (Mexico City). "Los Perniciosos," September 4, 1873. Hemeroteca Nacional Digital de México. https://hndm.iib.unam.mx/consulta/publicacion/visualizar/558075be7d1e63c9fea1a39a?pagina=558a36217d1ed64f16c31161.

El Porvenir. "Monterrey Sonríe," April 12, 1920. Hemeroteca Nacional Digital de México. https://hndm.iib.unam.mx/consulta/publicacion/visualizar/558075be7d1e63c9fea1a3e7?pagina=558a32af7d1ed64f168915ea.

El Siglo Diez y Nueve (Mexico City). "Giuditt-Cocktail," August 31, 1872. Hemeroteca Nacional Digital de México. https://hndm.iib.unam.mx/consulta/publicacion/visualizar/558075bf7d1e63c9fea1a43f?pagina=558a3e2c7d1ed64f17170bb7.

El Siglo Diez y Nueve (Mexico City). "Revista de Los Estados: Tabasco," October 3, 1868. Hemeroteca Nacional Digital de México. https://hndm.iib.unam.mx/consulta/publicacion/visualizar/558075bf7d1e63c9fea1a43f?pagina=558a3e1b7d1ed64f1716ae71.

El Sol. "Avisos," March 10, 1825, 634 ed. Hemeroteca Digital Nacional de México.

El Tiempo. “Higiene Publica,” July 12, 1905, num. 7419. Hemeroteca Nacional Digital de México. https://hndm.iib.unam.mx/consulta/publicacion/visualizar/558075bf7d1e63c9fea1a45b?pagina=558a35057d1ed64f16afab7b.

Enríquez, Gustavo A. *Curso sobre el cultivo del cacao*. Bib. Orton IICA/CATIE, 1985.

Escamilla-Hurtado, María de Lourdes, and María Guadalupe Escamilla-Hurtado. “Los alimentos fermentados que comían nuestros bisabuelos prehispánicos.” *Ciencia: Revista de la Academia Mexicana de Ciencias* 58, no. 2 75–84 (June 2007).

Feest, Christian F. “New Wines and Beers of Native North America.” *Journal of Ethnopharmacology* 9, nos. 2–3 (1983): 329–35.

Fernández Barberena, Maria Jose. “El patrimonio vitivinícola mexicano: historia, cultura y espacio económico.” Universidad de Córdoba, 2024.

Gante, Angélica de. “San Matías Cuijingo es un importante productor de manzanilla.” *Quadratin Edomex*, March 26, 2014. https://edomex.quadratin.com.mx/San-Matias-Cuijingo-es-un-importante-productor-de-manzanilla/.

García, Crescencio. “El Té Nurite.” *El Diario del Hogar* (Mexico City), July 28, 1891. Hemeroteca Nacional Digital de México. https://hndm.iib.unam.mx/consulta/resultados/visualizar/558a37377d1ed64f16d4e14b?resultado=1&tipo=pagina&intPagina=1.

García-Mendoza, Abisaí Josué. “México, País de Magueys.” *La Jornada Del Campo*, no. 53 (February 18, 2012). https://www.jornada.com.mx/2012/02/18/cam-pais.html.

Garza, Mercedes de la. *Sueño y alucinación en el mundo nahuatl y maya*. 1st ed. México: Instituto de Investigaciones Filológicas, Centro de Estudios Mayas, UNAM, 1990.

Gauss, Susan, and Edward Beatty. “The World’s Beer: The Historical Geography of Brewing in Mexico.” In *The Geography of Beer*, edited by Mark Patterson and Nancy Hoalst-Pullen, 57–65. Dordrecht: Springer, 2014. https://doi.org/10.1007/978-94-007-7787-3_6.

Génin, Auguste. *La cerveza entre los antiguos mexicanos y en la actualidad*. Mexico City: Tipografía Corral, 1924.

Gibson, Lorna F., Donald Olson, and Anne Olson. “Four Pame Texts.” *Tlalocan* 4, no. 2 (2016): 125–43. https://doi.org/10.19130/iifl.tlalocan.1963.316.

Godoy, Augusto, Teófilo Herrera, and Miguel Ulloa. *Más allá del pulque y el tepache: Las bebidas alcohólicas no destiladas indígenas de México*. Mexico City: UNAM Instituto de Investigaciones Antropológicas, 2003.

Goldstein, David J., and Jon B. Hageman. “Power Plants: Paleobotanical Evidence of Rural Feasting in Late Classic Belize.” In *Pre-Columbian Foodways: Interdisciplinary Approaches to Food, Culture, and Markets in Ancient Mesoamerica*, edited by J. E. Staller and M. D. Carrasco, 421–40. New York: Springer, 2009. http://doi.org/10.1007/978-1-4419-0471-3_17.

Gómez, Ana. “Alimentación cotidiana y especial en la comunidad de Pathuitz, Municipio de Chilón, Chiapas.” Master’s thesis, El Colegio de la Frontera Sur, 2017.

Gómez Martínez, Verónica. “Bebidas del cacao.” *Artes de México*, no. 103 (2011): 63. http://www.jstor.org/stable/24318967.

Gómez Ortega, Casimiro. “Prólogo de Don Casimiro Gómez Ortega, Profesor de Botánica, a Las Obras Del Dr. Francisco Hernández.” In *Historia de Las Plantas de Nueva España*, by Francisco Hernández, Vol. 1, Libros 1 y 2, xi–xxi. Imprenta Universitaria, UNAM, Instituto de Biología, bajo la dirección del Dr. Isaac Ochoterena, 1942.

Gómez Pérez, Ana Laura, and Erin Ingrid Jane Estrada Lugo. "Alimentación cotidiana y especial en la comunidad de Pathuitz, Municipio de Chilón, Chiapas." PhD diss., El Colegio de la Frontera Sur, 2017.

González Marín, María Luisa. *Producción de refrescos, tecnología y trabajo. Cuaderno de Investigación 5706*, 1989. https://ru.iiec.unam.mx/5706/1/cuarderno_investigaci%C3%B3n.pdf.

González-Stuart, Armando Enrique. "Use of Medicinal Plants in Monterrey, Mexico." *Notulae Scientia Biologicae* 2, no. 4 (2010): 07–11.

Griffiths, David, and Raleigh Frederick Hare. *The Tuna as Food for Man*. Vol. Issue: 64. Washington, DC: U.S. Government Printing Office, 1907. https://archive.org/details/tunaasfoodforma00haregoog.

Groark, Kevin P. "The Angel in the Gourd: Ritual, Therapeutic, and Protective Uses of Tobacco (Nicotiana Tabacum) among the Tzeltal and Tzotzil Maya of Chiapas, Mexico." *Journal of Ethnobiology* 30, no. 1 (2010): 5–30.

Guerrero Mills, Martha Beatriz. "Empresas y empresarios: El caso de la Cervecería Modelo, 1876–1955." Master's Thesis, Universidad Nacional Autónoma de México, 2006. http://hdl.handle.net/20.500.12525/1899.

Gust, John R., and Jennifer P. Mathews. *Sugarcane & Rum: The Bittersweet History of Labor and Life on the Yucatán Peninsula*. Tucson: University of Arizona Press, 2020.

Guzmán Gutiérrez, S. Laura, Ricardo Reyes Chilpa, and Herlinda Bonilla Jaime. "Medicinal Plants for the Treatment of 'Nervios,' Anxiety, and Depression in Mexican Traditional Medicine." *Revista Brasileira de Farmacognosia* 24, no. 5 (2014): 591–608.

Hamnett, Brian R. *A Concise History of Mexico*. 2nd ed. Cambridge; New York: Cambridge University Press, 2006.

Haro-Luna, Mara Ximena, Felipe Ruan-Soto, and Laura Guzmán-Dávalos. "Traditional Knowledge, Uses, and Perceptions of Mushrooms among the Wixaritari and Mestizos of Villa Guerrero, Jalisco, Mexico." *IMA Fungus* 10, no. 1 (2019): 16.

Heliodoro Valle , Rafael . "The History of Wine in Mexico." *American Journal of Enology and Viticulture* 9, no. 3 (1958): 146–54. https://doi.org/10.5344/ajev.1958.9.3.146.

Henderson, John S., Rosemary A. Joyce, Gretchen R. Hall, W. Jeffrey Hurst, and Patrick E. McGovern. "Chemical and Archaeological Evidence for the Earliest Cacao Beverages." *Proceedings of the National Academy of Sciences* 104, no. 48 (2007): 18937–40.

Hernández Palomo, José Jesús. *La renta del pulque en Nueva España: 1663–1810*. Sevilla: Escuela de Estudios Hispano-Americanos de Sevilla, 1979.

Hoppe, Walter A., Andres Medina, and Roberto J. Weitlaner. "The Popoloca." In *Ethnology*, edited by Robert Wauchope and Evon Z. Vogt, 489–98. New York: University of Texas Press, 1975. https://doi.org/10.7560/784192-025.

Instituto del Café de Chiapas. "Datos Importantes Del Café," n.d. https://incafech.gob.mx/assets/media/documentos/Datos%20cafe.pdf.

Instituto Nacional de Estadística y Geografía (INEGI). "Colección de estudios sectoriales y regionales: Conociendo la industria de la cerveza." Mexico City: INEGI, 2020. https://

www.inegi.org.mx/contenidos/productos/prod_serv/contenidos/espanol/bvinegi/productos/nueva_estruc/702825198428.pdf.

Irigoyen-Rascón, Fructuoso, and Alfonso Paredes. *Tarahumara Medicine: Ethnobotany and Healing among the Rarámuri of Mexico*. Norman: University of Oklahoma Press, 2015.

Iwadare, Miguel. *La cocina indígena de Huehuetlán: Tsubidhomtalab K'al an K'apnel ti tam ajab*. Mexico City: Secretaría de Cultura, 2015.

Iza, Leis G. "Origen de Algunas Palabras." *La Patria* (Mexico City), May 29, 1891. Hemeroteca Nacional Digital de México. https://www.hndm.unam.mx.

Jácome, Alba González, and Laura Reyes Montes. "El conocimiento agrícola tradicional, la milpa y la alimentación: el caso del Valle de Ixtlahuaca, Estado de México." *Revista de Geografía Agrícola* 52 (2014): 21–42.

Jaeger, Edmund C. "The Desert Bean Tree." *Desert Magazine* 22, no. 5 (May 1959): 14–16. https://swdeserts.com/index_htm_files/195905-DesertMagazine-1959-May.pdf.

Javier Luis, Diego. *The First Asians in the Americas: A Transpacific History*. 1st ed. Cambridge, MA: Harvard University Press, 2024.

Javier Quero, Julio César. *Bebidas y dulces tradicionales de Tabasco*. Vol. 23. Cuadernos Antropológicos. Mexico City: CONACULTA, 2000. https://issuu.com/editorialolmeca/docs/bebidas_y_dulces_tradicionales_de_tabasco.

Jiménez, Pedro Luna. *Nayarit: tres recorridos gastronómicos: y algunos secretos del fogón*. Tepic: Universidad Autónoma de Nayarit, 2004.

Kaufman, Terrence, and John Justeson. "The History of the Word for Cacao in Ancient Mesoamerica." *Ancient Mesoamerica* 18, no. 2 (2007): 193–237.

Knab, Timothy J. *A War of Witches: A Journey into the Underworld of the Contemporary Aztecs*. New York: Routledge, 2019.

Kolonitz, Paula. *Un viaje a México en 1864*. Mexico City: Secretaría de Educación Pública, 1976.

Kufer, Johanna, and Cameron L. Mcneil. "The Jaguar Tree (Theobroma Bicolor Bonpl.)." In *Chocolate in Mesoamerica: A Cultural History of Cacao*. University Press of Florida, 2006. https://doi.org/10.5744/florida/9780813029535.003.0004.

La Barre, Weston. "Native American Beers." *American Anthropologist* 40, no. 2 (1938): 224–34.

La Revista Universal y el Cosmopolita (Mexico City). "Hay Muertos Que No Hace Ruido." September 5, 1873. Hemeroteca Nacional Digital de México.

La Sociedad. "Nueva tienda de Abarrotes: Calle Melcros Num. 1," October 3, 1866. Hemeroteca Nacional Digital de México. https://hndm.iib.unam.mx/consulta/publicacion/visualizar/558075bf7d1e63c9fea1a445?pagina=558a3b017d1ed64f1701ff9d.

Lanaud, Claire, Hélène Vignes, José Utge, Gilles Valette, Bénédicte Rhoné, Mariella Garcia Caputi, and Natalia Sofía Angarita Nieto. "A Revisited History of Cacao Domestication in Pre-Columbian Times Revealed by Archaeogenomic Approaches." *Scientific Reports* 14, no. 1 (2024): 2972.

Lappe, Patricia, and Miguel Ulloa. *Estudios étnicos, microbianos y químicos del tesgüino tarahumara*. Mexico City: Universidad Nacional Autónoma de México, 1989.

Lara, Luis Fernando. "Africanismos en el español de México." *Nueva Revista de Filología Hispánica* LXIII, no. 2 (2015): 297–336. https://www.redalyc.org/articulo.oa?id=60246691001.

Lascurain-Rangel, Maite, Sergio Avendaño-Reyes, Richard Tan, Javier Caballero, Laura Cortés-Zárraga, Edelmira Linares-Mazari, Citlalli López-Binnqüist, and Alejandro Ávila. "Plantas americanas utilizadas como condimento en la cocina mexicana." *Revista Mexicana de Biodiversidad* 93 (2022): e933949.

Leander, Birgitta. "Mestizaje ecológico en México (Algunas frutas, legumbres y semillas)." *Journal de la Société des américanistes* 59 (1970): 65–89.

Lentz, David L., Trinity L. Hamilton, Stephanie A. Meyers, Nicholas P. Dunning, Kathryn Reese-Taylor, Armando Anaya Hernández, Debra S. Walker, Eric J. Tepe, Atasta Flores Esquivel, and Alison A. Weiss. "Psychoactive and Other Ceremonial Plants from a 2,000-Year-Old Maya Ritual Deposit at Yaxnohcah, Mexico." *Plos One* 19, no. 4 (2024): 0301497.

León-Payán, Feliciano. "Medicina precortesiana." *Boletín Clínico Hospital Infantil del Estado de Sonora* 22, no. 1 (2005): 34–9.

Linares, F. W. "Las antiguas uvas pasas de Norteamérica: Aporte indígena a la viticultura moderna." *Revista Cayey*, no. 90 (May 2010): 47–60.

Linares Mazari, Edelmira. *Tés curativos de México*. 1a ed. FONART, 1984.

López Barbosa, Lorenzo Alejandro. "El sotol en Coahuila, potencialidades y limitaciones." In *Bebidas y regiones: historia e impacto de la cultura etílica en México*, edited by Camilo Contreras Delgado and Isabel Ortega Ridaura, 63–84. México, D.F: Plaza y Valde, 2005.

López-De-Buen, Lorena, Eduardo Aquino-Rodríguez, Yessenia Maciel-Pérez, Concepción C. Ahuja-Aguirre, and Roberto Castillo-Tlapa. "Sobrevivencia de árboles nativos tropicales en un módulo silvopastoril en Veracruz, México." *Agrociencia* 53, no. 7 (2019): 969–86.

Lorente Fernández, David. "Hojas frías, flor de campana. Sobre el uso terapéutico del floripondio (Brugmansia) entre los nahuas." *Itinerarios* 36 (2022): 165–218.

Loyola Montemayor, Elías. *La industria del pulque*. Mexico City: Banco de México, Departamento de Investigaciones Industriales, 1956.

Lozano Armendares, Teresa. "De cómo el chinguirito y el mezcal enfrentaron al aguardiente de Castilla, durante la colonia." In *En torno a las bebidas alcohólicas mexicanas: Poder, prácticas culturales y configuraciones regionales*, edited by José Jesús Hernández López, 19–32. Universidad de Guadalajara, Centro Universitario de Los Altos (CuAltos), 2015.

Lozano Armendares, Teresa. *El chinguirito vindicado: El contrabando de aguardiente de caña y la política colonial*. 2nd ed. México City: UNAM Instituto de Investigaciones Históricas, 2005.

Lozoya, Javier, Abigail Aguilar, and Juan Raul Camacho. "Encuesta sobre el uso actual de plantas en la medicina tradicional mexicana." *Revista Médica del IMSS*, 1987, 283–91.

Lucio, Carlos. "Mezcales y diversidad biocultural en los alrededores del Volcán de Colima. El caso de los productores tradicionales de Zapotitlán de Vadillo." *EntreDiversidades* 5 (2015): 13–43.

Machuca Chávez, Paulina. *El vino de cocos en la Nueva España: Historia de una transculturación en el siglo XVII*. Zamora, Michoacán: El Colegio de Michoacán, 2018.

Madrazo Miranda, and Marco Urdapilleta Muñoz. "La fiesta patronal de Xico, Veracruz. Tradición oral y festividad." *CIENCIA ergo-sum, Revista Científica Multidisciplinaria de Prospectiva* 15, no. 1 (2008): 9–20.

Madrid-Solórzano, Juan Manuel, Jorge Luis García-Alcaraz, Emilio Jiménez Macías, Eduardo Martínez Cámara, and Julio Blanco Fernández. "Life Cycle Analysis of Sotol Production in Mexico." *Frontiers in Sustainable Food Systems* 5 (2021): 769478.

Marcos, Desiderio. *México y los españoles*. Mexico City: Tipografía El Autómovil en México S.A, 1915.

Marini, Elena. *Espuma: Bebidas de cacao de Oaxaca*. Photo series, n.d. Centro Cultural San Pablo,Oaxaca.

Marroquín, Jorge S., and Xorge A. Domínguez. "Las investigaciones fitoquímicas y sus relaciones con los herbarios." *Botanical Sciences* 34 (1975): 147–66.

Martin, Simon. "Cacao in Ancient Maya Religion: First Fruit from the Maize Tree and Other Tales from the Underworld." In *Chocolate in Mesoamerica: A Cultural History of Cacao*, edited by Cameron L. McNeil, 154–83. Gainesville: University Press of Florida, 2006.

Martínez-López, Liliana, Emma Zapata-Martelo, María Rosario Ayala-Carrillo, Beatriz Martínez-Corona, Gricelda Vázquez-Carrillo, Carmen Jacinto-Hernández, and Alejandro Espinosa-Calderón. "Conocimiento práctico y teórico de maíz y frijol en la región triqui Alta, Oaxaca." *Revista mexicana de ciencias agrícolas* 9, no. 1 (2018): 111–21.

McNamee, Gregory. *Tortillas, Tiswin & T-Bones: A Food History of the Southwest*. Albuquerque: University of New Mexico Press, 2017.

Mejía, Ana Johari. "Las casas prefabricadas de las fincas cafetaleras del Soconusco, México." *LIÑO: Revista Anual de Historia del Arte* 25 (2019): 127–38.

Mejía Prieto, Jorge. *Así habla el mexicano: diccionario básico de mexicanismos*. 11th reimpresión. Mexico City: Panorama Editorial, S.A, 2002.

Melgarejo Vivanco, José Luis. *Breve historia de Veracruz*. Xalapa, Mexico: Biblioteca de la Facultad de Filosofía y Letras, Universidad Veracruzana, 1960.

Mendieta, Fray Gerónimo. *Historia Eclesiástica Indiana: Obra escrita a fines del siglo XVI*. Edited by Joaquín García Icazbalceta. México: Antigua Librería, Portal de Agustinos número 3, 1870. https://archive.org/details/historiaeclesis00mendgoog/page/n8/mode/2up.

Mera Carrasco, Julio. *Entre Copy y Copa*. México: Editorial Diana S.A, 1973.

The Mexican Herald. "Advertisement," April 30, 1908. http://hndm.iib.unam.mx/consulta/publicacion/visualizar/558075be7d1e63c9fea1a34d?pagina=558a34847d1ed64f16a6d3e0.

México, Universidad Nacional Autónoma. "México, primer consumidor de refrescos en el mundo." *Boletín UNAM-DGCS-757*, October 26, 2019. https://www.dgcs.unam.mx/boletin/bdboletin/2019_757.html.

Meza Camacho, César. "Investigación del mercado de la industria refresquera en México y sus factores de éxito." Maestría en Administración de Empresas con Especialidad en

Mercadotecnia, Universidad Autónoma de Nuevo León, 2002. https://cdigital.dgb.uanl.mx/te/1020148191.PDF.

Morales, Ángel F. *La cultura del vino en México.* 1st ed. Monterrey, Mexico: Ediciones Castillo, 1980.

Moreno-Mata, Jesús. "Análisis discursivo del relato popular Haciendo tejuino, tradicional en la lengua y en la cultura wixárika." *Revista Lengua y Cultura* 4, no. 8 (2023): 43–52.

Muriá, María, Arturo Soberón Mora José, María Cristina Suárez, Teresa Lozano Armendares Farías, Laura Rueda, Luis Alberto Vargas, Paris Aguilar, et al. "Bebidas de la tradición." In *In Beber de tierra generosa: Historia de las bebidas alcohólicas en México,* 1:168–204. Fundación de Investigaciones Sociales, 1998.

Nava Martínez, Luis Humberto. "La triada del semidesierto: Características tecnológicas y nutricionales del maguey, nopal y mezquite en sociedades recolectoras cazadoras del centro norte de México: Un análisis comparativo." *Revista Chicomoztoc* 1, no. 2 (July 2019): 146–90.

Navarrete Pellicer, Sergio. *El aguardiente en una comunidad maya de los Altos de Chiapas.* Mexico City: INAH, 1988.

Navarro, Juan. "Nota o Informe al Virrey Don Matías de Gálvez, 29 de febrero de 1784." Originally in "Ramo de Aguardiente de Caña (1788–1789), tomo I, fs. 14–25v, Archivo General de la Nación, México. Reproduced in Brevajes en la colonia.—La fontana Mexicana del siglo XVIII en la mezcla de licores. Introduction by Manuel Carrera Stampa." *Memorias de la Academia Mexicana de la Historia: Correspondiente de la Real de Madrid,* no. 3 (July 1958): 310–36.

Navarro Ortíz, Davíd Ernesto. "Los Náhuas-Popolocas de San José Miahuatlán, Pue.: Endoculturación y educación formal en la escuela albergue." Master's Thesis, Universidad Veracruzana, Facultad de Antropología, 1983.

Negrin, Adam, Oswaldo Chinchilla Mazariegos, Cameron L. McNeil, W. Jeffrey Hurst, and Edward J. Kennelly. "Residue Analysis Suggests Ritual Use of Tobacco at the Ancient Mesoamerican City of Cotzumalhuapa, Guatemala." *Antiquity* 98, no. 398 (2024): 518–34.

Nesvig, Martin. "Forbidden Drugs of the Colonial Americas." In *The Oxford Handbook of Global Drug History,* 153–70. Oxford: Oxford University Press, 2022.

Nesvig, Martin. "Sandcastles of the Mind: Hallucinogens and Cultural Memory." In *Substance and Seduction,* edited by Stacey Schwartzkopf and Kathryn E. Sampeck, 27–54. New York: University of Texas Press, 2021. https://doi.org/10.7560/313862-004.

"Norma Oficial Mexicana NOM-070-SCFI-1994, Bebidas alcohólicas–Mezcal–Especificaciones" (1997).

Norton, Marcy. "Foreword." In *Substance and Seduction: Ingested Commodities in Early Modern Mesoamerica,* edited by Stacey Schwartzkopf and Kathryn E. Sampeck, vii–xiv. Austin: University of Texas Press, 2017.

Novo, Salvador. *Cocina mexicana, o, Historia gastronómica de la ciudad de México.* 8th ed. Mexico, D.F: Editorial Porrúa, 2002.

Núñez Bonifacio, Margarita, and Adriana Montserrat Pérez-Serrano. "Festival del Yolixpa, escenario turístico de claroscuros en Cuetzalan del Progreso, México." *RIVAR (Santiago)* 9, no. 26 (2022): 211–28.

Ojeda-Linares, César, et al "Traditional Fermented Beverages of Mexico: A Biocultural Unseen Foodscape." *Foods* 10, no. 10 (2021): 2390.

Ojeda-Linares, César Iván, Mariana Vallejo, and Alejandro Casas. "Disappearance and Survival of Fermented Beverages in the Biosphere Reserve Tehuacán-Cuicatlán, Mexico: The Cases of Tolonche and Lapo." *Frontiers in Sustainable Food Systems* 6 (2023). https://doi.org/10.3389/fsufs.2022.1067598.

Olea Franco, Rafael. *Un pulque literario*. (A la sombra de las pencas del maguey). México: El Colegio de México, Centro de Estudios Linguísticos y Literarios, 2020.

Olivas Sánchez, Martha Patricia. *Plantas medicinales del estado de Chihuahua*. Vol. 1. Ciudad Juárez: Universidad Autónoma de Ciudad Juárez, 1999.

Online Nahuatl Dictionary. "Ohuatl," 2000. https://nahuatl.wired-humanities.org/content/ohuatl.

Ortiz de Montellano, Bernardo. "Las Hierbas de Tláloc." *Estudios De Cultura Náhuatl* 14 (November 1980): 287–314. https://nahuatl.historicas.unam.mx/index.php/ecn/article/view/78429.

Otero Arnaiz, Adriano. *Coffee Annual: Mexico*. GAIN Report. Mexico City: U.S. Department of Agriculture, Foreign Agricultural Service, May 12, 2024. https://apps.fas.usda.gov/newgainapi/api/Report/DownloadReportByFileName?fileName=Coffee%20Annual_Mexico%20City_Mexico_MX2024-0025.pdf.

Padilla, Sisto Alberto. *Diccionario botánico y portátil de las tres Américas: tomo tercero*. Vol. 3. Ahuachapan, El Salvador: El Porvenir, 1923. https://www.biodiversitylibrary.org/page/55221022#page/8/mode/1up.

Padilla, Carlos Alberto Torreblanca. "Algunas notas en torno a los alimentos prehispánicos en el Cóporo, Ocampo, Guanajuato." *Diario de Campo* 12 (2013): 11–14.

Page Pliego, Jaime Tomás. "Sweet Extermination: Soda and Beer, as Trigger Cause and Complications in Diabetics, among High Land Mayans of Chiapas, Mexico." *Social Medicine* 12, no. 2 (2019): 79–83.

Palka, Joel W. "Real Tobacco for Real People: Nicotine and Lacandon Maya Trade." In *Substance and Seduction: Ingested Commodities in Early Modern Mesoamerica*, edited by Kathryn E. Sampeck and Stacey Schwartzkopf, 103–27. Austin: University of Texas Press, 2017.

Paris, Elizabeth H., Carlos Peraza Lope, Marilyn A. Masson, Pedro C. Delgado Kú, and Bárbara C. Escamilla Ojeda. "The Organization of Stingless Beekeeping (Meliponiculture) at Mayapán, Yucatan, Mexico." *Journal of Anthropological Archaeology* 52 (2018): 1–22.

Pat Fernández, Lucio Alberto, Francisco Anguebes Franceschi, Juan Manuel Pat Fernández, Pablo Hernández Bahena, and Rodimiro Ramos Reyes. "Condición y perspectivas de la meliponicultura en comunidades mayas de la reserva de la biósfera Los Petenes, Campeche, México." *Estudios de cultura maya* 52 (2018): 227–54.

Paz, Octavio. *The Other Mexico: Critique of the Pyramid*. Translated by Lysander Kemp. New York: Grove Press Inc., 1972.

Pérez Akaki, Pablo. "Los siglos XIX y XX en la cafeticultura nacional: de la bonanza a la crisis del grano de oro mexicano." *Revista de Historia* 67 (2013): 159–99.

Pérez-Flores, Julián, Víctor Córdova-Ávalos, Elsa Chávez-García, Efrén Hernández-Maldonado, Cristobal Enrique Córdova-Lázaro, Antonio Córdova-Ávalos, and José Antonio Hinojosa-Cuéllar. "Bebidas prehispánicas y novohispánicas de cacao y maíz en la Chontalpa, Tabasco." *Agro Productividad* 13, no. 7 3–8 (2020).

"Periódico Oficial del Estado de Baja California Norte," March 20, 1941. Hemeroteca Nacional Digital de México.

Periódico Oficial del Estado de Yucatán. "Circular," April 16, 1969. Hemeroteca Nacional Digital de México. https://hndm.iib.unam.mx/consulta/publicacion/visualizar/558075be7d1e63c9fea1a3d4?pagina=558a3a577d1ed64f16fc31f7.

Pilar Zazueta, María del. "De Coca-Cola a Vampi-Cola: políticas, negocios, y el consumo de refrescos y azúcar en México (1971–1982)." *Apuntes de Investigación del CECYP* 22 (2012): 35–55.

Piñón Jiménez, Gonzalo, and Jorge Hernández Díaz. *El café: crisis y organización: los pequeños productores en Oaxaca.* Oaxaca: Instituto de Investigaciones Sociológicas, Universidad Autónoma "Benito Juárez" de Oaxaca, 1998.

Plotto, Anne. "HIBISCUS: Post-Production Management for Improved Market Access." Edited by François Mazaud, Alexandra Röttger, and Katja Steffel. *Post-Harvest Compendium*, 2004. https://www.fao.org/fileadmin/user_upload/inpho/docs/Post_Harvest_Compendium_-_Hibiscus.pdf.

Pomar, Juan Bautista, and Alonso Zurita. "Pomar, Relación de Tezcoco; Zurita, Breve Relación de los Señores de la Nueva España." In *Nueva Colección de Documentos Para la Historia de Mexico: Pomar-Zurita-Relaciones Antiguas, Siglo XVI*, edited by Joaquín García Icazbalceta and F. D. Leon, Vol. III. Mexico City, 1891. Internet Archive, https://archive.org/details/pomaryzuritapom00icazgoog.

Pombo, Luis. *Mexico: 1876–1892.* Mexico: El Siglo Diez y Nueve, 1893.

Porraz Gómez, Iván Francisco, and Rafael Alonso Hernández. "¿'El costumbre' de los dioses o la imposición de los infieles? Cosmovisión y comercialización del posh en los Altos de Chiapas." In *En torno a las bebidas alcohólicas mexicanas: Poder, prácticas culturales y configuraciones regionales*, edited by José de Jesús Hernández López and Miguel Ángel Iwadare, 77–90. México: Universidad de Guadalajara, Centro Universitario de Los Altos (CuAltos), 2015.

Porter, Robert M. *The Coffee Farmers Revolt in Southern Mexico in the 1980s and 1990s.* Lewiston: Edwin Mellen Press, 2002.

Producción de uva en México 2022. Secretaría de Agricultura y Desarrollo Rural, 2022. https://www.gob.mx/cms/uploads/attachment/file/771603/Producci_n_Uva_en_M_xico.pdf.

Quintero-Salazar, Baciliza, Aldo Iván Bernáldez Camiruaga, V.Daniela Barrera García Octavio Dublán-García, and Héctor Javier Favila Cisneros. "Consumo y conocimiento actual de una bebida fermentada tradicional en Ixtapan del Oro, México: la sambumbia." *Alteridades* 22, no. 44 (2012): 115–29.

Rafferty, Sean M. *Native Intoxicants of North America.* 1st ed. Knoxville: The University of Tennessee Press, 2021.

Ramírez, García, Alicia Ortiz Fernando, and Alejandro Rosas. *A Company Through the Centuries: Cuauhtémoc Moctezuma Brewery.* México, D.F: Editorial Clío, 2006.

Ramírez Rancaño, Mario. *Ignacio Torres Adalid y la industria pulquera*. 1st ed. Mexico City: Plaza y Valdés; Instituto de Investigaciones Sociales de la UNAM, 2000. https://ru.iis.sociales.unam.mx/handle/IIS/5540.

Reed, Howard S. "An Account of Sixteenth-Century Agriculture on the Mexican Plateau." *Journal of the Washington Academy of Sciences* 34, no. 7 (1944): 209–13.

Renard, María Cristina. *El Soconusco: Una economía cafetalera*. Mexico: Universidad Autónoma Chapingo, Dirección de Difusión Cultural, 1993.

Reyes-Matamoros, Jenaro, J. G. Fuentes-López David Martínez-Moreno, and F. Basurto-Peña. "Importancia relativa de las especies medicinales ofertadas en el mercado de Tepeaca, Puebla, México." *Polibotánica* 54 (2022): 271–89.

Reyna, María del Carmen, and Jean-Paul Kramme. *Apuntes para la historia de la cerveza en México*. México, D.F: INAH, 2012.

Rodríguez Centeno, Mabel M. "Fiscalidad y café mexicano: El porfiriato y sus estrategias de fomento económico para la producción y comercialización del grano (1870–1910)." *Historia Mexicana vol. LIV, núm. 1, julio-septiembre* (2004): 93–128.

Rodríguez Pérez, Betania. "Tipos de bebidas alcohólicas novohispanas y variedad de nombres: Argumentos para desacreditar su producción y consumo." In *En torno a las bebidas alcohólicas mexicanas: Poder, prácticas culturales y configuraciones regionales*, edited by José Jesús Hernández López, 33–57. Guadalajara: Universidad de Guadalajara, 2015.

Rojas González, Francisco. *Ensayos indigenistas*. Zapopan, Jalisco: El Colegio de Jalisco, 1998.

Román Lagunas, Rosa. *Los atoles de Acapetlahuaya: Comidas y bebidas tradicionales*. Mexico City: Consejo Nacional para la Cultura y las Artes, Dirección General de Culturas Populares, 1991.

Romero, Matías. *Cultivo del café en la Costa Meridional de Chiapas*. 4th ed. Mexico: Oficina TIP de la Secretaría de Fomento, 1893.

Romero-Cerecero, Ofelia, María Lourdes Medina-Cordero, María Carmen Vázquez-Flota, and María Guadalupe Vargas-Arispuro. "Use of Medicinal Plants among Patients with Diabetes Mellitus Type 2 in Morelos, Mexico." *Boletín Latinoamericano y del Caribe de Plantas Medicinales y Aromáticas* 8, no. 5 (2009): 380–8.

Romero Contreras, Alejandro Tonatiuh, and Felipe Carlos Viesca González. "Formación del patrimonio gastronómico del Valle de Toluca, México." *CIENCIA ergo-sum* 17, no. 3 (2010): 239–52.

Ronquillo Arvizu, Martín. "La centralidad del kórima entre los rarámuri. Un recorrido de su tratamiento teórico etnográfico." *Diario de Campo* 2 (n.d.): 77–99. https://mediateca.inah.gob.mx/repositorio/islandora/object/articulo%3A17847.

Rosales, Genoveva R. Ocampo. "Medicinal Uses of Melipona Beecheii Honey, by the Ancient Maya." In *Pot-Honey: A Legacy of Stingless Bees*, edited by Patricia Vit, Silvia R. M. Pedro, and David Roubik, 229–40. New York: Springer, 2013. https://doi.org/10.1007/978-1-4614-4960-7_15.

Ruiz de Alarcón, Hernando. *Tratado de las supersticiones y costumbres gentílicas que hoy viven entre los indios naturales de esta Nueva España*. Edited by Francisco del Paso y Troncoso. Fuente Cultural de la Librería Navarro, 1953. https://www.cervantesvirtual.com/nd/ark:/59851/bmcdn423.

Sahagún, Bernardino de. "'Book 6: Rhetoric and Moral Philosophy,' Fol. 211v, Sahagún, Bernardino de. Florentine Codex: General History of the Things of New Spain. Transcribed and Translated with Notes by Arthur J. O. Anderson and Charles E. Dibble. 2nd Rev. Ed. Santa Fe, NM: School of American Research / University of Utah Press, 1950–82." Los Angeles, 2023. © J. Paul Getty Trust. https://florentinecodex.getty.edu/book/6/folio/211v.

Sahagún, Bernardino de. "'Book 6: Rhetoric and Moral Philosophy,' Fol. 212r, Sahagún, Bernardino de. Florentine Codex: General History of the Things of New Spain. Transcribed and Translated with Notes by Arthur J. O. Anderson and Charles E. Dibble. 2nd Rev. Ed. Santa Fe, NM: School of American Research / University of Utah Press, 1950–82." Los Angeles, 2023. © J. Paul Getty Trust. https://florentinecodex.getty.edu/en/book/6/folio/212r.

Sahagún, Bernardino de, Antonio Valeriano, Alonso Vegerano, Martín Jacobita, Pedro de San Buenaventura, Diego de Grado, Bonifacio Maximiliano, and Mateo Severino. *General History of the Things of New Spain: Books 1–11*. Edited by Kim N. Richter, Alicia Maria Houtrouw, Kevin Terraciano, Jeanette Peterson, Diana Magaloni, and Lisa Sousa. Translated by León García Garagarza. Vol. bk. 8, fol. 25r. Los Angeles: Getty Research Institute, 2023.

Salazar Solano, Vidal. "La industria del bacanora: historia y tradición de resistencia en la sierra sonorense." *Región y sociedad* 19, no. 39 (2007): 105–33.

Sampeck, Kathryn E., and Jonathan Thayn. "Translating Tastes: A Cartography of Chocolate Colonialism." In *Substance and Seduction: Ingested Commodities in Early Modern Mesoamerica*, edited by Stacey Schwartzkopf and Kathryn E. Sampeck, Austin: University of Texas Press, 72–100, 2017.

Sanchez Cortes, Maria Silva, Alma Gabriela Verdugo Valdez, Erika Judith Lopez Zuñiga, and Gilber Vela Gutierrez. "El atole agrio: su presencia y modo de preparación en la cultura alimentaria de Chiapas." *El Maíz: conocimiento de su patrimonio gastronómico y cultural*, 2019, 87–94. https://hdl.handle.net/20.500.12753/1498.

Sánchez Dirzo, María Guadalupe, Clementina Esmeralda López Ferrer, Martha Flores Valadez, Ana Luisa Jofre Garfia, José Antonio Aguirre Rodríguez, Erika Jazmine Morales Cruz, and Ricardo Reyes Chilpa. "Estudio Preliminar Del Axokot, Bebida Tradicional Fermentada, Bajo Una Perspectiva Transdisciplinaria." *Investigación Universitaria Multidisciplinaria: Revista de Investigación de La Universidad Simón Bolívar* 9, no. 9 (2010): 113–24.

Sánchez Trinidad, Lesterloon. *Las flores en la cocina veracruzana*. México: Secretaría de Cultura, Dirección General de Culturas Populares, Indígenas y Urbanas, 2017.

Schultes, Richard Evans. "Iconography of New World plant hallucinogens." *Arnoldia* 41, no. 3 (1981): 80–125.

Schultes, Richard Evans. "The Plant Kingdom and Hallucinogens (Part III)." *Bulletin on Narcotics* 22, no. 1 (1970): 25–53.

Schwartzkopf, Stacey. "Alcohol and Commodity Succession in Colonial Maya Guatemala: From Mead to Aguardiente." In *Substance and Seduction: Ingested Commodities in Early Modern Mesoamerica*, 55–71. Austin: University of Texas Press, 2017.

Seler, Eduard. *Codex Borgia: Eine altmexikanische Bilderschrift der Bibliothek der Congregatio de Propaganda Fide*. Vol. 1. 3 vols. Berlin: Druck von Gebr. Unger, 1904. https://archive.org/details/codex-borgia_202209.

Semana Mercantil. "Camara de Comercio de México," March 13, 1905. Hemeroteca Nacional Digital de México. https://hndm.iib.unam.mx/consulta/resultados/visualizar/558a348c7d1ed64f16a75479?resultado=3&tipo=pagina&intPagina=4.

Silva Riquer, Jorge. *La Administracíon de Alcabalas y Pulques de Michoacán, 1776–1821*. 1. México, D.F: Instituto Mora, 1993.

Singelmann, Peter. "La transformación política de México y los gremios cañeros del PRI." *Revista mexicana de sociología* 65, no. 1 (2003): 117–52.

Smalley, John, and Michael Blake. "Sweet Beginnings: Stalk Sugar and the Domestication of Maize." *Current Anthropology* 44, no. 5 (2003): 675–703.

Soleri, Daniela, and David A. Cleveland. "Tejate: Theobroma Cacao and T. Bicolor in a Traditional Beverage from Oaxaca, Mexico." *Food and Foodways* 15, no. 1 (2007): 107–18. https://doi.org/10.1080/07409710701260131.

Spell, Lota M. "The Anglo-Saxon Press in Mexico, 1846–1848." *The American Historical Review* 38, no. 1 (1932): 20–31. https://doi.org/10.2307/1838062.

Thelmadatter, Leigh. "Exploring the Rise of Mexico's Craft Beer Industry." *Mexico News Daily*, September 30, 2023. https://mexiconewsdaily.com/food/exploring-the-rise-of-mexicos-craft-beer-industry/.

Thiemer-Sachse, Ursula. "Sobre higiene y medicina entre los zapotecas durante la época de la conquista española." *Indiana* 16 (2000): 185–209.

Torquemada, Juan de. "Capítulo XXIII." In *Monarquía Indiana*, Tercera edición (primera edición UNAM). Vol. Volumen I. México: Universidad Nacional Autónoma de México, Instituto de Investigaciones Históricas, 1975.

Torres, Eliseo, and Timothy L. Sawyer. *Healing with Herbs and Rituals: A Mexican Tradition*. 1st ed. Albuquerque, New Mexico: University of New Mexico Press, 2006.

Tozzer, Alfred M., ed. *Landa's Relación de Las Cosas de Yucatán: A Translation*. Reprint. Vol. 18. Papers of the Peabody Museum of American Archaeology and Ethnology. Cambridge, MA: Harvard University, 1941.

Trabanino, Felipe. "Sistema de manejo del bosque tropical en Chinikihá a través de la etnoecología y la paleoetnobotánica." In *XXV Simposio de Investigaciones Arqueológicas en Guatemala, 2011*, edited by B. Arroyo, L. Paiz, and H. Mejía, 798–804. Guatemala: Ministerio de Cultura y Deportes, Instituto de Antropología e Historia y Asociación Tikal, 2012. https://www.asociaciontikal.com/wp-content/uploads/2017/03/068_Trabanino.pdf.

Trejo Fuentes, Ignacio. *La Fiesta y La Muerte Enmascarada: El Distrito Federal de Noche*. México, D.F: Colibrí, 1999.

The Two Republics. "The Cacao of Mexico," August 31, 1895, XLI no 53 ed. Hemeroteca Nacional Digital de México. https://hndm.iib.unam.mx/consulta/publicacion/visualizar/558075bf7d1e63c9fea1a473?pagina=558a36277d1ed64f16c37412.

The Two Republics. "Saunterings," October 13, 1897. Hemeroteca Nacional Digital de México. https://hndm.iib.unam.mx/consulta/publicacion/visualizar/558075bf7d1e63c9fea1a473?pagina=558a364b7d1ed64f16c5d75e.

Tyler, Varro E. "DAMIANA — History of a Herbal Hoax." *Pharmacy in History* 25, no. 2 (1983): 55–60. http://www.jstor.org/stable/41109400.

Union Commercial. "Los Mezcales Mexicanos." *El Tiempo* (Mexico City), July 13, 1894. Hemeroteca Nacional Digital de México. https://hndm.iib.unam.mx/consulta/resultados/visualizar/558a34b27d1ed64f16aa202e?resultado=2&tipo=pagina&intPagina=2.

Uvence Navarro, Héctor. "Universo culinario: El atole, elixir de buenaventura en la vida." *El Informador* (Guadalajara), February 28, 1999. Hemeroteca Nacional Digital de México. https://hndm.iib.unam.mx/consulta/publicacion/visualizar/558075be7d1e63c9fea1a303?pagina=558a3cfb7d1ed64f17104584.

Valenzuela-Zapata, Ana G., Paul D. Buell, María Paz Solano-Pérez, and Hyunhee Park. "'Huichol' Stills: A Century of Anthropology–Technology Transfer and Innovation." *Crossroads* 8 (2013): 157–91.

Vargas, Jesús. "El sotol chihuahuense, la increíble historia de una torpeza sin fin." *Cuadernos Fronterizos* 8 25–8 (2007).

Vargas, Luis Alberto, Paris Aguilar, Guadalupe Esquivel, Montserrat Gispert, Armando Gomez, Hugo Rodriguez, Cristina Suarez, and Carmen Wacher. "Bebidas de la tradición." In *Beber de tierra generosa: Historia de las bebidas alcohólicas en México*, Muría J. M., editor, 1:168–204. Mexico City: FISAC, 1998.

Vázquez-García, J. A., B. M. J. Cházaro, V. G. Hernández, Y. L. Vargas-Rodríguez, and T. Ma P. Zamora. "Taxonomía del género Agave en el Occidente de México: Una panorámica preliminar." In *Los Agaves del Occidente de México*, edited by M. J. Vázquez-García, G. Cházaro, V. E. Hernández, Flores, and Y. L. Vargas-Rodríguez, 38–82. Guadalajara: Universidad de, 2007.

Velázquez de León, Josefina. *Cocktails*. Mexico City: Ediciones Josefina Velázquez de León, 1950.

Viera, Juan de. *Breve y compendiosa narración de la Ciudad de México*, 1778. https://gallica.bnf.fr/ark:/12148/btv1b100329980/f1.item.

Vilar, Albert. "Biografia–Artur Mundet." *Revista de Girona*, 2016.

Villatoro Vera, Ricardo A., Lorena Luna Cazares, and Alma Rosa Gonzales Esquincas. "El Cuaulote, Recurso Herbolario de Chiapas." *Ciencias* 0, no. 083 (October 5, 2009). https://www.revistas.unam.mx/index.php/cns/article/view/12063.

Weitlaner, Robert J. "Sobre la alimentación chinanteca." In *Anales del Instituto Nacional de Antropologia e Historia*, 177–95, 1952.

Wilson, Iris H., and Antonio Pineda. "Pineda's Report on the Beverages of New Spain." *Arizona and the West* 5, no. 1 (1963): 79–90. http://www.jstor.org/stable/40167046.

Wobeser, Gisela von. *La formación de la hacienda en la época colonial: El uso de la tierra y el agua*. México City: UNAM Instituto de Investigaciones Históricas, 2016. https://historicas.unam.mx/publicaciones/publicadigital/libros/formacion_hacienda/epoca_colonial.html.

Yankelevich, Pablo. "Extranjeros indeseables en México (1911–1940): Una aproximación cuantitativa a la aplicación del artículo 33 constitucional." *Historia Mexicana* 54, no. 4 (2004): 693–744.

Yocupicio Buitimea, Rosa. *Recetario indígena de Sonora: Mayo y Yaqui*. Edited by María Trinidad Ruiz Ruiz. Translated by Salustriano Matuz González and Ismael Castillo Rendón. Cocina Indígena y Popular 9. Mexico City: Consejo, 2000.

Zizumbo-Villarreal, Daniel, Fernando González-Zozaya, Angeles Olay-Barrientos, Rafael Platas-Ruíz, Mariza Cuevas-Sagardí, Laura Almendros-López, and Patricia Colunga-GarcíaMarín. "Archaeological Evidence of the Cultural Importance of Agave Spp. in Pre-Hispanic Colima, Mexico." *Economic Botany* 63, no. 3 (2009): 288–302.

NOTES

Chapter 1

1 Teresa Lozano Armendares, *El chinguirito vindicado: El contrabando de aguardiente de caña y la política colonial*, 2nd ed. (México City: UNAM Instituto de Investigaciones Históricas, 2005), 11.

2 A Citizen of the United States, *Notes on Mexico, Made in the Autumn of 1822, Accompanied by an Historical Sketch of the Revolution, and Translations of Official Reports of the Present State of That Country* (Philadelphia: H.C. Carey and I. Lea, 1824), 96.

Chapter 2

1 César Ojeda-Linares et al., "Traditional Fermented Beverages of Mexico: A Biocultural Unseen Foodscape," *Foods* 10, no. 10 (2021): 3.

2 María del Carmen Reyna and Jean-Paul Kramme, *Apuntes para la historia de la cerveza en México* (México, D.F: INAH, 2012), 111.

3 Weston La Barre, "Native American Beers," *American Anthropologist* 40, no. 2 (1938): 233.

4 Sean M. Rafferty, *Native Intoxicants of North America*, 1st ed. (Knoxville: The University of Tennessee Press, 2021), 142.

5 Christian F. Feest, "New Wines and Beers of Native North America," *Journal of Ethnopharmacology* 9, nos. 2–3 (1983): 329.

6 Jesús Moreno-Mata, "Análisis discursivo del relato popular Haciendo tejuino, tradicional en la lengua y en la cultura wixárika," *Revista Lengua y Cultura* 4, no. 8 (2023): 45.

7 Iván Francisco Porraz Gómez and Rafael Alonso Hernández, "¿'El costumbre' de los dioses o la imposición de los infieles? Cosmovisión y comercialización del posh en los Altos de Chiapas," in *En torno a las bebidas alcohólicas mexicanas: Poder, prácticas culturales y configuraciones regionales*, ed. José de Jesús Hernández López and Miguel

Ángel Iwadare (México: Universidad de Guadalajara, Centro Universitario de Los Altos (CuAltos), 2015), 78.

8 Alfred M. Tozzer, ed., *Landa's Relación de Las Cosas de Yucatán: A Translation* (Cambridge, MA: Harvard University, 1941), 18:193.

9 Elizabeth H. Paris et al., "The Organization of Stingless Beekeeping (Meliponiculture) at Mayapán, Yucatan, Mexico," *Journal of Anthropological Archaeology* 52 (2018): 6.

10 Rita Guadalupe Alfaro Bates et al., *Caracterización palinológica de las mieles de la península de Yucatán* (Mérida, Yucatán: Universidad Autónoma de Yucatán and Comisión Nacional para el Conocimiento y Uso de la Biodiversidad, 2010), 63.

11 Ibid., 70.

12 John R. Gust and Jennifer P. Mathews, *Sugarcane & Rum: The Bittersweet History of Labor and Life on the Yucatán Peninsula* (Tucson: University of Arizona Press, 2020), 95.

13 Martin Nesvig, "Sandcastles of the Mind: Hallucinogens and Cultural Memory," in *Substance and Seduction*, ed. Stacey Schwartzkopf and Kathryn E. Sampeck (New York: University of Texas Press, 2021), 47, https://doi.org/10.7560/313862-004.

14 María Muriá et al., "Bebidas de la tradición," in *In Beber de tierra generosa: Historia de las bebidas alcohólicas en México*, vol. 1 (Fundación de Investigaciones Sociales, 1998), 180.

15 Paris et al., "The Organization of Stingless Beekeeping (Meliponiculture) at Mayapán, Yucatan, Mexico," 15.

16 Quintero-Salazar et al., "Consumo y conocimiento actual de una bebida fermentada tradicional en Ixtapan del Oro, México: la sambumbia," *Alteridades* 22, no. 44 (2012): 118.

17 Anonymous Conqueror, *Narrative of Some Things of New Spain and of the Great City of Temestitan, Mexico*, trans. Marshall A. Saville (New York: The Cortes Society, 1917), 44, https://archive.org/details/narrativeofsomet00savi/mode/2up.

18 Lozano Armendares, *El chinguirito vindicado: El contrabando de aguardiente de caña y la política colonial*, 22.

19 Henry J. Bruman, *Alcohol in Ancient Mexico* (Salt Lake City: University of Utah Press, 2000), 85.

20 Lozano Armendares, *El chinguirito vindicado: El contrabando de aguardiente de caña y la política colonial*, 24.

21 Ibid.

22 Ojeda-Linares et al., "Traditional Fermented Beverages of Mexico: A Biocultural Unseen Foodscape."

23 Luis Fernando Lara, "Africanismos en el español de México," *Nueva Revista de Filología Hispánica* LXIII, no. 2 (2015): 333, https://www.redalyc.org/articulo.oa?id=60246691001.

24 Lorna F. Gibson, Donald Olson, and Anne Olson, "Four Pame Texts," *Tlalocan* 4, no. 2 (2016): 126, https://doi.org/10.19130/iifl.tlalocan.1963.316.

25 Davíd Ernesto Navarro Ortíz, "Los Náhuas-Popolocas de San José Miahuatlán, Pue.: Endoculturación y educación formal en la escuela albergue" (Master's Thesis, Universidad Veracruzana, Facultad de Antropología, 1983), 83.

26 Ojeda-Linares et al., "Traditional Fermented Beverages of Mexico: A Biocultural Unseen Foodscape."

27 Bruman, *Alcohol in Ancient Mexico*, 54.

28 Edmund C. Jaeger, "The Desert Bean Tree," *Desert Magazine* 22, no. 5 (May 1959): 15, https://swdeserts.com/index_htm_files/195905-DesertMagazine-1959-May.pdf.

29 Rafferty, *Native Intoxicants of North America*, 136.

30 Luis Humberto Nava Martínez, "La triada del semidesierto: Características tecnológicas y nutricionales del maguey, nopal y mezquite en sociedades recolectoras cazadoras del centro norte de México: Un análisis comparativo," *Revista Chicomoztoc* 1, no. 2 (July 2019): 170.

31 Juan Navarro, "Nota o Informe al Virrey Don Matías de Gálvez, 29 de febrero de 1784." Originally in "Ramo de Aguardiente de Caña (1788–1789), tomo I, fs. 14–25v, Archivo General de la Nación, México. Reproduced in Brevajes en la colonia.—La fontana Mexicana del siglo XVIII en la mezcla de licores. Introduction by Manuel Carrera Stampa," *Memorias de la Academia Mexicana de la Historia: Correspondiente de la Real de Madrid*, no. 3 (July 1958): 336.

32 Frank S. Crosswhite, "The Annual Saguaro Harvest and Crop Cycle of the Papago, with Reference to Ecology and Symbolism," *Desert Plants*, 1980, 4, http://hdl.handle.net/10150/550735.

33 John Smalley and Michael Blake, "Sweet Beginnings: Stalk Sugar and the Domestication of Maize," *Current Anthropology* 44, no. 5 (2003): 675–703.

34 Navarro, "Nota o Informe al Virrey Don Matías de Gálvez, 29 de febrero de 1784." Originally in "Ramo de Aguardiente de Caña (1788–1789), tomo I, fs. 14–25v, Archivo General de la Nación, México. Reproduced in Brevajes en la colonia.—La fontana Mexicana del siglo XVIII en la mezcla de licores. Introduction by Manuel Carrera Stampa."

35 Bruman, *Alcohol in Ancient Mexico*, 60.

36 Ibid., 58–9.

37 Francisco Rojas González, *Ensayos indigenistas* (Zapopan, Jalisco: El Colegio de Jalisco, 1998), 106.

38 Corcuera de Mancera, *El Fraile, El Indio Y El Pulque: Evangelización Y Embriaguez En La Nueva España; (1523–1548)* (Fondo de cultura económica, 1993), 21.

39 Eduard Seler, *Codex Borgia: Eine altmexikanische Bilderschrift der Bibliothek der Congregatio de Propaganda Fide*, vol. 1 (Berlin: Druck von Gebr. Unger, 1904), 116, https://archive.org/details/codex-borgia_202209. "dass diese Götter in der Hauptsache und ihrem Wesen nach Erntegötter waren. Denn wenn die Ernte eingebracht war, wenn es wieder Lebensmittel in Fülle gab, dann war es wieder Zeit Pulque oder andere berauschende Getränke zu bereiten und in wüsten Gelagen den neuen Erntesegen zu feiern."

40 José Jesús Hernández Palomo, *La renta del pulque en Nueva España: 1663–1810* (Sevilla: Escuela de Estudios Hispano-Americanos de Sevilla, 1979), 68.

41 Ibid., 33–4.

42 Gisela von Wobeser, *La formación de la hacienda en la época colonial: El uso de la tierra y el agua* (México City: UNAM Instituto de Investigaciones Históricas, 2016), 74 n. 12, https://historicas.unam.mx/publicaciones/publicadigital/libros/formacion_hacienda/epoca_colonial.html.

43 Brian R. Hamnett, *A Concise History of Mexico*, 2nd ed. (Cambridge; New York: Cambridge University Press, 2006), 116.

44 Manuel Carrera Stampa, "La Ciudad de México a Principios del Siglo XIX: Aspectos Económicos," *Memorias de la Academia Mexicana de la Historia: Correspondiente de la Real de Madrid* 2, no. Tomo XXVI (June 1967): 202.

45 Rafael Olea Franco, *Un pulque literario. (A la sombra de las pencas del maguey)* (México: El Colegio de México, Centro de Estudios Linguísticos y Literarios, 2020), 16.

46 Paula Kolonitz, *Un viaje a México en 1864* (Mexico City: Secretaría de Educación Pública, 1976), 108. "vino y la cerveza se beben poco, pero el puqlue jamas falta a las mesa de los ricos."

47 Loyola Montemayor, *La industria del pulque* (Mexico City: Banco de México, Departamento de Investigaciones Industriales, 1956), Figure 43.

48 Ibid.

49 Mario Ramírez Rancaño, *Ignacio Torres Adalid y la industria pulquera*, 1st ed. (Mexico City: Plaza y Valdés; Instituto de Investigaciones Sociales de la UNAM, 2000), 15, https://ru.iis.sociales.unam.mx/handle/IIS/5540.

50 "Higiene Publica," *El Tiempo*, July 12, 1905, 7419 ed., 1, Hemeroteca Nacional Digital de México, https://hndm.iib.unam.mx/consulta/publicacion/visualizar/558075bf7d1e63c9fea1a45b?pagina=558a35057d1ed64f16afab7b. "Hay una costumbre sobre la cual suponemos que habrá fiajado su atención el Consejo Superior de Salubridad, y es, la de mezclar el pulque que dejan en cada vaso los consumidores que acuden a la taberna, echándolo los encargados de ellas a los barriles para volverlo a vender al público."

51 Bruman, *Alcohol in Ancient Mexico*, 12. Reprinted courtesy of the University of Utah Press.

52 Auguste Génin, *La cerveza entre los antiguos mexicanos y en la actualidad* (Mexico City: Tipografía Corral, 1924), 15–16.

53 Marco Buenrostro, "¿Cuáles bebidas se pueden preparar con maíz?," in *Respuestas acerca del maíz: La voz de 72 autores*, ed. C. Morales-Valderrama et al., vol. III (Mexico City: INAH, 2021), 92; Betania Rodríguez Pérez, "Tipos de bebidas alcohólicas novohispanas y variedad de nombres: Argumentos para desacreditar su producción y consumo," in *En torno a las bebidas alcohólicas mexicanas: Poder, prácticas culturales y configuraciones regionales*, ed. José Jesús Hernández López (Guadalajara: Universidad de Guadalajara, n.d.), 33–57.

54 Beatriz Coutiño et al., "Tavern or Coyol Wine: A Beverage From Palm Sap With Biotechnological Potential," in *Biotechnological Progress and Beverage Consumption*, ed. Alexandru Mihai Grumezescu and Alina Maria Holban (Academic Press, 2020), 233–52, https://doi.org/10.1016/B978-0-12-816678-9.00007-2.

55 Heidi Chemín Bässler, *Recetario pame de San Luis Potosí y Querétaro*, 1 (México, D.F: CONACULTA, Dirección General de Culturas Populares e Indígenas, 2000), 104.

56 Ana Gómez, "Alimentación cotidiana y especial en la comunidad de Pathuitz, Municipio de Chilón, Chiapas" (Master's thesis, El Colegio de la Frontera Sur, 2017), 74.

57 Augusto Godoy, Teófilo Herrera, and Miguel Ulloa, *Más allá del pulque y el tepache: Las bebidas alcohólicas no destiladas indígenas de México* (Mexico City: UNAM Instituto de Investigaciones Antropológicas, 2003), 21.

58 Iris H. Wilson and Antonio Pineda, "Pineda's Report on the Beverages of New Spain," *Arizona and the West* 5, no. 1 (1963): 87, http://www.jstor.org/stable/40167046.

59 Patricia Lappe and Miguel Ulloa, *Estudios étnicos, microbianos y químicos del tesgüino tarahumara* (Mexico City: Universidad Nacional Autónoma de México, 1989), 19.

60 Ibid., 5.

61 Fructuoso Irigoyen-Rascón and Alfonso Paredes, *Tarahumara Medicine: Ethnobotany and Healing among the Rarámuri of Mexico* (Norman: University of Oklahoma Press, 2015), 88.

62 César Iván Ojeda-Linares, Mariana Vallejo, and Alejandro Casas, "Disappearance and Survival of Fermented Beverages in the Biosphere Reserve Tehuacán-Cuicatlán,

Mexico: The Cases of Tolonche and Lapo," *Frontiers in Sustainable Food Systems* 6 (2023), https://doi.org/1067598.

63 "El Arte de Matar En Un Cuarto de Hora: Boticarios, Curanderos, y Medicos de Oficio," *El Chisme*, March 18, 1899, 3, Hemeroteca Nacional Digital de México, https://hndm.iib.unam.mx/consulta/publicacion/visualizar/558075bd7d1e63c9fea1a199?pagina=558a333c7d1ed64f16926262.

64 Diego Javier Luis, *The First Asians in the Americas: A Transpacific History*, 1st ed. (Cambridge, MA: Harvard University Press, 2024), 68.

65 Ibid., 94.

66 Navarro, "Nota o Informe al Virrey Don Matías de Gálvez, 29 de febrero de 1784." Originally in "Ramo de Aguardiente de Caña (1788–1789), tomo I, fs. 14–25v, Archivo General de la Nación, México. Reproduced in Brevajes en la colonia.—La fontana Mexicana del siglo XVIII en la mezcla de licores. Introduction by Manuel Carrera Stampa," 314.

67 *El Museo Mexicano, Tomo IV (Mexico City)*, "Trages y Costumbres Nacionales: El Jarocho (Departamento de Veracruz)," 61 note *. "Zambumbia (que es piña fermentada con especias y endulzada con piloncillo)"

68 Quintero-Salazar et al., "Consumo y conocimiento actual de una bebida fermentada tradicional en Ixtapan del Oro, México: la sambumbia," 126.

Chapter 3

1 Instituto Nacional de Estadística y Geografía (INEGI), "Colección de estudios sectoriales y regionales: Conociendo la industria de la cerveza" (Mexico City: INEGI, 2020), https://www.inegi.org.mx/contenidos/productos/prod_serv/contenidos/espanol/bvinegi/productos/nueva_estruc/702825198428.pdf.

2 Génin, *La cerveza entre los antiguos mexicanos y en la actualidad*, 15. "El chile por su principio resinoide llamado capisna, contribuye a preservar el alcohol de la rapida acidificacion, como el lupuloa en la cerveza."

3 Reyna and Kramme, *Apuntes para la historia de la cerveza en México*, 35.

4 Juan Bautista Pomar and Alonso Zurita, "Pomar, Relación de Tezcoco; Zurita, Breve Relación de los Señores de la Nueva España," in *Nueva Colección de Documentos Para la Historia de Mexico: Pomar-Zurita-Relaciones Antiguas, Siglo XVI*, ed. Joaquín García Icazbalceta and F. D. Leon, vol. III (Mexico City, 1891. Internet Archive, n.d.), 64, https://archive.org/details/pomaryzuritapom00icazgoog. "El trigo, muchas suertes, y cebada se da muy maravilloso en labranzas y heredades de españoles, porque may pocos indios se dan á ello por no tener lugar, y aun apenas para sus propias sementeras, por estar de ordinario ocupados en servicio de los españoles."

5 Martha Beatriz Guerrero Mills, "Empresas y empresarios: El caso de la Cervecería Modelo, 1876–1955" (Master's Thesis, Universidad Nacional Autónoma de México, 2006), 40, http://hdl.handle.net/20.500.12525/1899.

6 Génin, *La cerveza entre los antiguos mexicanos y en la actualidad*, 17–18.

7 "Avisos," *Águila Mexicana*, August 22, 1824, Hemeroteca Digital Nacional de México.

8 "Avisos," *El Sol*, March 10, 1825, 634 edition, Hemeroteca Digital Nacional de México.

9 Guerrero Mills, "Empresas y empresarios: El caso de la Cervecería Modelo, 1876–1955," 41.

10 García Ramírez, Alicia Ortiz Fernando, and Alejandro Rosas, *A Company Through the Centuries: Cuauhtémoc Moctezuma Brewery* (México, D.F: Editorial Clío, 2006), 20.

11 Susan Gauss and Edward Beatty, "The World's Beer: The Historical Geography of Brewing in Mexico," in *The Geography of Beer*, ed. Mark Patterson and Nancy Hoalst-Pullen (Dordrecht: Springer, 2014), 60, https://doi.org/10.1007/978-94-007-7787-3_6.

12 José Domingo Schievenini, "A Small Distinction with a Big Difference: Prohibiting 'Drugs' but Not Alcohol, from the Conquest to Constitutional Law," *The Social History of Alcohol and Drugs* 34, no. 1 (2020): 43.

13 Albino Aguado, "El Pulquero," in *Los Mexicanos Pintados por Sí Mismos: Tipos y Costumbres Nacionales* (México: Imprenta de M. Murguía y Compañía, 1854), 19, https://archive.org/details/losmexicanospint00mexi. "Este individuo es el cervecero, cuya maldita cerveza ha desalojado al pulque de las mesas aristocráticas, compite con él en la clase media, y tiene ya algunos adeptos entre el pueblo bajo."

14 Salvador Novo, *Cocina mexicana, o, Historia gastronómica de la ciudad de México*, 8th ed. (Mexico, D.F: Editorial Porrúa, 2002), 34–5.

15 Guerrero Mills, "Empresas y empresarios: El caso de la Cervecería Modelo, 1876–1955," 145.

16 Ramírez, Fernando, and Rosas, *A Company Through the Centuries: Cuauhtémoc Moctezuma Brewery*, 32.

17 Reyna and Kramme, *Apuntes para la historia de la cerveza en México*, 126.

18 Ramírez, Fernando, and Rosas, *A Company Through the Centuries: Cuauhtémoc Moctezuma Brewery*, 66.

19 Ibid., 67.

20 Ibid., 74.

21 Ibid., 92.

22 Ibid., 98.

23 Gauss and Beatty, "The World's Beer: The Historical Geography of Brewing in Mexico," 62.

24 Ramírez, Fernando, and Rosas, *A Company Through the Centuries: Cuauhtémoc Moctezuma Brewery*, 79.

25 Jaime Tomás Page Pliego, "Sweet Extermination: Soda and Beer, as Trigger Cause and Complications in Diabetics, among High Land Mayans of Chiapas, Mexico," *Social Medicine* 12, no. 2 (2019): 82.

26 Reyna and Kramme, *Apuntes para la historia de la cerveza en México*, 133.

27 Guerrero Mills, "Empresas y empresarios: El caso de la Cervecería Modelo, 1876–1955," 94.

28 "Regreso de Nueva York El Sr. V. Fernandez de la Reguera," *El Mundo: Diario Vespertino de Política e Información*, September 6, 1922, Hemeroteca Nacional Digital de México. "La 'Gran Cerveceria Modelo,' contara con elementos de tal naturaleza y con maquinaria de tanta importancia, que podra considerarse como la segunda Cerveceria de la America."

29 Guerrero Mills, "Empresas y empresarios: El caso de la Cervecería Modelo, 1876–1955," 99.

30 Ibid., 124.

31 Reyna and Kramme, *Apuntes para la historia de la cerveza en México*, 138.

32 *Cervecería Cosaco, los pioneros de la cerveza artesanal en CDMX*, vol. 5 (El Universal, 2021), https://youtu.be/VtkI8XKjpAU?si=y2m7xNjCimhqQvHK.

33 Leigh Thelmadatter, "Exploring the Rise of Mexico's Craft Beer Industry," *Mexico News Daily*, September 30, 2023, https://mexiconewsdaily.com/food/exploring-the-rise-of-mexicos-craft-beer-industry/.

34 José Luis Melgarejo Vivanco, *Breve historia de Veracruz* (Xalapa, Mexico: Biblioteca de la Facultad de Filosofía y Letras, Universidad Veracruzana, 1960), 81.

35 G. Cabañas, "El comercio entre México y España," *El Trimestre Económico* 4, no. 13 (1937): 64.

36 Ibid.

37 Albert Vilar, "Biografia–Artur Mundet," *Revista de Girona*, 2016, 39.

Chapter 4

1 Ángel F. Morales, *La cultura del vino en México*, 1st ed. (Monterrey, Mexico: Ediciones Castillo, 1980), 19.

2 Leon D. Adams, *The Wines of America* (Boston: Houghton Mifflin, 1973), 20.

3 Toribio de Benavente Motolinía, *Historia de los indios de la Nueva España: Escrita a mediados del siglo XVI* (Barcelona: Herederos de J. Gili, 1914), 193, https://archive.org/details/historiadelosind00moto/page/n3/mode/2up. "parras bravas muy gruesas . . . Y algunos espanoles hace de ellas vinagre, y algunos han hecho vino, aunque sido muy poco."

4 F. W. Linares, "Las antiguas uvas pasas de Norteamérica: Aporte indígena a la viticultura moderna," *Revista Cayey*, no. 90 (May 2010): 53.

5 Felipe Trabanino, "Sistema de manejo del bosque tropical en Chinikihá a través de la etnoecología y la paleoetnobotánica," in *XXV Simposio de Investigaciones Arqueológicas en Guatemala, 2011*, ed. B. Arroyo, L. Paiz, and H. Mejía (Guatemala: Ministerio de Cultura y Deportes, Instituto de Antropología e Historia y Asociación Tikal, 2012), 801, https://www.asociaciontikal.com/wp-content/uploads/2017/03/068_Trabanino.pdf.

6 Gregory McNamee, *Tortillas, Tiswin & T-Bones: A Food History of the Southwest* (Albuquerque: University of New Mexico Press, 2017), 46.

7 Heliodoro Valle, "The History of Wine in Mexico," *American Journal of Enology and Viticulture* 9, no. 3 (1958): 149, https://doi.org/10.5344/ajev.1958.9.3.146.

8 Ibid.

9 Adams, *The Wines of America*, 371.

10 Birgitta Leander, "Mestizaje ecológico en México (Algunas frutas, legumbres y semillas)," *Journal de la Société des américanistes* 59 (1970): 81.

11 Corcuera de Mancera, *El Fraile, El Indio Y El Pulque: Evangelización Y Embriaguez En La Nueva España; (1523—1548)*, 127.

12 Rodrigo de Albornoz, "Carta del contador Rodrigo de Albornoz, al emperador," in *Colección de documentos para la historia de México, tomo primero*, ed. Joaquín García Icazbalceta (Mexico: García Icazbalceta, 1858), 488, https://archive.org/details/bub_gb_WJk6nlChEKYC. "y después que la tierra está en el dominio de V. M., con la conversación y trato de los cristianos . . . beben vino de España con mejor voluntad que el pulque que ellos tienen por vino, que parece un poco a cerveza, aunque no es tal."

13 Rojas González, *Ensayos indigenistas*, 43.

14 Fray Gerónimo Mendieta, *Historia Eclesiástica Indiana: Obra escrita a fines del siglo XVI*, ed. Joaquín García Icazbalceta (México: Antigua Librería, Portal de Agustinos número 3, 1870), 503, https://archive.org/details/historiaeclesis00mendgoog/page/n8/mode/2up. "Y así el ordinário entrar del español por convecino de los indios, es con una pipa de vino por delante."

15 Stacey Schwartzkopf, "Alcohol and Commodity Succession in Colonial Maya Guatemala: From Mead to Aguardiente," in *Substance and Seduction: Ingested Commodities in Early Modern Mesoamerica* (University of Texas Press, 2017), 60.

16 Heliodoro Valle, "The History of Wine in Mexico," 148.

17 Maria Jose Fernández Barberena, "El patrimonio vitivinícola mexicano: historia, cultura y espacio económico" (Universidad de Córdoba, 2024), 72.

18 Heliodoro Valle, "The History of Wine in Mexico," 153.

19 Hamnett, *A Concise History of Mexico*, 108.

20 Heliodoro Valle, "The History of Wine in Mexico," 153.

21 Juan José Calva González, "El movimiento de Independencia de México y su repercusión en las necesidades de información de los agricultores que cultivan Vitis vinífera," in *Procesos revolucionarios, bibliotecas y movimientos culturales*, ed. Jaime Ríos Ortega and César Augusto Ramírez Velázquez (Universidad Nacional Autónoma de México, 2011), 101.

22 Adams, *The Wines of America*, 372.

23 Ibid., 242.

24 Luis Pombo, *Mexico: 1876–1892* (Mexico: El Siglo Diez y Nueve, 1893), 32.

25 Adams, *The Wines of America*, 375.

26 Fernández de Córdoba, "Actualidad de La Vitivinicultura Mexicana," *El Informador (Guadalajara)*, May 27, 1991, Hemeroteca Nacional Digital de México, https://hndm.iib.unam.mx/consulta/publicacion/visualizar/558075be7d1e63c9fea1a303?pagina=558a3bf27d1ed64f1708f52e.

27 Adams, *The Wines of America*, 370.

28 Morales, *La cultura del vino en México*, 95.

29 *Producción de uva en México 2022* (Secretaría de Agricultura y Desarrollo Rural, 2022), https://www.gob.mx/cms/uploads/attachment/file/771603/Producci_n_Uva_en_M_xico.pdf.

30 Reyna and Kramme, *Apuntes para la historia de la cerveza en México*, 50.

31 Lorena López-De-Buen et al., "Sobrevivencia de árboles nativos tropicales en un módulo silvopastoril en Veracruz, México," *Agrociencia* 53, no. 7 (2019): 977.

Chapter 5

1 Daniel Zizumbo-Villarreal et al., "Archaeological Evidence of the Cultural Importance of Agave Spp. in Pre-Hispanic Colima, Mexico," *Economic Botany* 63, no. 3 (2009): 288–302.

2 Javier Luis, *The First Asians in the Americas: A Transpacific History*, 94.

3 Ibid., 95.

4 Ana G. Valenzuela-Zapata et al., "'Huichol' Stills: A Century of Anthropology–Technology Transfer and Innovation," *Crossroads* 8 (2013): 175.

5 Teresa Lozano Armendares, "De cómo el chinguirito y el mezcal enfrentaron al aguardiente de Castilla, durante la colonia," in *En torno a las bebidas alcohólicas mexicanas: Poder, prácticas culturales y configuraciones regionales*, ed. José Jesús Hernández López (Universidad de Guadalajara, Centro Universitario de Los Altos (CuAltos), 2015), 20.

6 Lozano Armendares, *El chinguirito vindicado: El contrabando de aguardiente de caña y la política colonial*, 25.

7 Lozano Armendares, "De cómo el chinguirito y el mezcal enfrentaron al aguardiente de Castilla, durante la colonia," 21.

8 Henry J. Bruman, "Early Coconut Culture in Western Mexico," *The Hispanic American Historical Review* 25, no. 2 (1945): 219.

9 Vidal Salazar Solano, "La industria del bacanora: historia y tradición de resistencia en la sierra sonorense," *Región y sociedad* 19, no. 39 (2007): 106.

10 Union Commercial, "Los Mezcales Mexicanos," *El Tiempo (Mexico City)*, July 13, 1894, Hemeroteca Nacional Digital de México, https://hndm.iib.unam.mx/consulta/resultados/visualizar/558a34b27d1ed64f16aa202e?resultado=2&tipo=pagina&intPagina=2.

11 "Camara de Comercio de México," *Semana Mercantil*, March 13, 1905, Hemeroteca Nacional Digital de México, https://hndm.iib.unam.mx/consulta/resultados/visualizar/558a348c7d1ed64f16a75479?resultado=3&tipo=pagina&intPagina=4. "El <<comiteco>> y el <<tequila>> son muy conocidos y muy apreciados aqui; y en general, los nobres todas las bebidas alcoholicas que e fabrican en Mexico, se ostentan pomposamente anuncios e las cantinas y expendios e licores, y son muy solicitadas por los consumidores."

12 Abisaí Josué García-Mendoza, "México, País de Magueys," *La Jornada Del Campo*, no. 53 (February 18, 2012), https://www.jornada.com.mx/2012/02/18/cam-pais.html.

13 Lucio, "Mezcales y diversidad biocultural en los alrededores del Volcán de Colima. El caso de los productores tradicionales de Zapotitlán de Vadillo," 17.

14 Lozano Armendares, *El chinguirito vindicado: El contrabando de aguardiente de caña y la política colonial*, 29.

15 "Norma Oficial Mexicana NOM-070-SCFI-1994, Bebidas alcohólicas–Mezcal–Especificaciones" (1997).

16 J. A. Vázquez-García et al., "Taxonomía del género Agave en el Occidente de México: Una panorámica preliminar," in *Los Agaves del Occidente de México*, ed. M. J. Vázquez-García et al. (Guadalajara: Universidad de, 2007), 51.

17 Carlos Lucio, "Mezcales y diversidad biocultural en los alrededores del Volcán de Colima. El caso de los productores tradicionales de Zapotitlán de Vadillo," *EntreDiversidades* 5 (2015): 15 note 2.

18 Adams, *The Wines of America*, 382.

19 "Madero," *El Informador (Guadalajara)*, August 29, 1964, Hemeroteca Nacional Digital de México, https://hndm.iib.unam.mx/consulta/publicacion/visualizar/558075be7d1e63c9fea1a303?pagina=558a381a7d1ed64f16e19cc8.

20 Navarro, "Nota o Informe al Virrey Don Matías de Gálvez, 29 de febrero de 1784." Originally in "Ramo de Aguardiente de Caña (1788–1789), tomo I, fs. 14–25v, Archivo General de la Nación, México. Reproduced in Brevajes en la colonia.—La fontana Mexicana del siglo XVIII en la mezcla de licores. Introduction by Manuel Carrera Stampa," 316.

21 Adams, *The Wines of America*, 382.

22 Morales, *Là cultura del vino en México*, 114.

23 Ibid., 49

24 Kevin P. Groark, "The Angel in the Gourd: Ritual, Therapeutic, and Protective Uses of Tobacco (Nicotiana Tabacum) among the Tzeltal and Tzotzil Maya of Chiapas, Mexico," *Journal of Ethnobiology* 30, no. 1 (2010): 14.

25 Sergio Navarrete Pellicer, *El aguardiente en una comunidad maya de los Altos de Chiapas* (Mexico City: INAH, 1988).

26 Bruman, *Alcohol in Ancient Mexico*, 57. Reprinted courtesy of the University of Utah Press.

27 "Ohuatl," *Online Nahuatl Dictionary*, 2000, https://nahuatl.wired-humanities.org/content/ohuatl.

28 Navarro, "Nota o Informe al Virrey Don Matías de Gálvez, 29 de febrero de 1784." Originally in "Ramo de Aguardiente de Caña (1788–1789), tomo I, fs. 14–25v, Archivo General de la Nación, México. Reproduced in Brevajes en la colonia.—La fontana Mexicana del siglo XVIII en la mezcla de licores. Introduction by Manuel Carrera Stampa," 317; Bruman, *Alcohol in Ancient Mexico*, 60.

29 Navarro, "Nota o Informe al Virrey Don Matías de Gálvez, 29 de febrero de 1784." Originally in "Ramo de Aguardiente de Caña (1788–1789), tomo I, fs. 14–25v, Archivo General de la Nación, México. Reproduced in Brevajes en la colonia.—La fontana Mexicana del siglo XVIII en la mezcla de licores. Introduction by Manuel Carrera Stampa," 310.

30 Gust and Mathews, *Sugarcane & Rum: The Bittersweet History of Labor and Life on the Yucatán Peninsula*, 41.

31 Ibid., 5, 37, 52.

32 Ibid., 37.

33 Reyna and Kramme, *Apuntes para la historia de la cerveza en México*, 104.

34 "Periódico Oficial del Estado de Baja California Norte," March 20, 1941, Hemeroteca Nacional Digital de México.

35 Chemín Bässler, *Recetario pame de San Luis Potosí y Querétaro*, 104.

36 Jorge Silva Riquer, *La Administracíon de Alcabalas y Pulques de Michoacán, 1776–1821*, 1 (México, D.F: Instituto Mora, 1993), 85.

37 Juan Manuel Madrid-Solórzano et al., "Life Cycle Analysis of Sotol Production in Mexico," *Frontiers in Sustainable Food Systems* 5 (2021): 2.

38 Lorenzo Alejandro López Barbosa, "El sotol en Coahuila, potencialidades y limitaciones," in *Bebidas y regiones: historia e impacto de la cultura etílica en México*, ed. Camilo Contreras Delgado and Isabel Ortega Ridaura (México, D.F: Plaza y Valde, 2005), 73.

39 Jesús Vargas, "El sotol chihuahuense, la increíble historia de una torpeza sin fin," *Cuadernos Fronterizos* 8 (2007): 27.

40 David Griffiths and Raleigh Frederick Hare, *The Tuna as Food for Man*, vol. Issue: 64 (Washington, DC: US Government Printing Office, 1907), 27, https://archive.org/details/tunaasfoodforma00haregoog.

41 Paulina Machuca Chávez, *El vino de cocos en la Nueva España: Historia de una transculturación en el siglo XVII* (Zamora, Michoacán: El Colegio de Michoacán, 2018).

42 Bruman, "Early Coconut Culture in Western Mexico."

43 Javier Luis, *The First Asians in the Americas: A Transpacific History*, 62.

44 Ibid., 221.

Chapter 6

1 Reyna and Kramme, *Apuntes para la historia de la cerveza en México*, 52.

2 Lozano Armendares, *El chinguirito vindicado: El contrabando de aguardiente de caña y la política colonial*, 29.

3 Walter A. Hoppe, Andres Medina, and Roberto J. Weitlaner, "The Popoloca," in *Ethnology*, ed. Robert Wauchope and Evon Z. Vogt (New York: University of Texas Press, 1975), 489, https://doi.org/10.7560/784192-025.

4 Martha Patricia Olivas Sánchez, *Plantas medicinales del estado de Chihuahua*, vol. 1 (Ciudad Juárez: Universidad Autónoma de Ciudad Juárez, 1999), 109–10.

5 Crescencio García, "El Té Nurite," *El Diario del Hogar (Mexico City)*, July 28, 1891, Hemeroteca Nacional Digital de México, https://hndm.iib.unam.mx/consulta/resultados/visualizar/558a37377d1ed64f16d4e14b?resultado=1&tipo=pagina&intPagina=1.

6 Clementina Díaz y de Ovando, *Los cafés en México en el siglo XIX* (México: Universidad Nacional Autónoma de México, 2000), 20.

7 María Cristina Renard, *El Soconusco: Una economía cafetalera* (Mexico: Universidad Autónoma Chapingo, Dirección de Difusión Cultural, 1993), 19.

8 Jorge S. Marroquín and Xorge A. Domínguez, "Las investigaciones fitoquímicas y sus relaciones con los herbarios," *Botanical Sciences* 34 (1975): 154.

9 Bruman, *Alcohol in Ancient Mexico*, 78.

10 Ibid., 128, n. 93. Reprinted courtesy of the University of Utah Press.

11 Departamento de Salubridad Pública, "Relación de los productos comestibles, bebidas, y similares, aprobados durante los meses de diciembre de 1937 y enero y febrero del presente año," *Periódico Oficial del Estado de Baja California Norte*, October 30, 1938, LI, 30 ed., Hemeroteca Nacional Digital de México.

12 Rojas González, *Ensayos indigenistas*, 48.

13 Alejandro Tonatiuh Romero Contreras and Felipe Carlos Viesca González, "Formación del patrimonio gastronómico del Valle de Toluca, México," *CIENCIA ergo-sum* 17, no. 3 (2010): 246.

14 María De Los Angeles De Las Vilas, "La Puebla de los Ángeles y su Arte Culinario," *Artes de México*, no. 81/82 (1966): 17, http://www.jstor.org/stable/24314048. "licor de pasas estilo muscatel"

15 Madrazo Miranda and Marco Urdapilleta Muñoz, "La fiesta patronal de Xico, Veracruz. Tradición oral y festividad," *CIENCIA ergo-sum, Revista Científica Multidisciplinaria de Prospectiva* 15, no. 1 (2008): 13.

16 Francisca Aparicio Prudente, *Sazón de la cocina afromestiza de Guerrero*, 1 (México, D.F: Consejo Nacional para la Cultura y las Artes, 2007), 123.

17 David L. Lentz et al., "Psychoactive and Other Ceremonial Plants from a 2,000-Year-Old Maya Ritual Deposit at Yaxnohcah, Mexico," *Plos One* 19, no. 4 (2024): 0301497.

18 Margarita Núñez Bonifacio and Adriana Montserrat Pérez-Serrano, "Festival del Yolixpa, escenario turístico de claroscuros en Cuetzalan del Progreso, México," *RIVAR (Santiago)* 9, no. 26 (2022): 216.

19 Ibid., 216; Timothy J. Knab, *A War of Witches: A Journey into the Underworld of the Contemporary Aztecs* (New York: Routledge, 2019), 12.

Chapter 7

1 Lota M. Spell, "The Anglo-Saxon Press in Mexico, 1846–1848," *The American Historical Review* 38, no. 1 (1932): 20–31, https://doi.org/10.2307/1838062.

2 "Theater Coffee House," *The American Star (Mexico City)*, December 30, 1847, 30 ed., 3, Hemeroteca Nacional Digital de México, https://hndm.iib.unam.mx/consulta/publicacion/visualizar/558075bd7d1e63c9fea1a108?pagina=558a34187d1ed64f16a05f53.

3 "Nueva tienda de Abarrotes: Calle Melcros Num. 1," *La Sociedad*, October 3, 1866, 4, Hemeroteca Nacional Digital de México, https://hndm.iib.unam.mx/consulta/publicacion/visualizar/558075bf7d1e63c9fea1a445?pagina=558a3b017d1ed64f1701ff9d.

4 "Giuditt-Cocktail," *El Siglo Diez y Nueve (Mexico City)*, August 31, 1872, 3, Hemeroteca Nacional Digital de México, https://hndm.iib.unam.mx/consulta/publicacion/visualizar/558075bf7d1e63c9fea1a43f?pagina=558a3e2c7d1ed64f17170bb7.

5 "Hay Muertos Que No Hace Ruido," *La Revista Universal y el Cosmopolita (Mexico City)*, September 5, 1873, Hemeroteca Nacional Digital de México. Ibid., 3. "La fama que en estos últimos días ha conquistado Jorge es una fama usurpada: a Orfeo, y a nadie más, es a quien de derecho pertenece. Él fue el inventor de esa deliciosísima bebida cuyo legítimo nombre es 'Orfeo Cocktail.' Llamarla de otro modo en lo sucesivo será una punible injusticia."

6 "Los Perniciosos," *El Padre Cobos (Mexico City)*, September 4, 1873, 2, Hemeroteca Nacional Digital de México, https://hndm.iib.unam.mx/consulta/publicacion/visualizar/558075be7d1e63c9fea1a39a?pagina=558a36217d1ed64f16c31161. "Entren uds a los cafes y encontraran por donde quiera, en los rincones se entiende, a los americanos, ingleses, franceses y alemanes, enjaretindose un ponche 8tras otro ponche o un cocktail tras otro cocktail pero siempre con el pico caido."

7 "Saunterings," *The Two Republics*, October 13, 1897, 5, Hemeroteca Nacional Digital de México, https://hndm.iib.unam.mx/consulta/publicacion/visualizar/558075bf7d1e63c9fea1a473?pagina=558a364b7d1ed64f16c5d75e.

8 Desiderio Marcos, *México y los españoles* (Mexico City: Tipografía El Autómovil en México S.A, 1915), 5. "Se calcula que hay en esta Republica, de cuarente a cincuenta mil espanoles, dedicados a la agriculture, la industria, y el comercio, estando casi por completo en mano de nuestros compatriotas, los almacenes de tiendes de comestibles u bebidas, las panaderias y las casa de prestasmos."

9 Pablo Yankelevich, "Extranjeros indeseables en México (1911–1940): Una aproximación cuantitativa a la aplicación del artículo 33 constitucional," *Historia Mexicana* 54, no. 4 (2004): 720.

10 "Circular," *Periódico Oficial del Estado de Yucatán*, April 16, 1969, Hemeroteca Nacional Digital de México, https://hndm.iib.unam.mx/consulta/publicacion/visualizar/558075be7d1e63c9fea1a3d4?pagina=558a3a577d1ed64f16fc31f7.

11 "El Brandy 'Presidente' Hace la Felicidad de un Barman Mexicano, al Ganar Valioso Premio," *El Informador (Guadalajara)*, October 12, 1970, https://hndm.iib.unam.mx/consulta/publicacion/visualizar/558075be7d1e63c9fea1a303?pagina=558a38db7d1ed64f16eae54e.

12 Gust and Mathews, *Sugarcane & Rum: The Bittersweet History of Labor and Life on the Yucatán Peninsula*, 8.

13 Julio Mera Carrasco, *Entre Copy y Copa* (México: Editorial Diana S.A, 1973), 25.

14 Carlos Alberto Torreblanca Padilla, "Algunas notas en torno a los alimentos prehispánicos en el Cóporo, Ocampo, Guanajuato," *Diario de Campo* 12 (2013): 14.

15 Mera Carrasco, *Entre Copy y Copa*, 27.

16 Víctor M. Castillo Girón, Alfredo M. Coelho, and Suhey Ayala Ramírez, "Las marcas, la denominación de origen y la región de origen:¿ Qué estrategias de marketing en la globalización de la industria tequilera?," *Mercados y Negocios* 12 (2005): 31.

17 "Aviso Importante," *El Informador (Guadalajara)*, July 4, 1940, 2, Hemeroteca Nacional Digital de México, https://hndm.iib.unam.mx/consulta/publicacion/visualizar/558075be7d1e63c9fea1a303?pagina=558a34b97d1ed64f16aaa724. "Los dueños de Tiendas mercantiles, Tendejones, Restaurants, Puesto de refrescos y lugares en general donde se expende la bebida 'CHANGUIRONGO,' las serán exigidos los pagos correspondientes de permiso y contribuciones como Cantinas." © EL INFORMADOR® Todos los derechos reservados sobre las notas del periódico EL INFORMADOR a favor de UNIÓN EDITORIALISTA, S.A. DE C.V., por lo que se prohíbe su uso y/o reproducción total o parcial sin su consentimiento. ®EL

INFORMADOR es una marca registrada propiedad de UNIÓN EDITORIALISTA, S.A. DE C.V.

18 "Al Día," *El Informador (Guadalajara)*, July 5, 1940, 3, Hemeroteca Nacional Digital de México, https://hndm.iib.unam.mx/consulta/publicacion/visualizar/558075be7d1e63c9fea1a303?pagina=558a34b97d1ed64f16aaa909. "Otras drogas de una bebida yanki." © EL INFORMADOR® Todos los derechos reservados sobre las notas del periódico EL INFORMADOR a favor de UNIÓN EDITORIALISTA, S.A. DE C.V., por lo que se prohíbe su uso y/o reproducción total o parcial sin su consentimiento. ®EL INFORMADOR es una marca registrada propiedad de UNIÓN EDITORIALISTA, S.A. DE C.V.

19 Josefina Velázquez de León, *Cocktails* (Mexico City: Ediciones Josefina Velázquez de León, 1950), 24.

20 "Literatura: Reeleccionista," *El Continente Americano*, November 29, 1899, 232 ed., https://hndm.iib.unam.mx/consulta/publicacion/visualizar/558075be7d1e63c9fea1a1c1?pagina=558a35e87d1ed64f16bf7171.

21 Ignacio Trejo Fuentes, *La Fiesta y La Muerte Enmascarada: El Distrito Federal de Noche* (México, D.F: Colibrí, 1999), 24–5. "Lo distintivo de las cantinas es la botana espléndida que sirve principalmente en el día y aun en las noches por un par de cervezas uno puede comer igual o todavía mejor que en su propia casa. (Hace un par de décadas, cuando la cantina era espacio exclusivo de hombres, cuando estaba prohibida la entrada a las mujeres y las que entraba eran tan solo de una clase: las prostitutas; en ese tiempo, decía, la cantina era el rival más peligroso de las novias y las amas de casa: no podían comprender qué diablos había detrás esas puertas que sus hombres corrían hacia ellas a la menor provocación, no se explicaban cuál era el gancho mágico. Y es que ignoraban las delicias de la privacidad, el espacio macho y la bondad maravillosa de las botanas.)"

Chapter 8

1 Hamnett, *A Concise History of Mexico*, 27.

2 Pomar and Zurita, "Pomar, Relación de Tezcoco; Zurita, Breve Relación de los Señores de la Nueva España," 14. "en él había de todas semillas de la que usan y se mantienen los naturales, como era maíz blanco, negro, colorado y amarillo, y fríjoles muchos géneros y colores, chía, huauhtli y michhuautli, y ají de todas las suertes que podían haber los que lo tenían a cargo, renovándole cada año a cierto tiempo."

3 Juan de Viera, *Breve y compendiosa narración de la Ciudad de México*, 1778, 17, https://gallica.bnf.fr/ark:/12148/btv1b100329980/f1.item. "Tambien hai otra Calle donde estan las Tamaleras, que venden sus Tamales, que son compuestos de maiz cofido y molido con sal y manteca, y algunos rellenos de carne de erdo y pimiento molido, ordos de dulce, de camaron y Pezcado, y eftas mifmas venden el Atole, que es una especie de mais molido, y colado, y hecho ael modo dela Poleada, que queda mas blanco que la Almenda molida, y es el regular desayuno dela Gente pobre, y desvalida."

4 Francisco Javier Clavijero, *Historia antigua de México: Sacada de los mejores historiadores españoles, y de los manuscritos y de las pinturas antiguas de los indios: Dividida en diez libros . . . e ilustrada con disertaciones sobre la tierra, los animales y los habitantes*, trans. Joaquin de Mora (Mexico: Departamento Editorial de la Dirección General de Bellas Artes, 1917), 436, https://archive.org/details/historiaantiguadem01clav/page/n7/mode/2up. "El atolli es una especie de poleadas, que se hace con la masa del maíz bien molida, cocida, desleída en agua y colada. Ponen al fuego el líquido, después de esta última operación, y lo cuecen hasta darle la consistencia necesaria. Es insípido al paladar de los españoles; pero lo usan en sus enfermedades, endulzándolo con azúcar, en lugar de miel que los indios emplean. Para éstos es manjar tan grato, que no pueden vivir sin él."

5 Hamnett, *A Concise History of Mexico*, 62–3.

6 Clavijero, *Historia antigua de México: Sacada de los mejores historiadores españoles, y de los manuscritos y de las pinturas antiguas de los indios: Dividida en diez libros . . . e ilustrada con disertaciones sobre la tierra, los animales y los habitantes*, 436.

7 Danièle Dehouve, "Simbolismo de las técnicas de preparación del maíz. Análisis de unos platillos tlapanecos (me'phaa) del estado de Guerrero (México)," *Itinerarios* 29 (2019): 101.

8 Ricardo Ávila, Martín Tena, and Peter Hubbard, "Lime as the Key Element: A 'Non-Food' in Food for Subsistence," in *Consuming the Inedible: Neglected Dimensions of Food Choice*, ed. Jeremy MacClancy, Jeya Henry, and Helen Macbeth, vol. 6 (New York: Berghahn Books, 2009), 114.

9 Dehouve, "Simbolismo de las técnicas de preparación del maíz. Análisis de unos platillos tlapanecos (me'phaa) del estado de Guerrero (México)," 101.

10 Ibid.

11 Ibid., 102.

12 Dehouve, "Simbolismo de las técnicas de preparación del maíz. Análisis de unos platillos tlapanecos (me'phaa) del estado de Guerrero (México)."

13 Rosa Román Lagunas, *Los atoles de Acapetlahuaya: Comidas y bebidas tradicionales* (Mexico City: Consejo Nacional para la Cultura y las Artes, Dirección General de Culturas Populares, 1991), 17.

14 Héctor Uvence Navarro, "Universo culinario: El atole, elixir de buenaventura en la vida," *El Informador (Guadalajara)*, February 28, 1999, Hemeroteca Nacional Digital

de México, https://hndm.iib.unam.mx/consulta/publicacion/visualizar/558075be7d1e63c9fea1a303?pagina=558a3cfb7d1ed64f17104584.

15 Miguel Iwadare, *La cocina indígena de Huehuetlán: Tsubidhomtalab K'al an K'apnel ti tam ajab* (Mexico City: Secretaría de Cultura, 2015).

16 Román Lagunas, *Los atoles de Acapetlahuaya: Comidas y bebidas tradicionales*, 25 and 29.

17 Rosa Yocupicio Buitimea, *Recetario indígena de Sonora: Mayo y Yaqui*, ed. María Trinidad Ruiz Ruiz, trans. Salustriano Matuz González and Ismael Castillo Rendón, Cocina Indígena y Popular 9 (Mexico City: Consejo, 2000), 16–22.

18 Chemín Bässler, *Recetario pame de San Luis Potosí y Querétaro*, 112.

19 José Corona Núñez, "Religiones indígenas y cristianismo," *Historia mexicana* 10, no. 4 (1961): 567.

20 René Crocker-Sagástume, J. L. Vázquez-Castellanos, and V. G. García-Serrano, "La identidad etnocultural en la formación de multiplicadores en salud y nutrición maternoinfantil con el pueblo wixárika," *Revista Española de Nutrición Comunitaria* 16, no. 2 (2010): 110.

21 Lozano Armendares, *El chinguirito vindicado: El contrabando de aguardiente de caña y la política colonial*, 23. "se ponía maíz al fuego hasta que reventaba y entonces se molía en metate y se dejaba acedar con agua hasta tres o cuatro días."

22 Dehouve, "Simbolismo de las técnicas de preparación del maíz. Análisis de unos platillos tlapanecos (me'phaa) del estado de Guerrero (México)," 103.

23 Maria Silva Sanchez Cortes et al., "El atole agrio: su presencia y modo de preparación en la cultura alimentaria de Chiapas," *El Maíz: conocimiento de su patrimonio gastronómico y cultural*, 2019, 94, https://hdl.handle.net/20.500.12753/1498.

24 Iwadare, *La cocina indígena de Huehuetlán: Tsubidhomtalab K'al an K'apnel ti tam ajab*.

25 Sisto Alberto Padilla, *Diccionario botánico y portátil de las tres Américas: tomo tercero*, vol. 3 (Ahuachapan, El Salvador: El Porvenir, 1923), 564, https://www.biodiversitylibrary.org/page/55221022#page/8/mode/1up.

26 Pomar and Zurita, "Pomar, Relación de Tezcoco; Zurita, Breve Relación de los Señores de la Nueva España," 63. "Tienen michhuauhtli, que es otra semilla blanca y más menuda: de esta hacen bollos por la propia orden que se ha dicho del huahutli, y de este suelen beber después de tostada y molida y deshecha en agua miel."

27 Liliana Martínez-López et al., "Conocimiento práctico y teórico de maíz y frijol en la región triqui Alta, Oaxaca," *Revista mexicana de ciencias agrícolas* 9, no. 1 (2018): 116.

28 "Imp. y Lit. del Gobierno en la Escuela de Artes, a cargo de José Rosario Bravo," *Anales del Museo Michoacano*, January 1, 1888, https://hndm.iib.unam.mx/consulta

/publicacion/visualizar/558a32d97d1ed64f168be6b8?intPagina=103&tipo=pagina&anio=1888&mes=01&dia=01&butIr=Ir. "Maiz cocido convenientemente para hacer tortillas . . . Dase tambien esta nombre a una bebida de mayz cocido."

29 Chemín Bässler, *Recetario pame de San Luis Potosí y Querétaro*, 119.

30 Alba González Jácome and Laura Reyes Montes, "El conocimiento agrícola tradicional, la milpa y la alimentación: el caso del Valle de Ixtlahuaca, Estado de México," *Revista de Geografía Agrícola* 52 (2014): 30.

31 María Guadalupe Sánchez Dirzo et al., "Estudio Preliminar Del Axokot, Bebida Tradicional Fermentada, Bajo Una Perspectiva Transdisciplinaria," *Investigación Universitaria Multidisciplinaria: Revista de Investigación de La Universidad Simón Bolívar* 9, no. 9 (2010): 116.

32 Ibid., 114.

33 Howard S. Reed, "An Account of Sixteenth-Century Agriculture on the Mexican Plateau," *Journal of the Washington Academy of Sciences* 34, no. 7 (1944): 210.

34 Mercedes de la Garza, *Sueño y alucinación en el mundo nahuatl y maya*, 1st ed. (México: Instituto de Investigaciones Filológicas, Centro de Estudios Mayas, UNAM, 1990), 81.

35 Ana Laura Gómez Pérez and Erin Ingrid Jane Estrada Lugo, "Alimentación cotidiana y especial en la comunidad de Pathuitz, Municipio de Chilón, Chiapas" (PhD diss., El Colegio de la Frontera Sur, 2017), 74.

36 Ronquillo Arvizu, "La centralidad del kórima entre los rarámuri. Un recorrido de su tratamiento teórico etnográfico," *Diario de Campo* 2 (n.d.): 83, https://mediateca.inah.gob.mx/repositorio/islandora/object/articulo%3A17847.

37 Pedro Luna Jiménez, *Nayarit: tres recorridos gastronómicos: y algunos secretos del fogón* (Tepic: Universidad Autónoma de Nayarit, 2004), 138.

38 Buenrostro, "¿Cuáles bebidas se pueden preparar con maíz?," 91.

39 Julio César Javier Quero, *Bebidas y dulces tradicionales de Tabasco*, vol. 23, Cuadernos Antropológicos (Mexico City: CONACULTA, 2000), 49, https://issuu.com/editorialolmeca/docs/bebidas_y_dulces_tradicionales_de_tabasco.

40 Alicia Inés Bernard Menna and Maribel Lozano Cortés, "Las bebidas sagradas mayas: el balché y el saká," *Sincronía* 28 (2003): 5.

41 Lucio Alberto Pat Fernández et al., "Condición y perspectivas de la meliponicultura en comunidades mayas de la reserva de la biósfera Los Petenes, Campeche, México," *Estudios de cultura maya* 52 (2018): 240.

42 Moreno-Mata, "Análisis discursivo del relato popular Haciendo tejuino, tradicional en la lengua y en la cultura wixárika."

43 Mara Ximena Haro-Luna, Felipe Ruan-Soto, and Laura Guzmán-Dávalos, "Traditional Knowledge, Uses, and Perceptions of Mushrooms among the Wixaritari and Mestizos of Villa Guerrero, Jalisco, Mexico," *IMA Fungus* 10, no. 1 (2019): 7.

Chapter 9

1 Hamnett, *A Concise History of Mexico*, 53.

2 Don Fernando de Alva Ixtlilxóchitl et al., *History of the Chichimeca Nation: Don Fernando de Alva Ixtlilxóchitl's Seventeenth-Century Chronicle of Ancient Mexico* (Norman: University of Oklahoma Press, 2019), 262.

3 Claire Lanaud et al., "A Revisited History of Cacao Domestication in Pre-Columbian Times Revealed by Archaeogenomic Approaches," *Scientific Reports* 14, no. 1 (2024): 2.

4 John S. Henderson et al., "Chemical and Archaeological Evidence for the Earliest Cacao Beverages," *Proceedings of the National Academy of Sciences* 104, no. 48 (2007): 158.

5 Terrence Kaufman and John Justeson, "The History of the Word for Cacao in Ancient Mesoamerica," *Ancient Mesoamerica* 18, no. 2 (2007): 199.

6 Simon Martin, "Cacao in Ancient Maya Religion: First Fruit from the Maize Tree and Other Tales from the Underworld," in *Chocolate in Mesoamerica: A Cultural History of Cacao*, ed. Cameron L. McNeil (Gainesville: University Press of Florida, 2006), 170.

7 Kaufman and Justeson, "The History of the Word for Cacao in Ancient Mesoamerica," 194.

8 Johanna Kufer and Cameron L. Mcneil, "The Jaguar Tree (Theobroma Bicolor Bonpl.)," in *Chocolate in Mesoamerica: A Cultural History of Cacao* (University Press of Florida, 2006), 94, https://doi.org/10.5744/florida/9780813029535.003.0004.

9 de Alva Ixtlilxóchitl et al., *History of the Chichimeca Nation: Don Fernando de Alva Ixtlilxóchitl's Seventeenth-Century Chronicle of Ancient Mexico*, 148.

10 Bernardino de Sahagún, "'Book 6: Rhetoric and Moral Philosophy,' Fol. 211v, Sahagún, Bernardino de. Florentine Codex: General History of the Things of New Spain. Transcribed and Translated with Notes by Arthur J. O. Anderson and Charles E. Dibble. 2nd rev. ed. Santa Fe: School of American Research / University of Utah Press, 1950–82" (Los Angeles, 2023), fol. 211v, © J. Paul Getty Trust, https://florentinecodex.getty.edu/book/6/folio/211v.

11 John F. Bergmann, "The Distribution of Cacao Cultivation in Pre-Columbian America," *Annals of the Association of American Geographers* 59, no. 1 (1969): 87.

12 Henry Bruman, "The Culture History of Mexican Vanilla," *The Hispanic American Historical Review* 28, no. 3 (1948): 365.

13 Javier Quero, *Bebidas y dulces tradicionales de Tabasco*, 23:46.

14 Henderson et al., "Chemical and Archaeological Evidence for the Earliest Cacao Beverages."

15 Girolamo Benzoni, *History of the New World*, trans. Rear-Admiral W. H. Smyth (London: Printed for the Hakluyt Society, 1857), 149–50, https://archive.org/details/historynewworld00smytgoog/page/n12/mode/2up.

16 Clavijero, *Historia antigua de México: Sacada de los mejores historiadores españoles, y de los manuscritos y de las pinturas antiguas de los indios: Dividida en diez libros . . . e ilustrada con disertaciones sobre la tierra, los animales y los habitantes*, 437.

17 María de Lourdes Escamilla-Hurtado and María Guadalupe Escamilla-Hurtado, "Los alimentos fermentados que comían nuestros bisabuelos prehispánicos," *Ciencia: Revista de la Academia Mexicana de Ciencias* 58, no. 2 (June 2007): 83.

18 Dmitri Beliaev, Albert Davletshin, and Alexandre Tokovinine, "Sweet Cacao and Sour Atole: Mixed Drinks on Classic Maya Ceramic Vases," in *Pre-Columbian Foodways: Interdisciplinary Approaches to Food, Culture, and Markets in Ancient Mesoamerica* (New York: Springer, 2009), 262.

19 Meredith L. Dreiss and Sharon Greenhill, *Chocolate: Pathway to the Gods*, 1st ed. (Tucson: University of Arizona Press, 2008), 141.

20 Javier Luis, *The First Asians in the Americas: A Transpacific History*, 86.

21 Kaufman and Justeson, "The History of the Word for Cacao in Ancient Mesoamerica," 219.

22 Kathryn E. Sampeck and Jonathan Thayn, "Translating Tastes: A Cartography of Chocolate Colonialism," in *Substance and Seduction: Ingested Commodities in Early Modern Mesoamerica*, ed. Stacey Schwartzkopf and Kathryn E. Sampeck, n.d., 78. University of Texas Press, 2017. *Project MUSE*, https://muse.jhu.edu/book/126289.

23 Gustavo A. Enríquez, *Curso sobre el cultivo del cacao* (Bib. Orton IICA/CATIE, 1985), 9.

24 Hamnett, *A Concise History of Mexico*, 83.

25 *Cuatro Bebidas Típicas Nicaragüenses* (Managua: Banco Central de Nicaragua, 1997).

26 Julián Pérez-Flores et al., "Bebidas prehispánicas y novohispánicas de cacao y maíz en la Chontalpa, Tabasco," *Agro Productividad* 13, no. 7 (2020): 5.

27 Martin, "Cacao in Ancient Maya Religion: First Fruit from the Maize Tree and Other Tales from the Underworld," 176.

28 Beliaev, Davletshin, and Tokovinine, "Sweet Cacao and Sour Atole: Mixed Drinks on Classic Maya Ceramic Vases," 257.

29 Dreiss and Greenhill, *Chocolate: Pathway to the Gods*, 58.

30 Pérez-Flores et al., "Bebidas prehispánicas y novohispánicas de cacao y maíz en la Chontalpa, Tabasco," 5.

31 Lesterloon Sánchez Trinidad, *Las flores en la cocina veracruzana* (México: Secretaría de Cultura, Dirección General de Culturas Populares, Indígenas y Urbanas, 2017), 233–4.

32 Kufer and Mcneil, "The Jaguar Tree (Theobroma Bicolor Bonpl.)," 94.

33 Cristina Barros and Marco Buenrostro, "Pozol, popo, champurrado," *Revista Digital Universitaria* 12, no. 4 (2011): 6, https://revista.unam.mx/vol.12/num4/art41/art41.pdf.

34 Luis Alberto Vargas et al., "Bebidas de la tradición," in *Beber de tierra generosa: Historia de las bebidas alcohólicas en México*, vol. 1 (Mexico City: FISAC, 1998), 194.

35 Ibid., 195.

36 Javier Quero, *Bebidas y dulces tradicionales de Tabasco*, 23:40.

37 "Revista de Los Estados: Tabasco," *El Siglo Diez y Nueve (Mexico City)*, October 3, 1868, Hemeroteca Nacional Digital de México, https://hndm.iib.unam.mx/consulta/publicacion/visualizar/558075bf7d1e63c9fea1a43f?pagina=558a3e1b7d1ed64f1716ae71. "El chorote o tlascalote es una horchata de maíz bien recocido, quebrado con un poco de cacao del país, acompañándole una cantidad corta de polvos de la nuez tostada del zapote colorado, o de la canela."

38 "The Cacao of Mexico," *The Two Republics*, August 31, 1895, XLI no 53 ed., Hemeroteca Nacional Digital de México, https://hndm.iib.unam.mx/consulta/publicacion/visualizar/558075bf7d1e63c9fea1a473?pagina=558a36277d1ed64f16c37412.

39 Javier Quero, *Bebidas y dulces tradicionales de Tabasco*, 23:39.

40 Dora Centurión-Hidalgo et al., "Comidas y bebidas en celebraciones y ritos como rasgo de identidad cultural tabasqueña," *Estudios sociales. Revista de alimentación contemporánea y desarrollo regional* 31, no. 57 (2021), 12.

41 Jorge Mejía Prieto, *Así habla el mexicano: diccionario básico de mexicanismos*. 11th reimpresión (Mexico City: Panorama Editorial, S.A, 2002), 59.

42 Javier Quero, *Bebidas y dulces tradicionales de Tabasco*, 23:56.

43 Barros and Buenrostro, "Pozol, popo, champurrado," 7.

44 Verónica Gómez Martínez, "Bebidas del cacao," *Artes de México*, no. 103 (2011): 63, http://www.jstor.org/stable/24318967.

45 Maite Lascurain-Rangel et al., "Plantas americanas utilizadas como condimento en la cocina mexicana," *Revista Mexicana de Biodiversidad* 93 (2022): 28.

46 Gómez Martínez, "Bebidas del cacao," 63.

47 Javier Quero, *Bebidas y dulces tradicionales de Tabasco*, 23:58.

48 Daniela Soleri and David A. Cleveland, "Tejate: Theobroma Cacao and T. Bicolor in a Traditional Beverage from Oaxaca, Mexico," *Food and Foodways* 15, no. 1 (2007): 112, https://doi.org/10.1080/07409710701260131.

49 Marcy Norton, "Foreword," in *Substance and Seduction: Ingested Commodities in Early Modern Mesoamerica*, ed. Stacey Schwartzkopf and Kathryn E. Sampeck (Austin: University of Texas Press, 2017), viii.

50 Soleri and Cleveland, "Tejate: Theobroma Cacao and T. Bicolor in a Traditional Beverage from Oaxaca, Mexico," 112.

51 Javier Quero, *Bebidas y dulces tradicionales de Tabasco*, 23:42.

52 Elena Marini, *Espuma: Bebidas de cacao de Oaxaca. Photo series*, n.d., Centro Cultural San Pablo.

53 Kufer and Mcneil, "The Jaguar Tree (Theobroma Bicolor Bonpl.)," 102.

54 Bernardino de Sahagún et al., *General History of the Things of New Spain: Books 1–11*, ed. Kim N. Richter et al., trans. León García Garagarza, vol. bk. 8, fol. 25r. (Los Angeles: Getty Research Institute, 2023).

Chapter 10

1 Adriano Otero Arnaiz, *Coffee Annual: Mexico*, GAIN Report (Mexico City: US Department of Agriculture, Foreign Agricultural Service, May 12, 2024), https://apps.fas.usda.gov/newgainapi/api/Report/DownloadReportByFileName?fileName=Coffee%20Annual_Mexico%20City_Mexico_MX2024-0025.pdf.

2 Díaz y de Ovando, *Los cafés en México en el siglo XIX*, 7.

3 Novo, *Cocina mexicana, o, Historia gastronómica de la ciudad de México*, 84.

4 Mabel M. Rodríguez Centeno, "Fiscalidad y café mexicano: El porfiriato y sus estrategias de fomento económico para la producción y comercialización del grano (1870–1910)," *Historia Mexicana* vol. 54, no. 1, 2004, pp. 93–128.

5 Renard, *El Soconusco: Una economía cafetalera*, 17–18.

6 Ibid., 16.

7 Ibid., 18.

8 Ibid.

9 Ana Johari Mejía, "Las casas prefabricadas de las fincas cafetaleras del Soconusco, México," *LIÑO: Revista Anual de Historia del Arte* 25 (2019): 133.

10 Gonzalo Piñón Jiménez and Jorge Hernández Díaz, *El café: crisis y organización: los pequeños productores en Oaxaca* (Oaxaca: Instituto de Investigaciones Sociológicas, Universidad Autónoma "Benito Juárez" de Oaxaca, 1998), 67.

11 Ibid.

12 Pablo Pérez Akaki, "Los siglos XIX y XX en la cafeticultura nacional: de la bonanza a la crisis del grano de oro mexicano," *Revista de Historia* 67 (2013): 172.

13 Rodríguez Centeno, "Fiscalidad y café mexicano: El porfiriato y sus estrategias de fomento económico para la producción y comercialización del grano (1870–1910)," 101.

14 Matías Romero, *Cultivo del café en la Costa Meridional de Chiapas*, 4th ed. (Mexico: Oficina TIP de la Secretaría de Fomento, 1893), 9. "hace pocos años que apenas se tomaba el café en la República, mientras que ahora empieza á competir con el cacao y hasta con el maíz."

15 Robert J. Weitlaner, "Sobre la alimentación chinanteca," in *Anales del Instituto Nacional de Antropologia e Historia, 6(5). Instituto Nacional de Antropología e Historia, Secretaría de Educación Pública*, 1952, 177–195.

16 Novo, *Cocina mexicana, o, Historia gastronómica de la ciudad de México*, 154.

17 Ibid., 338.

18 Piñón Jiménez and Hernández Díaz, *El café: crisis y organización: los pequeños productores en Oaxaca*, xvii.

19 Robert M. Porter, *The Coffee Farmers Revolt in Southern Mexico in the 1980s and 1990s* (Lewiston: Edwin Mellen Press, 2002), 87.

20 Otero Arnaiz, *Coffee Annual: Mexico*, 5.

21 Ibid., 4.

22 "Datos Importantes Del Café," *Instituto Del Café de Chiapas*, n.d., https://incafech.gob.mx/assets/media/documentos/Datos%20cafe.pdf.

23 Otero Arnaiz, *Coffee Annual: Mexico*, 6.

Chapter 11

1 Universidad Nacional Autónoma México, "México, primer consumidor de refrescos en el mundo," *Boletín UNAM-DGCS-757*, October 26, 2019, https://www.dgcs.unam.mx/boletin/bdboletin/2019_757.html.

2 Page Pliego, "Sweet Extermination: Soda and Beer, as Trigger Cause and Complications in Diabetics, among High Land Mayans of Chiapas, Mexico," 80.

3 México, "México, primer consumidor de refrescos en el mundo."

4 Ehécatl Cabrera, "El alto consumo de refrescos en México es resultado del entramado de procesos económicos, políticos y culturales," October 24, 2019, https://www.iis.unam.mx/blog/el-alto-consumo-de-refrescos-en-mexico-es-resultado-del-entramado-de-procesos-economicos-politicos-y-culturales/.

5 México, "México, primer consumidor de refrescos en el mundo."

6 María Luisa González Marín, *Producción de refrescos, tecnología y trabajo. Cuaderno de Investigación 5706*, 1989, 27, https://ru.iiec.unam.mx/5706/1/cuarderno_investigaci%C3%B3n.pdf.

7 Ibid.

8 César Meza Camacho, "Investigación del mercado de la industria refresquera en México y sus factores de éxito." (Maestría en Administración de Empresas con Especialidad en Mercadotecnia, Universidad Autónoma de Nuevo León, 2002), 26, https://cdigital.dgb.uanl.mx/te/1020148191.PDF.

9 Tania Alemán Saavedra, "Chaparritas, el refresco de nuestra infancia," *México Desconocido*, February 27, 2020, https://www.mexicodesconocido.com.mx/chaparritas-el-refresco-de-nuestra-infancia.html.

10 González Marín, *Producción de refrescos, tecnología y trabajo. Cuaderno de Investigación 5706*, 6.

11 "Advertisement," *The Mexican Herald*, April 30, 1908, http://hndm.iib.unam.mx/consulta/publicacion/visualizar/558075be7d1e63c9fea1a34d?pagina=558a34847d1ed64f16a6d3e0.

12 "Monterrey Sonríe," *El Porvenir*, April 12, 1920, Hemeroteca Nacional Digital de México, https://hndm.iib.unam.mx/consulta/publicacion/visualizar/558075be7d1e63c9fea1a3e7?pagina=558a32af7d1ed64f168915ea; "Ventas," *El Informador (Guadalajara)*, September 23, 1928, sec. SECOND, https://hndm.iib.unam.mx/consulta/publicacion/visualizar/558075be7d1e63c9fea1a303?pagina=558a33b97d1ed64f169a32eb.

13 "Familia Fleishman, Cuatro Generaciones Engrandeciendo Nuestro País," *Dentral de Noticias Diario Judío*, June 21, 2012, https://diariojudio.com/comunidad-judia-mexico/familia-fleishman-cuatro-generaciones-engrandeciendo-nuestro-pais/8837/.

14 María del Pilar Zazueta, "De Coca-Cola a Vampi-Cola: políticas, negocios, y el consumo de refrescos y azúcar en México (1971–1982)," *Apuntes de Investigación del CECYP* 22 (2012): 36.

15 Ibid., 37.

16 Peter Singelmann, "La transformación política de México y los gremios cañeros del PRI," *Revista mexicana de sociología* 65, no. 1 (2003): 118.

17 Ibid., 121.

18 Porter, *The Coffee Farmers Revolt in Southern Mexico in the 1980s and 1990s*, 34.

19 Singelmann, "La transformación política de México y los gremios cañeros del PRI," 126.

20 Yocupicio Buitimea, *Recetario indígena de Sonora: Mayo y Yaqui*, 39.

21 Anne Plotto, "HIBISCUS: Post-Production Management for Improved Market Access," ed. François Mazaud, Alexandra Röttger, and Katja Steffel, *Post-Harvest Compendium*, 2004, 13, https://www.fao.org/fileadmin/user_upload/inpho/docs/Post_Harvest_Compendium_-_Hibiscus.pdf.

22 Oscar Montaño Arango et al., "Evaluación del nivel competitivo de un desinfectante de alimentos desarrollado a partir de cálices de flor de Jamaica," *Revista CEA* 9, no. 19 (2023): 10.

23 Rafael Ariza-Flores et al., "Variedades mexicanas de jamaica (Hibiscus sabdariffa L.) Alma Blanca y Rosalíz de color claro, y Cotzaltzin y Tecoanapa de color rojo," *Revista fitotecnia mexicana* 37, no. 2 (2014): 181.

Chapter 12

1 Lola Bahena, "Tés e infusiones: bebidas que se han adaptado al gusto de México," February 23, 2024, https://thefoodtech.com/tendencias-de-consumo/el-te-una-bebida-que-se-ha-adaptado-al-gusto-de-mexico/.

2 Casimiro Gómez Ortega, "Prólogo de Don Casimiro Gómez Ortega, Profesor de Botánica, a Las Obras Del Dr. Francisco Hernández," in *Historia de Las Plantas de Nueva España, by Francisco Hernández, Vol. 1, Libros 1 y 2* (Imprenta Universitaria, UNAM, Instituto de Biología, bajo la dirección del Dr. Isaac Ochoterena, 1942), xiii.

3 Hernández Palomo, *La renta del pulque en Nueva España: 1663–1810*, 11. "los indios sanaban mejor con sus hierbas «que con medicamentos de botica que los matan."

4 Irigoyen-Rascón and Paredes, *Tarahumara Medicine: Ethnobotany and Healing among the Rarámuri of Mexico*, 4.

5 Leonardo Beltrán-Rodríguez, Ignacio García-Madrid, and Alfredo Saynes-Vásquez, "Apropiación cultural de una planta europea en la herbolaria tradicional mexicana: el caso del Ajenjo (Artemisia absinthium L. Asteraceae)," *Etnobiología* 15, no. 2 (2017): 50.

6 Francisco Alberto Basurto Peña et al., "Uso actual de las plantas del Libellus de Medicinalibus Indorum Herbis o Códice de la Cruz-Badiano en México," *Anales del Jardín Botánico de Madrid* 80, no. 1 (2023): fig. 2.

7 Edelmira Linares Mazari, *Tés curativos de México*, 1a ed. (FONART, 1984), 38 and 66.

8 de Benavente Motolinía, *Historia de los indios de la Nueva España: Escrita a mediados del siglo XVI*, 250. "Todas las medicinas que se han de beber se dan a los enfermos con este vino; puesto en su taza o copa echan sobre el la medicina que aplican para la cura y salud del enfermo."

9 Joan Bristol, "Health Food and Diabolic Vice: Pulque Discourse in New Spain," in *Substance and Seduction: Ingested Commodities in Early Modern Mesoamerica* (Austin: University of Texas Press, 2017), 131.

10 Feliciano León-Payán, "Medicina precortesiana," *Boletín Clínico Hospital Infantil del Estado de Sonora* 22, no. 1 (2005): 37.

11 Basurto Peña et al., "Uso actual de las plantas del Libellus de Medicinalibus Indorum Herbis o Códice de la Cruz-Badiano en México," 3.

12 León-Payán, "Medicina precortesiana," 35.

13 Armando Enrique González-Stuart, "Use of medicinal plants in Monterrey, Mexico," *Notulae Scientia Biologicae* 2, no. 4 (2010): 7.

14 Jenaro Reyes-Matamoros, J. G. Fuentes-López David Martínez-Moreno, and F. Basurto-Peña, "Importancia relativa de las especies medicinales ofertadas en el mercado de Tepeaca, Puebla, México," *Polibotánica* 54 (2022): 271–89.

15 S. Laura Guzmán Gutiérrez, Ricardo Reyes Chilpa, and Herlinda Bonilla Jaime, "Medicinal Plants for the Treatment of 'Nervios,' Anxiety, and Depression in Mexican Traditional Medicine," *Revista Brasileira de Farmacognosia* 24, no. 5 (2014): 591–608.

16 Javier Lozoya, Abigail Aguilar, and Juan Raul Camacho, "Encuesta sobre el uso actual de plantas en la medicina tradicional mexicana," *Revista Médica del IMSS*, 1987, 289.

17 Rosita Arvigo, Nadine Epstein, and Marilyn Yaquinto, *Sastun: My Apprenticeship with a Maya Healer*, 1st ed. (San Francisco: HarperSanFrancisco, 1995), 17.

18 Leis G. Iza, "Origen de Algunas Palabras," *La Patria (Mexico City)*, May 29, 1891, Hemeroteca Nacional Digital de México, https://www.hndm.unam.mx.

19 Varro E. Tyler, "DAMIANA—History of a Herbal Hoax," *Pharmacy in History* 25, no. 2 (1983): 55, http://www.jstor.org/stable/41109400.

20 Eliseo Torres and Timothy L. Sawyer, *Healing with Herbs and Rituals: A Mexican Tradition*, 1st ed. (Albuquerque, New Mexico: University of New Mexico Press, 2006), 141.

21 Domingo Asencio, *Tes Curativos Mexicanos: Recetario de Herbolaria para la Salud* (Mexico City: Selector, S.A. de C.V., 1995), 19.

22 Bernardo Ortiz de Montellano, "Las Hierbas de Tláloc," *Estudios de Cultura Náhuatl* 14 (November 1980): 287–314, https://nahuatl.historicas.unam.mx/index.php/ecn/article/view/78429.

23 Linares Mazari, *Tés curativos de México*, 34.

24 Guzmán Gutiérrez, Chilpa, and Jaime, "Medicinal Plants for the Treatment of 'Nervios,' Anxiety, and Depression in Mexican Traditional Medicine," 603.

25 Ricardo A. Villatoro Vera, Lorena Luna Cazares, and Alma Rosa Gonzales Esquincas, "El Cuaulote, Recurso Herbolario de Chiapas," *Ciencias* 0, no. 083 (October 5, 2009): 21, https://www.revistas.unam.mx/index.php/cns/article/view/12063.

26 David J. Goldstein and Jon B. Hageman, "Power Plants: Paleobotanical Evidence of Rural Feasting in Late Classic Belize," in *Pre-Columbian Foodways: Interdisciplinary Approaches to Food, Culture, and Markets in Ancient Mesoamerica*, ed. J. E. Staller and M. D. Carrasco (New York: Springer, 2009), 429, https://doi.org/10.1007/978-1-4419-0471-3_17.

27 Villatoro Vera, Luna Cazares, and Gonzales Esquincas, "El Cuaulote, Recurso Herbolario de Chiapas," 23.

28 Genoveva R. Ocampo Rosales, "Medicinal Uses of Melipona Beecheii Honey, by the Ancient Maya," in *Pot-Honey: A Legacy of Stingless Bees*, ed. Patricia Vit, Silvia R. M. Pedro, and David Roubik (New York: Springer New York, 2013), 236, https://doi.org/10.1007/978-1-4614-4960-7_15.

29 Arvigo, Epstein, and Yaquinto, *Sastun: My Apprenticeship with a Maya Healer*, 189.

30 Angélica de Gante, "San Matías Cuijingo es un importante productor de manzanilla," *Quadratin Edomex*, March 26, 2014, https://edomex.quadratin.com.mx/San-Matias-Cuijingo-es-un-importante-productor-de-manzanilla/.

31 Linares Mazari, *Tés curativos de México*, 40.

32 Lozoya, Aguilar, and Camacho, "Encuesta sobre el uso actual de plantas en la medicina tradicional mexicana," 287.

33 Arvigo, Epstein, and Yaquinto, *Sastun: My Apprenticeship with a Maya Healer*, 187.

34 Lascurain-Rangel et al., “Plantas americanas utilizadas como condimento en la cocina mexicana,” 29.

35 Linares Mazari, *Tés curativos de México*, 56; Ortiz de Montellano, “Las Hierbas de Tláloc,” 289.

36 Ortiz de Montellano, “Las Hierbas de Tláloc,” 306–7.

37 Ofelia Romero-Cerecero et al., “Use of Medicinal Plants among Patients with Diabetes Mellitus Type 2 in Morelos, Mexico,” *Boletín Latinoamericano y del Caribe de Plantas Medicinales y Aromáticas* 8, no. 5 (2009): 382.

38 García, “El Té Nurite.”

39 Guzmán Gutiérrez, Chilpa, and Jaime, “Medicinal Plants for the Treatment of ‘Nervios,’ Anxiety, and Depression in Mexican Traditional Medicine,” fig. 1.

Chapter 13

1 Richard Evans Schultes, “Iconography of New World Plant Hallucinogens,” *Arnoldia* 41, no. 3 (1981): 81.

2 Ibid., 103.

3 Nesvig, “Sandcastles of the Mind: Hallucinogens and Cultural Memory,” 30; Richard Evans Schultes, “The Plant Kingdom and Hallucinogens (Part III),” *Bulletin on Narcotics* 22, no. 1 (1970): 25–53.

4 Bernardino de Sahagún, “‘Book 6: Rhetoric and Moral Philosophy,’ Fol. 212r, Sahagún, Bernardino de. Florentine Codex: General History of the Things of New Spain. Transcribed and Translated with Notes by Arthur J. O. Anderson and Charles E. Dibble. 2nd Rev. Ed. Santa Fe, NM: School of American Research / University of Utah Press, 1950–82” (Los Angeles, 2023), fols. 211r&212r, © J. Paul Getty Trust, https://florentinecodex.getty.edu/en/book/6/folio/212r.

5 Bruman, *Alcohol in Ancient Mexico*, 105. Reprinted courtesy of the University of Utah Press.

6 Ibid., 106.

7 de la Garza, *Sueño y alucinación en el mundo nahuatl y maya*, 81.

8 Ibid.

9 Domingo Schievenini, “A Small Distinction with a Big Difference: Prohibiting ‘Drugs’ but Not Alcohol, from the Conquest to Constitutional Law,” 22.

10 Martin Nesvig, "Forbidden Drugs of the Colonial Americas," in *The Oxford Handbook of Global Drug History* (Oxford: Oxford University Press, 2022), 162.

11 Irigoyen-Rascón and Paredes, *Tarahumara Medicine: Ethnobotany and Healing among the Rarámuri of Mexico*, 52.

12 Domingo Schievenini, "A Small Distinction with a Big Difference: Prohibiting 'Drugs' but Not Alcohol, from the Conquest to Constitutional Law," 39.

13 Hernando Ruiz de Alarcón, *Tratado de las supersticiones y costumbres gentílicas que hoy viven entre los indios naturales de esta Nueva España*, ed. Francisco del Paso y Troncoso (Fuente Cultural de la Librería Navarro, 1953), https://www.cervantesvirtual.com/nd/ark:/59851/bmcdn423. "el ololuhqui es vn genero de semilla como lantejas, que la produce vn genero de yedra desta tierra, y veuida esta semilla priua del juicio, porque es muy vehemente; y por este medio comunican al demonio."

14 Nesvig, "Sandcastles of the Mind: Hallucinogens and Cultural Memory," 48.

15 Javier Luis, *The First Asians in the Americas: A Transpacific History*, 160.

16 Lozano Armendares, *El chinguirito vindicado: El contrabando de aguardiente de caña y la política colonial*, 23; Génin, *La cerveza entre los antiguos mexicanos y en la actualidad*, 18.

17 Gonzalo Aguirre Beltrán, *Medicina y magia: el proceso de aculturación en la estructura colonial*, 3a reimpresión (México: Instituto Nacional Indigenista, 1987), 151. "el peyote se molía en metate hasta convertirlo en polvo o masa y así es ingerido. Las más de las veces, sin embargo, se acude a la dilución del polvo o masa en agua . . . o en vino, nombre genérico que por lo común califica el licor destilado del agave que produce el mezcal."

18 Ibid., 142.

19 Irigoyen-Rascón and Paredes, *Tarahumara Medicine: Ethnobotany and Healing among the Rarámuri of Mexico*, 69.

20 Schultes, "The Plant Kingdom and Hallucinogens (Part III)."

21 Adam Negrin et al., "Residue Analysis Suggests Ritual Use of Tobacco at the Ancient Mesoamerican City of Cotzumalhuapa, Guatemala," *Antiquity* 98, no. 398 (2024): 526.

22 Ursula Thiemer-Sachse, "Sobre higiene y medicina entre los zapotecas durante la época de la conquista española," *Indiana* 16 (2000): 200.

23 Bruman, *Alcohol in Ancient Mexico*, 104.

24 Negrin et al., "Residue Analysis Suggests Ritual Use of Tobacco at the Ancient Mesoamerican City of Cotzumalhuapa, Guatemala," 529.

25 Joel W. Palka, "Real Tobacco for Real People: Nicotine and Lacandon Maya Trade," in *Substance and Seduction: Ingested Commodities in Early Modern Mesoamerica*, ed.

Kathryn E. Sampeck and Stacey Schwartzkopf (Austin: University of Texas Press, 2017), 106.

26 Negrin et al., "Residue Analysis Suggests Ritual Use of Tobacco at the Ancient Mesoamerican City of Cotzumalhuapa, Guatemala," 519.

27 Schultes, "The Plant Kingdom and Hallucinogens (Part III)."

28 de la Garza, *Sueño y alucinación en el mundo nahuatl y maya*, 61.

29 Florentine Codex, Book 11 fol. 142v.

30 de la Garza, *Sueño y alucinación en el mundo nahuatl y maya*, 77.

31 David Lorente Fernández, "Hojas frías, flor de campana. Sobre el uso terapéutico del floripondio (Brugmansia) entre los nahuas," *Itinerarios* 36 (2022): 176.

Chapter 14

1 Octavio Paz, *The Other Mexico: Critique of the Pyramid*, trans. Lysander Kemp (New York: Grove Press Inc., 1972), 85.

2 Juan de Torquemada, "Capítulo XXIII," in *Monarquía Indiana*, Tercera edición (primera edición UNAM), vol. Volumen I (México: Universidad Nacional Autónoma de México, Instituto de Investigaciones Históricas, 1975), 402.

DRINKS INDEX

SUBJECT INDEX

About the Author

N. C. Stevens writes about the role beverages play in communities and cultures around the world. He has published on a range of topics, including the native tea gods of ethnic minorities in Yunnan, China, the genetic diversity of coffee in Madagascar, and sacramental winemaking for the Catholic church in the Finger Lakes of New York.

He endeavors to approach research and writing about beverages holistically to remove silos between categories of drinks that the media has traditionally treated separately. His aim is to form a more complete and cohesive understanding of the drink as a phenomenon of material culture distinct from food.

He developed an interest in beverage culture after living on the East Coast of Madagascar with the Betsimisaraka people, who ferment and drink an artisanal bark-hopped sugarcane wine called *betsabetsa*. When he returned home to Massachusetts, he fell into the legally ambiguous hobby of home distilling with his oldest brother. He has traveled extensively in Latin America in search of local beverages, including several month-long stints in Mexico, Honduras, and Guatemala. He typically couch-surfs with locals wherever he travels.

His writing has appeared in the *Financial Times*, *BBC Travel*, *Slate*, *Wine Enthusiast*, and *Atlas Obscura*, among others. He maintains a self-curated website, DrinkingFolk.com.